Discover Historic Washington State

A Travel Guide to Hundreds of Historical
Places in the Evergreen State

George and Jan Roberts

Gem
Guides Book Co.

315 CLOVERLEAF DRIVE, SUITE F
BALDWIN PARK, CA 91706

First Edition 1999

Maps by Scott and Jan Roberts
County maps courtesy of Washington State Department of Transportation
Heritage Highway Markers text courtesy of Washington State Department of Transportation
Cover design and layout by Scott Roberts

Library of Congress Catalog Card Number: 99-73431

ISBN 1-889786-07-1

This book is dedicated to:

Our son, Jeff and his wife Kerry

Our grandchildren: Michael, Katie and Clare

Our son, Scott and his wife Jennifer

Our youngest son, Patrick

and

Our favorite daughter, Jennifer.

They made every trip a pleasant adventure.

TABLE OF CONTENTS

ACKNOWLEDGEMENTS

Hundreds of organizations and groups provided material that was used to write this travel guide. You'll find many of their names in the pages of this book. For they are the chambers of commerce and visitor centers that furnish historical tour information to those who visit their cities.

Staff and volunteers at community museums were extremely generous with their time and more than willing to explain the local history represented by their collections.

Libraries were an excellent source for research material. Staff in their reference departments made a special effort to help us.

Judy Menish, Skagit County Treasurer, furnished photographs of historic sites from her personal collection and updates on historic sites and museums across the state.

Barbara Jones led us on personal tours of Seattle and some of the surrounding communities.

Lee Hall introduced us to the impressive sites along the North Cascades Highway (Hwy 20) and led us on a tour of Winthrop.

Jana McCunn, Spokane Regional Convention and Visitors Bureau, was a great resource for Eastern Washington information. Also verified our research information.

Lisa Barksdale, Republic's Stonerose Interpretive Center, gave us an opportunity to experience the state's million-year-old fossil history hands-on.

Mark Bozanich, Washington State Department of Transportation, furnished an excellent map of the state we reproduced by county within this guide.

And the many people we met along the way who showed us the hospitality and friendship that made our visits enjoyable.

INTRODUCTION

Discovering places where Washington State history was made.

After Columbus' discovery of the New World in 1492, Spanish explorers began their search along Washington's coast for the *Strait of Anian,* a mythical river that connected the Atlantic to the Pacific through North America; a Northwest Passage. A hundred years later, Apostolos Valerianus, a Greek who took the Spanish name, Juan de Fuca, discovered the strait that now bears his name, believing it to be a passage to the Atlantic Ocean. Unable to convince Spanish officials of his discovery, he returned to Greece. It would be another two hundred years before the Spanish returned.

In 1775 a boat from the Bruno Heceta and Juan Francisco de la Bodega y Quadra expeditions went ashore at the mouth of the Hoh River; the first known landing in what is now Washington State. By the end of the eighteenth century, British and American captains were mapping the area, giving names to the places they discovered and trading with Coastal Indians for their valuable sea otter furs. The names of those early seamen, Fidalgo, Vancouver, Cook, Wilkes and Gray were forever etched into the journals of the state's history.

Exploration also came by way of overland voyagers in the early 1800s. Hudson Bay Company established a strong presence in the territory by building trading posts along the Snake and Columbia Rivers. Fort Vancouver Factor, John McLoughlin, managed an area for the Hudson Bay Company that covered the entire river system north of California and west of the Rockies.

At the same time, President Jefferson commissioned Meriwether Lewis and William Clark to explore the region between the Mississippi and the Rockies and find a route to the Pacific that would open the West to American fur trade. The impact their expedition had on the settlement of the Pacific Northwest has been forever memorialized in the cities and counties, colleges and schools that today bare their names.

Missionaries followed Lewis and Clark's trail with an aim to bring white civilization and Christianity to the northwestern Indian tribes. They built missions and schools and taught Native Americans to farm. Among those missionaries were Dr. Marcus Whitman and his wife Narcissa. Whitman's passion for his work, his tireless efforts to bring settlers to the Oregon territory and his guiding of a large party of immigrants across the Oregon Trail in 1843 helped to eventually secure the territory for the United States. A measles epidemic at Whitman's mission in 1847 cost the Whitman's their lives along with twelve other white people. They didn't die from measles. They were massacred by Indians because the Indians thought Whitman was either unable to cure their people or had deliberately poisoned them. In spite of the dangers, immigrants continued to follow the Oregon Trail to the Northwest. A year after the massacre, Oregon Territory was established.

By the middle of the ninteenth century, the region north of the Columbia was growing. Port Townsend, Whidbey Island, and Seattle (first called New York) were settled. Washington Territory was carved out of the Oregon Territory. Olympia became the seat of the new territory. The first territory road was built between Walla Walla and Fort Steilacoom.

Through the late 1870s, American Indian resistance to the intrusion of white men on their lands resulted in many conflicts, especially in the eastern part of the state where an increasing number of immigrants were settling. Miners heading for the Orofino gold fields swelled the non-Indian population even more. The need for military protection became the primary concern in many communities. Blockhouses were built to protect families. Army forts and posts were erected and manned.

Peace came with the signing of treaties. Attention then turned to defense from outside aggressors. Coastal artillery installations and shipyards were constructed.

The arrival of the railroad in the 1880s and the railroad's offer of free land quadrupled the territory's population in less than 10 years. On November 11, 1889 Washington became a state.

With the coming of the twentieth century, modern pioneers, Boeing, Hill, and Kaiser left evidence of their contribution to the state's history for others to see and put their names in the state's history books.

Today, much of the state's past has been preserved and identified. Historic markers line the state's roads. Lighthouses dot the coastline. Segments of the original Oregon Trail remain. Murals record historic events in many towns. In cities across the state, Victorian homes, grist mills, pioneer log cabins, covered bridges and historic sites remain to be seen. And, inside community museums are thousands of relics, antiques, memorabilia, photographs and artifacts that trace and record their region's history.

Come, Discover Historic Washington State.

Traveling with *Discover Historic Washington State*

Sites in this guide have been grouped by travel region. And, within each region, sites are listed in alphabetical order by county within that region.

Official Washington State Highway maps were used for each county. When a city or town has a listing in the guide, the city name is enlarged on the map. Site listings immediately follow each county map.

Some historic sites are on private property and not open or accessible to the public. Please respect the property owner's right to privacy.

State and National Parks, museums and privately operated facilities may be closed during certain times of the year, have limited days or hours of operation, shown only by appointment, or may be inaccessible under adverse weather conditions.

Telephone numbers have been included whenever possible. If you plan to make a special trip to see one particular site, it would be advisable to call ahead. Area codes also change.

Entrance fees are charged at some parks, museums and privately operated facilities to help defray expenses.

Extensive research was conducted to insure the accuracy of information included in this guide. Historic buildings are sometimes relocated, damaged by the elements or destroyed. Others are renovated, opened to the public for the first time, designated a state monument, etc. If you let us know when you find a change or a better address for a site, we'll include an update in the next printing of this guide.

Several publications are listed at the end of this guide that you can refer to for more history about the listed sites. Many chambers of commerce, visitor centers and historical societies are active throughout the state and are an excellent source for more information.

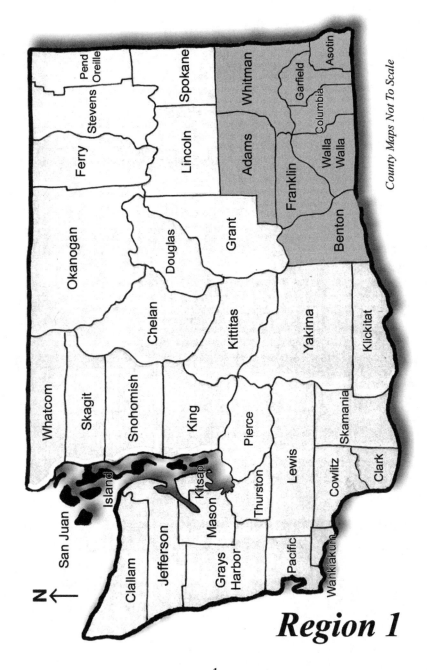

County Maps Not To Scale

Region 1

Adams County

REGION 1

ADAMS COUNTY

LIND

Adams County Historical Society Museum
Phillips Building, Downtown Lind (509) 677-3393

History of the 22,000-acre Phillips Farm, the largest wheat farm in the state, and the important role the community of Lind played as a shipping center is recorded at this museum. The positive impact of the Grand Coulee million-acre reclamation project on Adams County communities is also exhibited.

OTHELLO

Othello Community Museum and Arts Center
Third and Larch Sts., Othello (509) 488-2268 Leave message

This vast agricultural region has important ties to two major railroads: the Northern Pacific and the Chicago, Milwaukee and St. Paul. The land around Othello once belonged to the Northern Pacific Railroad. And the Chicago, Milwaukee and St.

Paul Railroad laid tracks for its transcontinental line through the city of Othello. The railroad's influence on the early growth of the city is underscored by the preservation of "The Abraham Lincoln," a Denver and Rio Grande Western Railroad business car which is listed on the National Register of Historic Places. The story of Othello and its railroad history is exhibited in this former Presbyterian Church building. The building, erected in 1908, was the city's first church and is listed on the National Register of Historic Places.

Bank safe at the Othello Community Museum

The Old Hotel Art Gallery
33 E. Larch St., Othello (509) 488-5936

The rooms of this former 1912 railroad-era boarding house are now filled with paintings, crafts, and other works by Northwestern artists. Othello's Chamber of Commerce also has its offices in this preserved building where visitors can get information about the region.

RITZVILLE

Dr. Frank R. Burroughs Historical Home
408 West Main St., Ritzville (509) 659-0698 Leave message

The restored 1889 home of Dr. Frank Burroughs, for years Ritzville's only physician, is maintained as a museum of local history. Many original Burroughs' family heirlooms can be seen throughout the home, including the doctor's office archives, which record the names of 5,000 babies he delivered between 1888 and 1925. Dr. Burroughs also served the community as city councilman, postmaster, and mayor. His home is listed on the National Register of Historic Places.

Dr. Frank R. Burroughs Museum - 1890
RITZVILLE, WASHINGTON

Burroughs Historical Home, Courtesy of Dr. Frank R. Burroughs Museum

Ritzville Carnegie Library
302 West Main St., Ritzville

Ritzville's Carnegie Library, built in 1907, is one of the few Carnegie libraries in the country still primarily used for its intended purpose: as a community library. The library also houses a collection of Ritzville memorabilia. This distinctive Carnegie-style building is an important local landmark and is listed in the National Register of Historic Places.

Both the Dr. Burroughs Home and the Carnegie Library are located within a three-block section of Ritzville's historic Main Street. This area of downtown Ritzville, which is listed on the National Register of Historic Places, features buildings that were constructed around the turn-of-the-century.

Ritzville Railroad Depot
Main Street Historic District, Downtown Ritzville

Northern Pacific Railroad built this red brick, mission-style depot building in 1910 as a replacement for the original wooden depot that stood across the street from this site for nearly thirty years. Many of the building's original interior features: terrazzo floors, freight and baggage room and floor scales have remained unchanged over the years. Today, the building, which is listed on the National Register of Historic Places, houses a museum of Ritzville memorabilia and the city's Chamber of Commerce.

Zion Congregational Church
305 East Broadway, Ritzville

The large number of Russian-German settlers who homesteaded this area erected Zion Congregational Church in 1888 to serve their cultural, social and religious needs. In 1901, they replaced the original wood-frame structure with this building, now a State Registered Landmark.

Nelson H. Green House
502 South Adams St., Ritzville

At the turn-of-the-century, when the Green home was being constructed, Ritzville was on its way to becoming the largest inland wheat shipping center in the world. At that time, more acres of wheat were produced here than in any other county in the state. The prosperity of the community's first settlers is reflected in the various architectural styles of homes built during the period that are now proudly maintained throughout the region. One of the finest examples of early twentieth century construction is the Green family's 1902 Queen Anne, Neo-Classical style house, with its nearby carriage house. Both are listed on the National Register of Historic Places. A self-guided tour guide to forty-eight of the city's other historic commercial and residential buildings is available from the Ritzville Preservation Society.

N. H. Greene - 1902
Ritzville, Washington

Nelson H. Green House, Courtesy of Dr. Frank R. Burroughs Museum

WASHTUCNA (wawsh-TUHK-nuh)

Marmes Rock Shelter
Lyons Ferry State Park, 8 miles northwest of Starbuck on Hwy. 261

In 1969, backwaters of Monumental Dam created the reservoir that now covers Marmes Rock Shelter, the location of a prehistoric Indian habitation and burial site. Excavations at Marmes, once considered the most outstanding archaeological site uncovered in the Northwest, revealed evidence that early man inhabited the area 10,000 years ago. Remains and artifacts from some of the earliest known inhabitants of the Western Hemisphere were uncovered at this National Historic Landmark. Relics and skull fragments unearthed here are displayed at the Washington State University Museum of Anthropology in Pullman.

Lyons Ferry State Park
8 miles northwest of Starbuck on Hwy. 261

The first civilian ferry licensed by the territorial legislature to operate on the Snake River was operated at this site in 1859. For more than a hundred years, emigrants, with their wagons and animals, local ranchers, and travelers crossed the Snake River at this historic spot. Dan Lyons' ferry last operated in 1968, and is now on permanent display near the upper end of the park's day-use area.

Palouse Falls
Palouse Falls State Park, off Hwy. 261, 9 miles south of junction with Hwy. 260, 17 miles southeast of Washtucna

In the massive flooding that followed the Ice Age, the Palouse River's course was altered. The river crossed the Continental Divide, carved hundreds of coulees and created a number of waterfalls. Only Palouse Falls remain today. Higher than Niagara, Palouse Falls plummets 198-feet down a sheer rock canyon on its rush to the Snake River. Between 1860 and 1883, thousands of settlers and miners passed through here while traveling this section of the 624-mile Mullan Road between Walla Walla and Fort Benton, Montana.

The Mullan Road Historical Marker
4 miles east of Washtucna on Hwy. 26

"This highway point intersects an historic 624-mile road between Walla Walla and Fort Benton, Montana, then the navigable limit of the Missouri River. Between 1855 and 1862, soldiers and civilians under Captain John Mullan, U.S. Army, hacked the 25-foot wide road through 125 miles of timber, dug 30 miles of excavation, built hundreds of bridges and scores of ferry boats using only horse and manpower. Immigrants poured westward over this route. In 1866, 10,000 pack mules shuttled between Walla Walla and Montana mining camps."

Asotin County

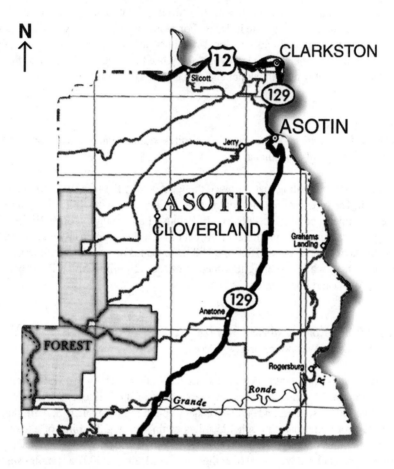

ASOTIN COUNTY

ASOTIN (uh-SOH-tin)

Asotin County Historical Museum
Third & Filmore Sts., Asotin (509) 243-4659

The first pole frame barn placed on the grounds of a Washington museum is located on this former Indian camp ground along with: a Salmon River barge; the preserved 1882 Forgey log cabin; one-room schoolhouse; working windmill, blacksmith shop; and other pioneer structures. Antique carriages and one of the largest collections of branding irons in the state are featured in the museum's outdoor displays. The history of the region is depicted inside the main museum building with sculptures of early frontier scenes, pioneer clothing and equipment, and ancient Native American artifacts.

Asotin Full Gospel Church
First and Monroe Sts., Asotin

In this community where a number of early 1900s brick buildings can be found, stands Asotin's Full Gospel Church, the second-oldest religious structure in the county. An attention to design detail and fine craftsmanship can been seen in the quality of this c.1890s Carpenter Gothic building with its well-proportioned octagonal steeple. This former Presbyterian Church is listed on the National Register of Historic Places.

CLARKSTON

Alpowai Interpretive Center
Chief Timothy State Park on Silcott Island, 8 miles west of Clarkston on Hwy. 12 (509) 758-9580

When the Lower Granite Dam was completed in 1975, the Snake River, backed up by the dam, flooded the valley leaving only this island as evidence of the pioneer town of Silcott and the ancient Indian village that once stood here. The interpretive center at this state park features exhibits of Nez Perce Indian artifacts and tells the history of Silcott and this valley where the Lewis and Clark expedition camped in 1805.

9

Valley Art Center
842 6th St., Clarkston (509) 758-8331

In addition to the historical and Indian art displayed in their permanent collections, the center presents antique shows and hosts the annual Pacific Northwest Heritage Art Exhibit.

While in the area, stop at the Clarkston Chamber of Commerce, 502 Bridge St., (800) 933-2128, for information about water excursions through Hells Canyon, the deepest river gorge in North America. In addition to the beauty of the rugged, unspoiled canyon, visitors get an up-close view of ancient Indian petroglyphs that were carved here thousands of years ago.

Chief Timothy's Grave
Beachview Park, Clarkston

Chief Timothy (1800-1891), was the head of a band of the Nez Perce Indian Nation who lived in this area. He befriended the early white settlers of this region and, with Chief Red Wolf, led his people into agriculture and farming. (Chief Red Wolf planted the first orchard in the Snake River Valley from apple seeds given to him in 1837 by missionary and explorer Henry H. Spalding.) Chief Timothy, a converted Christian, also aided Col. Steptoe in his campaign against the hostile Palouse Indians in 1858. His gravesite is in a remote corner of this busy city park, overlooking Alpowa Creek.

Chief Timothy's daughter, Jane Silcott, is also memorialized at this site. She married John Silcott and guided Captain E.D. Pierce around the Nez Perce Reservation to gold diggings near Pierce, Idaho. As a result of her efforts, gold mining began in Idaho.

C.C. Van Arsdol Home
15th and Chestnut Sts., Clarkston

Cassius Van Arsdol settled here in 1896 when Clarkston was a small ferry-landing community on the Snake River known as Jawbone Flat. Van Arsdol, a civil engineer and survey manager for the Northern Pacific Railroad, played a major role in the growth of the state's rail and highway network. An early entrepreneur, Van Arsdol designed and constructed an irrigation system that enabled him to develop and sell high-value real estate in this area. The original 1800s one-room cottage, now enlarged, is listed on the National Register of Historic Places.

A guide to historical sites in downtown Clarkston is available from the Chamber of Commerce.

Lewis and Clark Historical Marker
One mile west of Clarkston on US 12 near the Snake River

"Down this river in 1805 came a corps sent to realize the cherished plan of President Thomas Jefferson for exploring the Northwest and its rivers. This band of enlisted men and guides was led by Captain Meriwether Lewis and Captain William Clark on the pathless trek from St. Louis to the Pacific Ocean. The next year, hunting and trading for food as they went, this corps of discovery made their way east again. Their journey gave our country a claim, by right of exploration, to territory they crossed and rivers they mapped."

The travels and adventures of the American Corps of Discovery, led by Lewis and Clark through the Pacific Northwest in 1805-06, is commemorated here, and at other historic places along the Lewis and Clark National Historic Trail.

CLOVERLAND

Cloverland Garage
10 miles west of Asotin, Cloverland

This two-story building was erected in 1902 as a general store and dance hall when Cloverland was on the main road between Lewiston, Idaho and Wallowa, Oregon. As the town grew, the building took on more importance. The first telephone service in Asotin County was established here, then at the city's post office. The building later housed an auto dealership, garage and featured the town's first gasoline pump. Other than the Cloverland Garage, which is listed on the National Register of Historic Places, little remains at Cloverland today.

Nez Perce Trail

History of the Nez Perce Indian can be traced along Hwy. 129 between Clarkston and the Oregon border. The most noticeable evidence is the 5,000-6,000 year-old Indian petroglyphs still visible on the cliffs of the Snake River near Buffalo Eddy. Access to this historic spot can be made via River Road in Clarkston. The Nez Perce made their winter camp at Asotin at a site now housing the Asotin County Historic Museum. They traveled the route between Asotin and Anatone to the southwest when traveling from the Joseph area in Oregon to Lapwai, Idaho. And, two miles from the junction of Hwy. 129 and the Grande Ronde, at the mouth of Joseph Creek, is Chief Joseph's cave, the birthplace of the last great Nez Perce chief.

Benton County

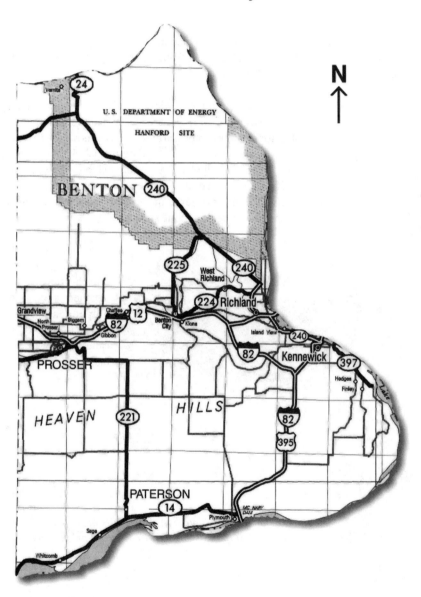

N
↑

BENTON COUNTY

KENNEWICK (KEN-uh-wik)

East Benton County Historical Society Museum
Keewaydin Park, 205 Keewaydin Dr., across from the senior center in Keewaydin Park, Kennewick (509) 582-7704

The story of Kennewick's history, from the heyday of railroad construction and irrigation projects to the Depression of 1893-97, are chronicled in this museum's exceptional collection of historical photographs, artifacts and memorabilia from the surrounding region. Displays of Native American culture include stone tools, arrowheads and Columbia River petroglyphs. Agriculture exhibits showcase the bounty of the area's wheat fields and fruit crops that the land began producing after irrigation projects turned wasteland into farmland. Today, this fertile land is considered the best grape-producing region in the state.

The beauty of the museum building, which features a petrified wood floor, helped earn it the distinction of being called "the best small museum in the state."

Indian carvings found in the vicinity of Kennewick,
Displayed at the East Benton County Historical Museum

PATERSON

Telegraph Island Petroglyphs
Telegraph Island, Columbia River, near Paterson

Prehistoric aboriginal drawings of unknown age are inscribed on rocks in the John Day Pool.

PLYMOUTH

McNary Locks and Dam
On the Columbia River east of intersection of Hwys. 82/395 and 14, east of Plymouth Visitor Center on Oregon side of Columbia River

One of a series of dams and locks constructed to control the mighty Columbia River and improve navigation was erected here by the Corps of Engineers in the late 1940s. The Dam's visitor center helps tourists understand how these dams and locks operate.

McNary Locks and Dam

PROSSER
Benton County Historical Museum
Prosser City Park, 7th St. and Patterson Ave., Prosser (509) 786-3842

The history of Benton County, the city of Prosser, and Native Americans of the region is displayed in life-like settings throughout this large museum. Original furnishings and collectibles are used to recreate a 1900s homestead shack, schoolroom, general store and Victorian parlor. Antique dolls, Indian artifacts, a substantial collection of gowns from 1843 to 1920, Edison phonographs, and an 1867 square grand piano are among the more than 2,000 items exhibited.

Benton County Historical Museum

Benton County Courthouse
Dudley Ave. at Market, Prosser

Col. William Prosser, for whom the town was named, homesteaded here in 1882. His town grew in importance with the coming of the railroad and development of hydroelectric power at nearby Tap-Tap Falls.   In 1903, two years before Prosser became the county seat, Col. Prosser published "History of the Puget Sound Country." The county courthouse was built in 1926 and is listed on the National Register of Historic Places.

Prosser Historical Home Tour
Prosser Visitor Information Center and Chamber of Commerce, 1230 Bennett Ave., Prosser (509) 786-3177

A guide to the homes built by eight pioneer Prosser families between 1899 and 1907 is available from the chamber of commerce. Queen Anne, Dutch and Colonial Revival, and Craftsman bungalow styles can be seen on this self-guided tour. Locally quarried stone and sandstone bricks are among the special features found in these early homes.

16

1003 Brown St., c.1903, Queen Anne cottage with turned spindle posts and ornamentation on the gables.

962 Court St., 1905, Craftsman sandstone bungalow with colonial-style columns.

818 Court St., 1902, features detailed woodwork around the doors and windows and under the eaves.

611 and 615 Court St., the Mahans family, who owned the Montana Restaurant on Meade Avenue, built two Queen Anne/Stick-Eastlake style homes.

801 Guernsey, 1906, many outstanding features including bay window in dining room, four styles of shingles, and gable ornamentation.

831 Guernsey, 1899, Dutch/Colonial Revival home with gambrel roof, decorative shingles and colonial-style columns.

1071 Spokana Ave., c.1905, Queen Anne Tower cottage with gently rolled roof, oval window under front eave and decorative shingles.

1019 Sixth St., 1907, constructed from locally quarried Prosser stone.

At Meade and Sixth Sts. a 12-foot by 48-foot mural, created for the nation's bicentennial, gives a pictorial history of the city.

RICHLAND

Hanford Science Center
Columbia River Exposition History Science Technology Center (CREST)
Richland Community House, Richland (509) 376-6374 or (509) 946-0951

World War II forever changed Richland. As the war raged in Europe and the Pacific, thousands were working on a top secret wartime project at the Hanford Reservation, 25 miles north of Richland. It was here, as part of the Manhattan Project, that plutonium was produced for the Atomic Bomb that would be dropped on Nagasaki. Today, activities at the Hanford Site are directed towards the peacetime use and development of nuclear energy. This science center exhibits the history of the Hanford Site, the B-reactor which has been designated a National Historic Mechanical Engineering Landmark, and present energy projects.

The town of Richland was home to many who worked at the Hanford Project in the mid-1940s. They lived in homes that were built by the U.S. government and maintained under contract by General Electric. It wasn't until the late 1950s that residents were able to buy their homes, and the city could again incorporate.

Fast Flux Test Facility Visitor Center
11 miles north of Richland via Stevens Dr., Jadwin Ave., or George Washington Way (509) 376-6374

The world's most advanced and versatile sodium-cooled nuclear test reactor is operated at this test facility by Westinghouse. The visitor center displays photographs, models and information about the testing of nuclear fuel and materials for fast breeder reactors.

Washington Public Power Supply System's Visitor Information Center
10 miles north of Richland off Stevens Dr. (509) 372-5860

Although visitors can't tour the state's first commercial nuclear power plant, they can get a bird's eye view of Plant 2 from the deck of this center. Inside the center, visitors can take a video tour of the plant and experience hands-on exhibits.

Three Rivers Children's Museum
650 George Washington Way, Richland (509) 946-5343

Through a number of fun activities and interactive exhibits, this museum introduces youngsters to events in local and national history. A Gold Rush Era general store and bank bring realism to the historical and cultural display on Alaska and the Yukon Gold Rush. A replica of the bi-plane "Swallow" tells about the first airmail flight from Pasco, Washington to Elko, Nevada. Communication devices, from the early telegraph to the telephone to the modern computer terminal, give children a hands-on history lesson. Other adventures also await visitors to this special museum.

Three Rivers Children's Museum

Columbia County

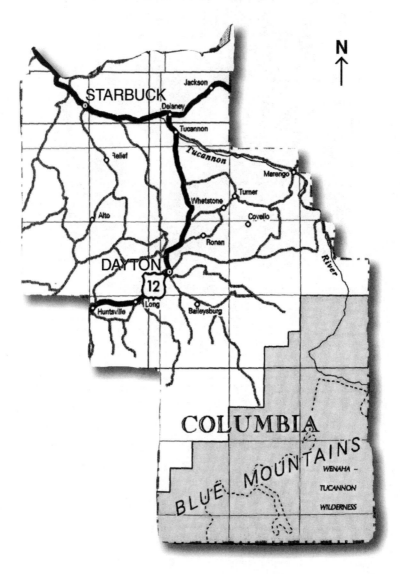

COLUMBIA COUNTY

DAYTON

Columbia County Courthouse
341 East Main St., Dayton

Columbia County's Courthouse has the distinction of being the oldest courthouse in the state that's still used for county government offices. The Italianate-style, 1886 building, which was constructed two years before Washington's Statehood, is considered one of the two most beautiful buildings in the state. During restoration in 1991-93, the cupola, exterior detail and the statues of Justice and the American eagle were permanently removed. But, the interior woodwork and central staircase remain almost unchanged. Historical documents and early photographs are displayed along the second-floor corridor.

Dayton Depot Museum
Second and Commercial Sts., Dayton, (509) 382-2026

The state's oldest existing railroad depot, erected in 1881 for the Oregon Railroad & Navigation Company, was purchased by the Northern Pacific and relocated to this site in 1889. It remained in operation until 1974 when the Northern Pacific Railroad donated it to the Dayton Historical Depot Society for a museum. The Society restored the two-story station and furnished it with antique furniture and railroad memorabilia. The working freight scale is original, as is the beaded wallboard and wainscoting that are featured in this historic structure. The importance of this station to this community's development was recognized in 1974 when it was placed on the National Register of Historic Places.

Dayton Depot Museum

Historic Dayton Walking Tour
Chamber of Commerce, 145 East Main St., Dayton (509) 382-4825

Dayton's pioneer settlers prospered from the rich, fertile farmland; the growth that came with the railroad; and selection as the seat of Columbia County. Evidence of Dayton's prosperity can be seen in the scores of well-preserved nineteenth century homes that line the city's streets. More than seventy structures of various architectural styles, including many that are listed on the National Register of Historic Places, are listed in a self-guided walking tour brochure that's available from the Dayton Chamber of Commerce.

Lewis and Clark Trail State Park
West of Dayton on U.S. 12

Lewis and Clark's expedition camped at this ancient Indian campground in May, 1806, on their return from the Pacific. A marker in the campground at the south side of the highway records their stay and the hardships they faced in providing provisions for the members of their party.

KAHLOTUS (kuh-LOH-tuhs)

Kahlotus Main Street
Junction of Hwys 21, 260 and 261

Visitors to Kahlotus, the gateway to the Lower Monumental Dam and Locks on the Snake River, will find a main street business district that's been restored to its original early 1900s appearance. In October 1805, Lewis and Clark, in their westward trek to the Pacific, camped near this spot on the Snake River and noted nearby Monumental Rock in their journal.

Franklin County

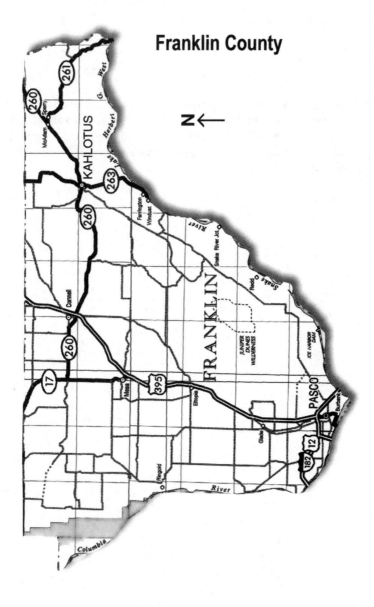

FRANKLIN COUNTY

PASCO

Franklin County Historical Museum
305 North Fourth St., Pasco (509) 547-3714

For 50 years, this 1910 Mission-style Carnegie building served as the city's library. Today, this impressive building, with its high ceilings and dark wood moldings, once again serves the community by preserving its past for future generations. Featured exhibits inside this restored building include: area photographs from 1900 to present depicting the history of Franklin County; homesteading relics from the turn-of-the-century; antique furnishings, dolls, toys and fashions; and displays that commemorate the important role railroad, water and air transportation played in the development of the region.

Franklin County Historical Museum

Franklin County Courthouse
1016 North Fourth St., Pasco

The arrival of the Northern Pacific Railway at this site in 1880 marked the beginning of the town of Pasco. Pasco was an important center for the railroad, and the presence of the railroad helped the city to grow. When the county seat moved here from Ainsworth, Franklin County's Courthouse was constructed. This imposing 1907 Neo-Classic structure, with its beautifully designed brick and limestone exterior, is listed on the National Register of Historic Places.

Franklin County Courthouse

Sacajawea State Park and Interpretive Center
Sacajawea State Park, Pasco (509) 545-2361

When Lewis and Clark and their Corps of Discovery stopped in North Dakota on the first leg of their expedition to the Pacific Ocean, they hired Frenchman, Toussaint Charbonneau as a guide. His Indian wife, Sacajawea, and their newborn son, Jean Baptiste, would also accompany the party. The interpretive center at this state park, honors Sacajawea and the contribution she made to the success of this famous expedition. A collection of Indian artifacts, interpretive displays and an exhibit commemorating the arrival of Lewis and Clark at this site in October 1805, is exhibited.

The U.S. Treasury further memorializes the accomplishments of Sacajawea by minting a new gold-colored one-dollar coin in the year 2000. The image of Sacajawea and her infant son on the face of the coin pay tribute to the contribution made by Native American women to the nation's culture.

Sacajawea Historical Marker
Southeast of Pasco on US 12 near the entrance to Sacajawea State Park

"Let us pause at this point along the Lewis and Clark trail of 1805 and pay tribute to the memory of the most dramatic female figure in the history of the Northwest:

26

Sacajawea, the Bird Woman. Enduring uncomplainingly all of the many hardships of 19 months of dangerous travel on foot, on horseback, and in boats, through an uncharted wilderness, this little Indian squaw, with her papoose in a net on her back, performed an invaluable aid as guide, interpreter, and symbol to the curious native tribes of the peaceful intentions of her strange band of white explorers."

Ainsworth Historical Marker
Southeast of Pasco on U.S. 12 near the entrance to Sacajawea State Park

"One of the most colorful of early Northwest railroad towns once existed near junction of the Snake and Columbia Rivers. Ainsworth was founded, 1879, when the railroad bridge was building over the Snake River. In its heyday it was a wild, lusty town, noted for brawls, gunfights and hangings. For a time a vital cog in the Northern Pacific railroad's extension to Puget Sound, it sank slowly into oblivion after opening of the bridge to traffic in 1884. The town was named for John C. Ainsworth, a prominent figure in transportation circles of the early Northwest."

Ainsworth was chosen by the Northern Pacific Railroad as a starting point for completion of its transcontinental railroad. While mills at Ainsworth turned-out railroad ties, crews were building supports for the iron superstructure that was being shipped around the Horn from the East Coast. When the bridge was completed in April, 1884, it would be the first to span the Snake River.

Ice Harbor Lock and Dam
9 miles east of Pasco, north of Hwy. 124

Ice Harbor Dam was the first of four dams built on the lower Snake River and one of the most impressive. Its navigational locks, the second largest in the world match the grandeur of the Dam's 100-foot spillway. Visitors can take a self-guided tour of the powerhouse, fish viewing room, and a Native American exhibit depicting the culture of the region's first inhabitants.

Garfield County

GARFIELD COUNTY

PATAHA (Pa-tah –hah)

Pataha Flour Mill
U.S. 12 east of Pataha

Flour milled at this site a century ago was of such high quality that it was marketed around the world. All that remains today of this once-thriving business is the abandoned Pataha Flour Mill.

Pataha Flour Mill, Courtesy of Garfield County Museum

POMEROY

Garfield County Courthouse
8th and Main Sts., Pomeroy

Residents of Pomeroy and the nearby town of Pataha fought a legal battle for three years over the location of the county seat. It took an Act of Congress to finally resolve the issue in Pomeroy's favor. Fire destroyed Garfield County's first courthouse and two-thirds of Pomeroy's Main Street in 1900. The following year, this magnificent brick and stone building, with Queen Anne features, was constructed. Atop the dome is an unblindfolded statue of justice holding her scales and sword. It is one of only five unblindfolded statues of justice in the country. The Victorian-era courthouse is listed on the National Register of Historic Places and is still in use by Garfield County.

*Garfield County Courthouse, Courtesy of Garfield County Museum,
E.V. Kuyendall Collection*

Garfield County Museum
7th and Columbia, Pomeroy (509) 843-3925

For more than a quarter of a century, local volunteers have collected, cataloged, and taken great care to preserve and display memorabilia that charts the history of Garfield County. Period rooms, household items from the "good old days," antique dolls and early 1900s collectibles fill the museum. One of the museum's prized pieces is an original oil painting of President James A. Garfield, for whom the county was named. President Garfield died from an assassin's bullet two months before the county was formed.

Inside display at Garfield County Museum

Pioneer kitchen display inside Garfield County Museum

Pomeroy Historic Tour
Chamber of Commerce, Pomeroy

Sixty homes, buildings and sites of historic interest in Pomeroy are listed in self-guided heritage tour brochure published for the city's Centennial in 1989. Each listing gives a background on the owners, special features or a little history. A former stage stop, the city's first hospital, a house of seven gables, and the virtually unchanged 1883 St. Peter's Episcopal Church, are among the sites listed.

1910 street scene at southeast corner of Main and Third Streets in Pomeroy, Courtesy of Garfield County Museum

31

Lewis and Clark Trail and Travois Road
10 miles east of Pomeroy on the north side of U.S. 12

This ancient Indian road was used by the Lewis and Clark expedition on their return trip to Missouri in 1806. It's one of the last sections of original Indian trails remaining in the state.

Walla Walla County

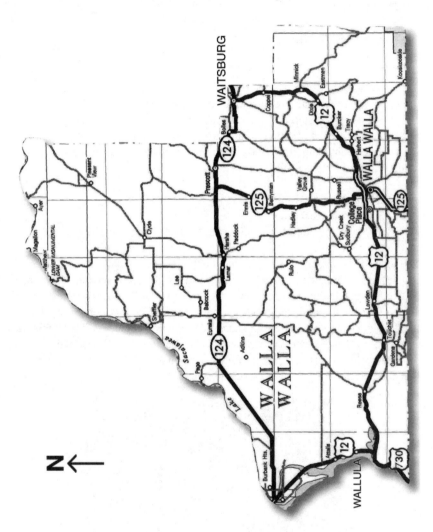

WALLA WALLA COUNTY

WAITSBURG

Waitsburg Historic District
Main St., Waitsburg

Although William Bruce was the first to settle here, the town would be named for Sylvester Wait, who established a water-powered gristmill at the Touchet River in 1865. When the mill closed in 1957, its millstones were moved to Coppei Park for preservation. In 1889, the first Grange to be charted in the state was begun here. The town's quaint Main Street, with its many turn-of-the-century buildings, is listed on the National Register of Historic Places.

William Perry Bruce Home
Bruce Memorial Museum
318 Main St., Waitsburg. By appointment (509) 337-6582 or 337-6287

The town of Waitsburg grew-up around William Bruce's homesteader log cabin that he built at this site in 1861. Bruce played a significant role in the development of Waitsburg. He contributed money and property for the town's first flourmill, helped found a Republican newspaper and served as county commissioner. The family's Italianate-style home, built here in 1883, was the center of William Bruce's social, political and business activities until his death in 1888. His restored Victorian mansion is listed on the National Register of Historic Places and is the site of Waitsburg's annual September Pioneer Festival.

William Perry Bruce House, Courtesy of Bruce Memorial Museum

WALLA WALLA (WAW-luh-WAW-luh)

Fort Walla Walla Museum Complex
Fort Walla Walla Park, 755 Myra Rd. (509) 525-7703

The third and final Fort Walla Walla was built at this site by the U.S. Army in 1858 to provide security for southeastern Washington settlers and to protect travel routes. A replica of the old fort, along with a reconstructed pioneer village, early military cemetery and agricultural museum, can be seen on this former military reservation. Original buildings from the old fort are preserved in a section of the reservation now administered by the Department of Veterans Affairs Medical Center.

Pioneer Village includes 16 original and replica buildings that date from 1859 to the turn-of-the-century. Among the historic buildings are the c.1880 **Babcock Railway Station**, 1867 **Union one-room schoolhouse**, and 1859 **Ransom Clark cabin**. Exhibits are drawn from a collection of over 26,000 artifacts that tell the story of the settlement from the time of the Oregon Trail pioneers to the conversion from horse-drawn to mechanical farming.

Headstones in the military cemetery mark the burial sites of men who served in every campaign in the fort's history. Included are the graves of the six enlisted men that were killed in the Steptoe Battle of 1858. Near the cemetery a marker commemorates the building of the Mullan Road, the vital military roadway that connected Walla Walla and other Eastern Washington cities to Montana and Idaho during the 1860s Gold Rush.

Pioneer life and equipment of the horse-era farming days is displayed in five, 4,000 square-foot buildings adjacent to the Pioneer Village. These five buildings house the largest collection of horse-era antique agricultural implements in the Northwest. One of the featured exhibits, in Agricultural Building #3, is a large, 1919, side hill combine that's harnessed to thirty-three life-size fiberglass mules using the famous Shenandoah (Shandoney) hitch.

Department of Veterans Affairs Medical Center
West Chestnut St., Walla Walla (509) 525-5200

Preserved on the grounds of this Veterans Hospital, are buildings that were once part of the last Fort Walla Walla.

Dacres Hotel
Fourth and West Main Sts., Walla Walla

The Stine House, Walla Walla County's first and best-known hotel, stood at this site nearly 20 years until it and most of the block, were destroyed by fire in 1892. From the ruins, George Dacres built one of the finest hotels in the country. The magnificent, three-story Dacres Hotel was the center of the city's social, political and business activity, and served travelers for 64 years. The renovated 1899 building, with its distinctive exterior, is listed on the National Register of Historic Places.

Kirkman House Museum
214 North Colville St., Walla Walla (509) 529-4373

This c.1880 brick house, the oldest residence in Walla Walla, was home to the Kirkman's, one of the city's first and most prominent families. William Kirkman raised cattle, established a meat packing plant, and was director of Whitman College. He pioneered shipments of livestock via rail out of the territory and was instrumental in stimulating the city's early economic growth. His fourteen-room, Italianate-style mansion, the city's only period house museum, was restored by the Historical Architecture Development Corporation, and is listed on the National Register of Historic Places. Victorian period furnishings and accessories, including Mr. Kirkman's original desk, piano and family photographs, are featured throughout the home.

Kirkman House Museum

Historical Downtown Walla Walla Tours,
Walla Walla Area Chamber of Commerce, 29 East Sumach, Walla Walla
(509) 525-0850

Just a few blocks south of the Kirkman Mansion is the city's old downtown district containing vintage buildings of various architectural styles. Along the city's Main Street, which was built on the original Nez Perce Indian Trail, is the old **Liberty Theater**. A plaque on that building identifies it as the location where the second Fort Walla Walla once stood. The Chamber's guide lists this, and other significant buildings within this district, and tells their history.

Walla Walla's Places of Historic Interest

Walla Walla's emergence as the most prominent city in Washington Territory began with the 1859 gold rush. Merchants prospered. The first bank and first college in the territory were established. And a railroad was built. As the gold played-out, agriculture became the new "gold mine." Many grand residences, commercial buildings and churches from the period remain today.

H. P. Isaacs c.1865 Home, 107 Brookside
Dr. Isaacs, a former military officer built and operated a successful flourmill at this site. By the 1880s his flour was being shipped to mid-western cities and foreign markets. Several times he remodeled this original adobe house, now one of the oldest homes in Walla Walla.

Small-Elliott 1879 House, Newell and Catherine Sts.
The Small and Elliott families' role in the development of Walla Walla was significant. David and Ira Small helped manage the building of the Columbia and Walla Walla Railroad; Alfred Small ran the Stine House. The Elliots, who purchased this home in 1892 from the Smalls, donated land and raised money for construction of the Carnegie Library. The house is listed on the National Register of Historic Places.

Miles Conway Moore 1883 Mansion, 725 Bryant St.
Retailing, transportation and banking brought the family its wealth, but politics brought fame. Moore served as Walla Walla's mayor, and the last territorial governor. His large, three-story home features four chimneys, tall windows and unusual exterior ornamentation.

Ben Stone 1909 House, 1415 Modoc St.
The design of this "$5,000 fireproof home" was based on a work by Frank Lloyd Wright that was featured in "Ladies Home Journal."

Carnegie Center of the Arts, 109 South Palouse St. (509) 525-4270
This distinctive, red-brick building opened in 1905 as the Walla Walla Public Library. It was similar in style to the other 2,800 libraries that a Carnegie grant help found throughout the country. The library housed thousands of volumes and a special Northwest history collection. When the library outgrew this building, it became a community art museum. It was one of the first buildings in the city to be placed on the National Register of Historic Places. A monument behind the building commemorates the 1855 Indian Council organized by Territorial Governor Issac Stevens.

Sharpstein School
410 Howard, Walla Walla (509) 527-3098

Walla Walla students attended classes in this 1898 building for the last hundred years. Today, grades kindergarten through fifth are taught here. Pictures, books and other memorabilia are displayed on the school's main floor. Murals that students have painted over the years are also preserved.

St. Patrick's Roman Catholic Church
425 W. Adler, Walla Walla (509) 525-1602

This building was constructed in 1881 as St. Patrick's Church and was the original cathedral of the now repressed Diocese of Walla Walla.

Memorial Building
Whitman College, 345 Boyer Ave., Walla Walla

Washington State's oldest, and for some time its largest, post-secondary school, was founded at this site in 1859 by Congregational missionary, Cushing Eells. Eells named the school Whitman Seminary in honor of his fellow missionaries, Marcus and Narcissa Whitman, who were killed by Cayuse Indians in 1847 at nearby Wai-I-Lat-Pu. The 1889 Romanesque Revival Whitman Memorial Building, the college's oldest and most notable landmark is listed on the National Register of Historic Places.

On campus, near the Stanton Street entrance to the campus amphitheater, stands a monument to Hol-Lol-Sote-Tote a Nez Perce Indian chief known to the Americans as Chief Lawyer. This great chief provided protection and prevented an attack on Territorial Governor and Superintendent of Indian Affairs, Isaac Stevens when he attended a council meeting at this site in 1855 with thousands of Native Americans from nearby tribes.

An Oregon Trail Marker outside Prentiss Hall honors Narcissa Prentiss Whitman. Mrs. Whitman and Eliza Spalding, both missionaries' wives, made history in 1836 as the first women to cross the continent.

Wai-I-Lat-Pu Historical Marker
5 miles west of Walla Walla on U.S. 12

"A short distance to the south on the Walla Walla River at Wai-I-Lat-Pu, meaning 'The Place of Rye Grass,' is the site of a mission established by the reverend Doctor Marcus Whitman and his courageous wife, Narcissa. Faced with hardships in this new land, they brought the religion of the white man to the Indians and sought to teach them and administer to their ills until, during a period of Indian suspicion and skepticism, on the afternoon of November 29, 1847, Doctor Whitman and his wife with a number of others were massacred by Cayuse Indians."

Whitman Mission National Historic Site
6 miles west of Walla Walla on U.S. 12 (509) 522-6360

Dr. Marcus Whitman and his wife Narcissa came to the Oregon country in 1836 as Protestant missionaries to convert Native Americans to Christianity. At this site, they established a mission among the Cayuse, with a gristmill, sawmill and blacksmith shop. They grew wheat and corn; raised sheep, hogs and cattle; and harvested peaches and apples from their orchard. Their mission served as a way station on the Oregon Trail where immigrants were given refuge and their sick were treated. But, transforming the nomadic Indian into a Christian farmer, the primary purpose of the mission, met with little success.

As more immigrants came to the mission, the Cayuse became suspicious of the Whitmans, and began to doubt the true purpose of their ministry. In 1847, a wagon train of sick immigrants brought a measles epidemic to the mission. Indians, who had no resistance to the disease, began to die at an alarming rate. Although Dr.

Whitman's medicine helped white children, he couldn't cure the affected Indians. With half their number dead, the Cayuse attacked the mission and killed the Whitmans and eleven others.

The Whitman's courage would forever change the West. Narcissa Whitman, with Eliza Spalding, another missionary's wife, were the first white women to cross the continent overland.

Their bravery inspired others to also make the journey. Marcus Whitman led the first wagon train on the Oregon Trail from his mission to the Columbia River. His success in farming and ranching encouraged more settlers to come West. And, their deaths sparked Congress to create the Oregon Territory, the first territorial government west of the Rockies.

Artifacts recovered from the mission ruins, a segment of the original Oregon Trail, the foundation of the mission's adobe building, the common grave of those who perished in the massacre, and a memorial to the Whitmans can be seen here. Those who tour this historic site can get a sense for the hardships the Whitmans had to overcome and what they accomplished during their eleven years among the Cayuse. And they will know why, when the state of Washington was asked to send statues of the two most inspirational people in the state's history to Statuary Hall in Washington, DC, Dr. Whitman was one of the two selected. A replica of the statue can be seen in Walla Walla at the intersection of Main and Boyer Sts.

Drawing of scene at Whitman Mission,
Courtesy of Whitman Mission National Historic Site

Replica covered wagon on section of Oregon Trail, Whitman Mission National Historic Site

WALLULA (wuh-LOO-luh)

Fort Walla Walla Historical Marker
South of Wallula on the west side of U.S. 12

"To the west, at the junction of the Walla Walla and Columbia Rivers, is the site of a trading post built in 1818. Fort Walla Walla was a vital link in the region's fur trade, and helped open up the Northwest to the white man. From this post traders and trappers pushed into the rich Snake River Basin. Pioneers on the overland trek to the Oregon country in the 1840s found its farms a source of supply, and employees of the fort were among the area's first permanent settlers. The fort was abandoned by the Hudson's Bay Company at the start of the Indian War in 1855."

41

When the first wooden fort built at this site, originally called Fort Nez Perce, burned down in the early 1840s, the Hudson Bay Company using adobe made from local clay and ryegrass rebuilt the fort. Abandoned in 1855, the walls stood nearly 40 years until the 1894 flood of the Columbia River destroyed the fort leaving only the rock foundations to be seen today.

During the Idaho and Montana gold rush era in the early 1860s, this site, the first Wallula townsite, was a busy port of entry for thousands of prospectors who steamed up the Columbia River en route to the gold rush center in Walla Walla.

Whitman County

WHITMAN COUNTY

ALBION

Guy-Albion Historical Society Museum
Albion (509) 332-5609 Open by appointment only

Two rooms of the former brick school building now house the Historical Society's collections. Old photographs, clothing, tools and numerous small artifacts from early Albion families comprise the majority of items on display.

COLFAX

Manning Rye Covered Bridge
On Green Hollow Rd., at the outskirts of Colfax

One of the state's oldest covered railroad bridges now sits on private property. Although the century-old bridge, which is listed on the National Register of Historic Places, remains relatively intact, its fair condition makes it is only accessible by foot.

Manning Rye Covered Bridge

Perkins House
623 North Perkins St., Colfax (509) 397-2555 or (509) 397-3712

James A. Perkins settled here in 1870, built a squared-log cabin, and established the first homestead in this part of the Palouse River valley. He constructed the first sawmill in Colfax, used his cabin for the site of the first Republican convention in Whitman County and his sawmill for the first Democratic convention, opened the town's first bank, was elected mayor five times and served in the state legislature. In 1884, he began building this two-story Italianate-style frame house. The home, which is listed on the National Register of Historic Places, features four balconies, bay windows and extensive Italianate detail. Although the house was built without imported glass or wood, the fine attention to detail and sound construction from local material make it a treasure from the past. Many original and period furnishings can be found throughout the home that is being maintained by the Whitman County Historical Society. Perkins' original homestead cabin is also on the grounds.

Perkins' original homestead cabin

Colfax's Historic Main Street

Preserved along the main street of Colfax are several turn-of-the-century commercial buildings. Many owners used material from the local area when they constructed their buildings. Of particular interest is the brick, three-story 1889 Fraternity Block building. A horse in the building's basement powered its elevator.

Codger Pole
John Crawford Blvd. and Main St., Colfax (509) 397-3712

In the center of the town's business district stands the towering "Codger Pole, " the world's largest chainsaw carving. It was erected in honor of the men (the old codgers) who replayed a football game on the same field where they played 50

years before. Features of the players are carved around the pole with a statue of one of the players, in his 1938 uniform, standing on top. Their complete story has been etched in the granite blocks that surround the pole. One of the plaques reads, "The real stars were those brave souls who went back on to the field after fifty years, the Codgers."

Codger Pole

GARFIELD

McCroskey House
803 Fourth St., Garfield (509) 635-1459 or 878-1688 (Tours are available by calling in advance)

This large, two-story Victorian home was designed and built for State Senator Robert C. McCroskey and his family in 1897. The McCroskey family home served as headquarters for their 2000-acre wheat farm, and as a center for entertaining their many guests. McCroskey, a banker and one of Whitman County's most influential men, served as regent for the State College of Washington, the predecessor of Washington State University. This well-preserved mansion is listed on the National Register of Historic Places and is now operated as a day care center.

McCroskey House

OAKESDALE

Joseph Barron Flour Mill
103 East Jackson, Oakesdale (509) 285-4652

Piece-by-piece, this 1900s mill was moved from Illinois and reconstructed at this site by Joseph Barron. Grain was milled into flour until 1939. From then, until the mill closed in 1960, it was used for cleaning and storing grain. Barron's preserved mill is listed on the National Register of Historic Places and still houses the original milling and sifting equipment. Tours are available by appointment only.

Joseph Barron Flour Mill

McCoy Valley Museum

Fifth St. off Whitman, Oakesdale   Visits can be arranged by calling (509) 285-4691 or (509) 285-4239

James McCoy originally founded the town of Oakesdale in 1888 under the name, "McCoy Valley." The town became a central railroad hub when three major rail lines converged here: The Great Northern, Northern Pacific and Union Pacific. Today, Oakesdale is a farming community. But its past hasn't been forgotten. It's being preserved here in the form of artifacts, antiques, photographs, old books and memorabilia contributed by families who started it all. Information about tours to some of the city's historic neighborhoods can also be obtained form museum staff.

The Hanford Castle Bed & Breakfast

1/2 mile east of Oakesdale at the end of Roberts and Montana Rds. (509) 285-4120

The same architects who designed Spokane's Our Lady of Lourdes Cathedral and the Gonzaga University Administration Building were commissioned by Oakesdale banker, Edwin Hanford, in 1892 to draw plans for his impressive Victorian home. Owners of the "Castle," who are completely restoring the former mansion, offer tours that showcase the original conservatory and fountain. Guests at this Bed & Breakfast Inn stay in one of the home's restored rooms that have been appointed with furnishings of the period.

PALOUSE (puh-LOOS)

Boomerang Newspaper Museum

110 East Main, Palouse (509) 878-1688 or (509) 878-1309

Linotype machines and a 1900s flatbed letterpress are among the printing equipment on display from the county's first newspaper. The history of letterpress printing, old newspapers and other publications are exhibited.

Palouse Historic Main Street District

Main Street between "K" and Mary Sts., Palouse (800) 562-4570 (within Washington only)

Commercial businesses, industrial plants, mills, the railroad, and river commerce once made Palouse the commercial hub of the North Palouse River Valley. Trade with Idaho's gold mining and logging camps also contributed to the growth of the city in the 1880s. The central core of historic Palouse, its 19th century Main Street, features many one and two-story brick buildings that are listed on the National Register of Historic Places.

Kamiak Butte Historic Marker
3 miles southwest of Palouse on Hwy. 27

"Kamiak Butte was named for a famous Yakima chieftain. Its hard quartzite rock was once sand on the bottom of an ancient sea. Lifted by powerful forces, that ocean floor became this mountainous land. A few of the peaks rose far above the surrounding crests. Later, lava poured from fissures in the earth, slowly burying all but the highest parts of these mountains. In turn, during the ice age, a blanket of fine silt covered this lava, creating the fertile wheat lands of the Palouse."

Kamiak Butte County Park has been designated a National Natural Landmark. The park features a nature walk through the only forested area in this region. Plants and wild flowers line the trail to the top of the butte, which provides panoramic view of the Palouse Valley. Evening programs on the history of the area are presented during summer months

PULLMAN

Three Forks Pioneer Village Museum
Rossebo Pioneer Village Museum
Take Hwy. 27 one-half mile north from Pullman to Albion Rd. Turn left and follow Albion Road two miles to Anderson Rd. Turn right and stay on Anderson Road three miles to the Rossebo family farm and museum. Call (509) 332-3889 for appointment

By 1882, the settlement of "Three Forks" was an established townsite at the confluence of the Missouri Flat Creek, Dry Fork Creek and South Fork branch of the Palouse River. The history of Three Forks, renamed Pullman in 1884, is preserved in this restored pioneer village. Lining the main street are old store fronts of a general store, bank, blacksmith shop, saloon, harness and leather shop, hardware store, barber shop, jail, dentist/eye doctor's office, millinery and dry goods shoppe, doctor's office and an 1883 log cabin. And, the buildings are filled with thousands of antiques and artifacts from the 1800s, all of which are displayed in realistic settings. This outstanding private museum has been called "the Smithsonian of the Palouse."

Hardware Store and Jail at Rossebo's Pioneer Village Museum,
Courtesy Rossebo's Pioneer Village Museum

Washington State University
Thatuna St. and Campus Ave., Pullman

The "Washington Agricultural College, Experiment Station and School of Science" was established at this site in 1892 with sixty students. Today, it is the second-largest educational institution in the state. The two oldest buildings: Thompson Hall, erected in 1895; and Stevens Hall, erected in 1896, were both designed by the Seattle architectural firm of Stephen & Josenhans and are listed on the National Register of Historic Places. Sixteen museums are housed on campus including:

Museum of Anthropology, 110 College Hall (509) 335-8556. Discoveries of Pacific Northwest Indian culture made by WSU archaeologists are exhibited including skull fragments and artifacts from the Marmes Rock Shelter.

Heritage House, between Owen Library and Cleveland Hall (509) 335-8681. Artifacts that chronicle the history and achievements of Black Americans are showcased in the building's entrance hall.

A guide to campus buildings, museums, research laboratories, and the observatory may be obtained at the information kiosk or the Office of Information, 448 French Administration Building.

Clock tower, Washington State University

ROSALIA

Steptoe Memorial Park
Seventh St., Rosalia

A 26-foot-tall granite obelisk commemorates the site of the 1858 battle between Lt. Col. Steptoe's company of 158 First Dragoons, and 600-1200 Indians of the Spokane, Palouse and Coeur D'Alene tribes. On this battlefield, the Army suffered one of its worse defeats by Indians. Two officers, six enlisted men and an unknown number of Native Americans lost their lives.

51

Rosalia Museum
City Hall Building on 5th St. off Whitman, Rosalia

In 1858, fourteen years before the first settlers arrived to found the town of Rosalia, Major Edward J. Steptoe and his 156-man calvary unit fought hundreds of hostile Spokane, Palouse and Coeur D'Alene American Indians about a half-mile south of here in the battle of Te-Hots-Nim-Me. The American Army lost that fight and suffered one of the worse defeats of the 1858 Indian Wars. The story of that battle is told in the collections of the museum along with the history of Whitman County.

Rosalia Museum

Antique office equipment displayed at the Rosalia Museum

Steptoe Battlefield Historical Marker
1/2 Mile south of Rosalia on U.S. 195

"Here on May 17, 1858, 159 American soldiers, commanded by Lt. Col. E.J. Steptoe, engaged in a running fight with a large band of Spokane, Palouse and Coeur D'Alene Indians. Taking cover on a nearby hill, they beat off a series of attacks until night halted the battle. With ammunition almost gone and facing disaster, they retreated hurriedly with their wounded, and under cover of darkness, toward Fort Walla Walla. Steptoe's defeat was among the results of unenlightened dealings with the Indian tribes in this region. Later in the year the Indians were ruthlessly subjugated in a full-scale campaign."

STEPTOE

Steptoe Butte Historical Marker
South of Steptoe, 1/2 mile from the junction of Hwy. 23 and U.S. 195

"This butte was first called Pyramid Peak. It was named "Steptoe" for a commander (Lt. Col. Edward J. Steptoe) in the Indian wars at a battle in 1858 near the present town of Rosalia. In the 1880s James H. Davis built a resort and observatory on the Butte's top. A powerful telescope stood on the roof. He was called Cashup Davis, as he gave credit to no man. The town of Cashup was named for him. After Davis' death the hotel was lost by fire. In 1945 Virgil T. McCroskey donated the land to form Steptoe State Park. A road winds to the summit and a panoramic view of the Palouse Country."

A Registered National Landmark plaque is located at the summit of this peak.

TEKOA

Tekoa Museum
Crosby St., Tekoa (509) 284-2753 Open by appointment only

Relics from the towns' early days are exhibited in this former J.C. Penny building, now turned into a city library and museum. Included among the museum's exhibits are many household items, clothing from several periods, a horse-drawn buggy and the town's old jail. A large mural above the entrance guides visitors to the museum.

UNIONTOWN

St. Boniface Catholic Church
Uniontown (509) 229-3359

This imposing twin tower, brick structure is a symbol of the faith of the German Catholics who settled here in 1875. They laid the foundation for St. Boniface in 1893, but the depression that hit the country between 1893 and 1897 delayed its completion. Construction was completed in 1905, and, five years later, St. Boniface became the first consecrated church in the state. Its original stained glass windows have been preserved along with five altars, wooden pews and oil painted stations of the cross.

Ruddy-Collins House
5 miles southeast of Uniontown on US 95

Michael Ruddy built Whitman County's oldest house, in 1870-71. It was both a family home and a station for the Northwestern Stage Company until it was purchased by Orville Collins in 1884. Collins, a successful wheat farmer, also owned a feed store, manufactured bricks, and served as President of a bank in Idaho. The home is still owned by the Collins family.

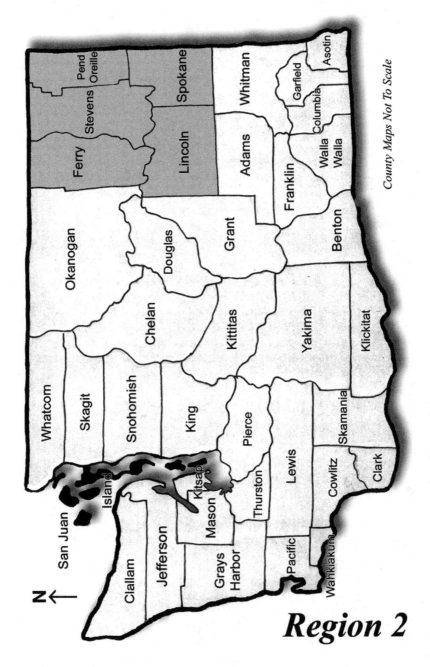

County Maps Not To Scale

Region 2

Ferry County

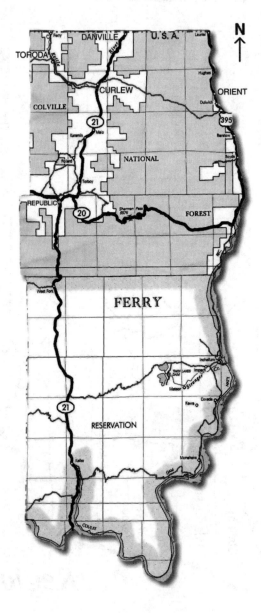

REGION 2

FERRY COUNTY

CURLEW (KER-loo)

Ansorge Hotel Museum
River St. and Railroad Ave., Curlew (509) 779-4955

Homesteaders, prospectors and travelers on the Great Northern Railroad who stopped at the Ansorge Hotel in the early 1900s were treated to an elegant stay. The 1903, thirteen-room hotel, now listed on the National Register of Historic Places, featured such luxuries as a gravity-fed water system and long-distance telephone service. One of the hotel's best-known guests was Henry Ford, who stayed here in 1917. Original furnishings have been preserved and can be seen throughout the hotel.

Interesting places to see in the Curlew area are: **St. Patrick's Catholic Church**, built in 1903; the home and grave site of **Chief Tonasket**, Chief of the Okanogan Indians; and two structures listed on the National Register of Historic Places: the **city's first schoolhouse** and the single-lane, **plank bridge** that spans the Kettle River.

DANVILLE

The Antique Car & Truck Museum
Hwy. 21 North, Danville (509) 779-4787, (509) 779-4204 or (509) 779-4648

The Kettle River History Club operates this museum, the first non-profit museum in the state, where fifty vintage cars and trucks are exhibited. Among the museum's treasures are: a 1913 Ford Brass Touring car in its original state; A Howard Cooper, one of four ever built; the late Walter Brennen's 1928 Ford Phaeton; and a 1926 Yellow Knight, one of five in existence.

ORIENT

Orient Historic District

Gold ore from the First Thought, Big Nine, Gold Stake, Easter Sunday and Little Gem mines brought prosperity and a boom to the town of Orient in the early 1900s. Although the mines produced millions (The **First Thought Mine** was a major producer of lode gold for nearly 40 years), it wasn't enough to keep the town viable once the gold played out. A scattering of buildings remains from the period. The 1910 **brick schoolhouse**, one of the town's finest structures, is listed on the National Register of Historic Places.

REPUBLIC

Stonerose Interpretive Center
61 N. Kean St., Republic (509) 775-2295

In prehistoric times, the land around today's town of Republic was the bottom of an ancient lake bed. For millions of years, layers of volcanic ash, sediment, and everything that fell into the lake built up on the lake bottom. As the layers hardened, leaves, insects, fish and other organisms left their impressions in the rocks that formed. Examples of fossils discovered in this area and the geological history of the region is exhibited in the Center. Visitors who want to dig for fossils at nearby Boot Hill Fossil Site can get a permit at the Center where tools are also available to rent.

Million-year-old fossil, Courtesy of Stonerose Interpretive Center

Ferry County Historical Society Museum
Kean and 6th Sts., Republic (509) 775-3888

The 1911 home of Dr. and Mrs. Fred Whitaker, Republic's physician and surgeon from 1911-17, now houses the Ferry County Historical Society, **Stonerose Interpretive Center**, Eureka Arts and the Tourist Information Center. The historical society exhibits a pictorial history of the city that includes the "boom and bust" 1890s gold rush period and the devastating fires that plagued the city from 1899 until well into the twentieth century.

Republic's oldest surviving structure, the 1896 **Kaufman squared-log cabin**, is preserved on the grounds. Kaufman, a local miner, helped form the city of Eureka (which was later renamed Republic).

Historic Republic Walking Tour
Ferry County Historical Society, Kean and 6th Sts., Republic (509) 775-3888

The interesting history of more than four dozen of Republic's pioneer businesses and homes is well-documented by the historical society in their guide, "Historic Republic Walking Tour." In those cases where a replacement building was erected, the guide includes the history and description of the original building.

TORODA

Ranald MacDonald's Grave
Indian cemetery, one mile north of Toroda on the West Side of the Kettle River.

Ranald MacDonald, the son of a Hudson's Bay Company factor and an Indian chief's daughter, traveled to Japan in the late 1840s, a time when that country was closed to most foreigners. To get on Japanese soil, MacDonald faked a shipwreck and rowed a small boat to shore. While under house arrest in Nagasaki, he taught English to Japanese youth and a small class of interpreters. His students acted as interpreters when Commodore Perry arrived in Japan in 1853 to negotiate a trade treaty. MacDonald is credited with helping to open Japan to the rest of the world.

Lincoln County

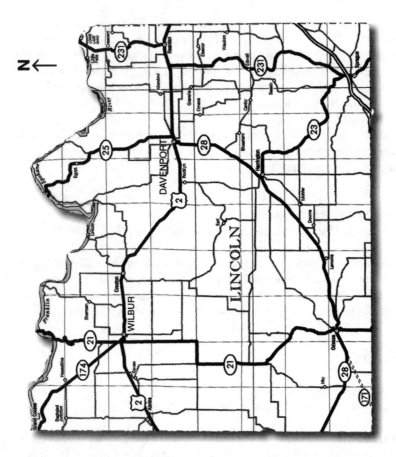

LINCOLN COUNTY

DAVENPORT

Lincoln County Historical Museum
Park and 7th Sts., Davenport (509) 725-6711

Long before settlers turned this area into fields of wheat, local Indians would camp here, and prospectors would pass this way on their way to the gold fields of Montana. Indian artifacts, period furniture, tools, old photographs, and one of the finest collections of steam engines and horse-powered agricultural equipment in the state tell the history of the region from its earliest times to the present.

Nearby is a well-preserved 1879 log building, the county's first schoolhouse. Originally built as a homestead cabin, the owner, W. G. McClure, moved out in 1883 so it could be used as a schoolhouse. Several years later the school district constructed a new building and McClure moved back into the cabin. In 1954, the Davenport High School student body made preservation of the old schoolhouse a class project. Through their efforts a part of history that touched the lives of so many of the town's families has been preserved.

Lincoln County School District No. 1 First Schoolhouse, Courtesy of Lincoln County Historical Museum and the Davenport Visitor Information Center

Lincoln County Courthouse
4th and Logan Sts., Davenport

A bitter dispute over the county seat raged for several years between Davenport and Sprague. Charges of election fraud, armed confrontations and theft of county records brought the issue before the state legislature, which named Davenport the county seat in 1896. A year later, this brick and limestone, Classic Revival-style courthouse was erected.

Several striking turn-of-the-century houses can be seen in the older residential area across the highway from the courthouse including: the grand 1899 McInnis Queen Anne-style home at 1001 Morgan Street; the Fry house at 9th and Marshall, with three-foot thick walls, and the c.1896 Hoople house and its elaborately trimmed front porch

Fort Spokane
44304 State Route 25 North
21 miles north of Davenport on the west side of Hwy. 25 (509) 725-2715

The task of keeping Indians on reservations, and keeping settlers off Indian grounds fell to the troops of the 2nd, 4th and 16th Infantry and 2nd Calvary who were stationed here between 1880 and 1898. When the United States went to war with Spain in 1898, the entire garrison was moved to Fort George Wright near Spokane. During the next 30 years the fort was used as an Indian agency headquarters, school and hospital.

Only four of the original 45 buildings remained intact when the fort was transferred to the National Park Service in 1960 for restoration. Today, the 1892 brick guardhouse serves as the fort's visitor center and museum. A 1 1/2-mile self-guided interpretive trail includes several trail side exhibits: the 1884 quartermaster mule stable, a massive structure that housed 94 mules; 1888 powder magazine; and an 1889, 150,000-gallon water reservoir. Original historic documents, early photographs, uniforms and Indian artifacts are exhibited at this state registered historic landmark.

WILBUR

Big Bend Historical Society Museum
One block north of Main St. at the West End of town, Wilbur (509) 647-5772

"Wild Goose" Bill Condon, the town's founding father, was killed in a shoot-out over a woman in January 1895. His gun, and other local memorabilia, is displayed in this former church building-turned-museum. More than 100 years of the town's history can be traced in the collection of newspapers maintained in the museum's archives.

Pend Oreille County

PEND OREILLE COUNTY *(PAHN-do-RAY)*

NEWPORT

Pend Oreille County Historical Society Museum
4th and Washington Sts., Newport (509) 447-5388

Newport, the seat of Pend Oreille County, began as a settlement in 1889 around a small store in Idaho. Three years later, the Great Northern Railway established a station near the original store. On the other side of town, which happened to be in Washington State, the I&WN (Idaho & Washington Northern Railroad) built this depot. When the Great Northern's first station burned, they erected their new depot in Washington next to the I&WN depot, and the town of Newport officially "moved" to Washington.

The history of the I&WN, one of the most elegant lines in the Pacific Northwest, and a vast collection of Pend Oreille County memorabilia is exhibited by the historical society in the former 1908, I&WN depot and other museum buildings at this site. An original settler's log cabin and one-room log schoolhouse were re-erected here and have been completely furnished with period pieces. A train caboose houses the museum's railroad display. Pioneer farm and logging machines can also be seen on the grounds.

The 1910 Great Northern depot, now home to the Stimson Lumber Company, is located in nearby Centennial Plaza.

2236 I. & W. N. Depot, Newport, Wash.

Historic photo of I. & W.N. Depot, Courtesy of Pend Oreille County Historical Society Museum

The Big Wheel
W. 4th St., one block east of Hwy. 2, Newport

Timber from Idaho and Northeast Washington was cut into a billion feet of lumber at the sawmill powered by this Corliss steam engine and its 16-foot flywheel.

Settler's Log Home Museum
Pend Oreille County Fairgrounds, 18 miles west of Newport on Hwy. 20, Cusick

Furnishings, housewares and clothing from the early twentieth century is displayed in this two-story homesteader's log cabin and is open to the public during the annual pioneer picnic (first Sunday after July 4th) and the five-day county fair in late August.

RUBY

David Thompson Historical Marker
Hwy. 20, one mile north of Ruby

"In the historic race between British and American fur traders for control of Columbia River trading, David Thompson, a partner of North West Company, was first to travel the Columbia from source to mouth. Energetic explorer, surveyor and mapper, he founded Kootenay House in Canada, the first trading post on the Columbia, in 1807, Spokane House in 1810, and first mapped the Pend Oreille, Snake and other rivers in the Columbia Basin, claiming the entire region for Great Britain."

When Thompson retired in 1812, at the age of forty-two, he had spent more than half his life exploring the Pacific Northwest. In addition to his accomplishments in what is now the State of Washington, he mapped the Thompson River in British Columbia, which was named in his honor, and built Kullyspell House, Idaho's first building erected by white men.

USK   (UHSK)

Kalispel Indian Caves
5 miles north of Usk on the side of a cliff along the LeClerc Hwy., on the Kalispel Indian Reservation

These natural rock caves were used as a gathering place by local Indians, and for missionary work by Father Peter Jean de Smet in 1840-41. Father de Smet and Father Hoecken also built St. Ignatius Mission near here on the bank of the Pend Oreille River, only to have it washed away by heavy spring rains. The caves are listed on the National Register of Historic Places.

Spokane County

SPOKANE COUNTY

CHENEY

F.M. Martin Milling Company
601 First St., Cheney

During the 1900s the Martin Flour Mill was the largest and most productive flour mill of its type in the state. By the end of World War I in 1918, the mill was producing 1,000 barrels a day. This structure, erected in 1918-19, was the second mill built in Cheney by the Martin family. The most prominent member of the Martin family, and one-time owner of the mill, was Clarence Martin, governor of the state from 1932 to 1940.

Cheney Interurban Depot
505 Second St., Cheney

In the years before automobile travel became popular, and practical, Washington Water Power Company operated an electric commuter railroad between Cheney, Spokane and the well-known summer resort at Medical Lake. From 1907 to 1922, thousands of passengers crossed the platform of this historic station. In 1979, the depot was added to the National Register of Historic Places.

Sutton Barn
Eastern Washington University campus, Washington and Seventh Sts., Cheney

Eastern Washington University's roots can be traced to 1881 when the Benjamin P. Cheney Academy was founded. In 1890, when the academy became a state-supported training institution for teachers, its name was changed to Cheney Normal School. This c.1884 double-walled barn, which was once part of the estate of State Senator William Sutton, vice-president of the school, now houses the university's information office and campus police department. The impressive "Big Red Barn" is listed on the National Register of Historic Places.

Showalter Hall was constructed on the original academy site in 1915. The entryway to this Renaissance-style building contains stones from the granite foundation of the original Cheney Normal School building that was destroyed by fire in 1912.

Also on the campus is the **Museum of Anthropology** (509) 359-6200. Exhibits illustrate the history of American Indian and Eskimo settlement in North America.

David Lowe House
306 "F" St., Cheney

One of the city's most imposing homes is this Queen Anne-style Victorian, built in 1904 by David Lowe. Lowe was a successful farmer who was also active in Cheney's real estate market. Lowe's home and carriage house is listed on the National Register of Historic Places.

Cheney Electric Light Works
Liefer Apartments, 701 1st St., Cheney

Cheney established itself as major agriculture, railroad and education center in the late 1800s. Sparking the growth of the city was its first electric generating station, which was established with the construction of this plant in 1890-91. Its smokestack, generator and dynamos have long since been removed, and the building renovated into apartments. But the important role it played in the development of the city has been underscored by its preservation as a local historic landmark.

*Electric Light Works, Courtesy of Office of Archaeology and
Historic Preservation, City of Cheney*

Cheney Historical Museum
614 3rd St., Cheney

Cheney Historical Museum was founded in 1935 by the ladies of the Tillicum Club and is often referred to as the "Cheney Tillicum Museum." Displays featuring pioneer items from Cheney and the surrounding area tell the history of the first settlers, higher education, and the region's commerce and industry.

Cheney's Historic Properties
Community Development Department, 609 Second St., Cheney (509) 235-7315

The Cheney Historic Preservation Commission and Cheney Planning Office list private and public city buildings of historic interest in their "Guide to Historic Cheney." Among the structures listed is: the Northern Pacific Depot, one of the few Mission Revival-style stations in the state; the boyhood home and office of former governor Clarence Martin; and buildings listed on the State and National Register of Historic Places.

FOUR LAKES

Battle of Four Lakes Monument
One block west of the Cheney Hwy., one block north of the Medical Lake-Four Lakes Road, across the intersection from the post office, Four Lakes

Near this site, on September 1, 1858, Col. George Wright and his company of 700 American soldiers were attacked by a large band of Indian braves. The four-day running battle that ensued involved more than a thousand Indians and covered over 40 miles. The Indians were defeated September 5th, on the Spokane Plains Battlefield, west of Spokane. Four Lakes Battlefield is listed on the State Register of Historic Places.

LATAH (LAY-tah)

William McEachern Home
Pine and Fifth Sts., Latah

The Bank of Latah was founded in 1906 by William McEachern, who owned this showcase Queen Anne-style Victorian home. McEachern's home, the grandest in the area, is listed on the National Register of Historic Places. Several c.1900s commercial buildings and the White Swan Hotel can be seen along the town's Market Street. Nearby, at the crown of a hill, is an abandoned brick, 2-story schoolhouse.

MEDICAL LAKE

Hallett's Castle
1900 East 623 Lake St., Medical Lake

Tourists traveled to Medical Lake in the early 1900s on electric commuter trains from Cheney and Spokane for recreational and health reasons. Some came for the medical benefits of the salt lake; others for the big band entertainment at the city's dance halls. In 1900, an English emigrant and the town's first mayor, Stanley Hallett, designed and built this three-story brick "castle" as his residence and the center of his political activities. The third floor had a ballroom with a grand piano that had been shipped around the Horn. On the grounds were a tennis court, ice house and barn. Hallett went on to become a Spokane County Commissioner and Washington State Senator.

MICA (MEYE-kuh)

California Ranch
East of Mica on Jackson and Belmont Rds., Mica

One of the oldest farms in Spokane County was established at this site along the Kentuck Trail around 1864. It was one of the few places where settlers, and miners who followed this trail between Walla Walla and the Montana gold mines, could get supplies and lodging. The hand-hewn, c.1870-80s log barn still stands at this ranch which is listed on the National Register of Historic Places.

71

SPOKANE *(spoh-KAN)*

Spokane Visitor Information Center

West 926 Sprague Ave., Spokane (800) 248-3230

Guides to places to visit in the local area, historic sites, detailed maps, day trips, restaurants, hotels, motels, camping areas, entertainment, local events and other helpful information is available here.

Spokane House Interpretive Center

Riverside State Park, one mile north of Ninemile Falls on Hwy. 291 (12 miles northwest of Spokane) (509) 456-3964

The first permanent white settlement in what is now Washington State was established at this site in 1810 with the construction of Spokane House. The white men who built this fur trading post were under the direction of David Thompson, a Canadian and partner in the North West Company. For nearly 16 years furs from the wilderness were traded and expeditions outfitted at this post. Furs were shipped from here down the Columbia River to ships that would take them to China and north through Canada to Lake Superior for shipment to England. The Interpretive Center exhibits the history of fur trade in the Pacific Northwest and the Spokane House, which is listed on the National Register of Historic Places.

Just northwest of the Center is a c.1850-60 log building, considered to be the oldest existing log structure in Spokane County.

Drumheller Springs

Euclid Ave. and Maple St., Spokane

The springs at this site were an important source of water for Indians and settlers traveling between Spokane House and the falls on the Spokane River. The site is listed on the National Register of Historic Places.

Peaceful Valley Historic District
Between the Monroe and Maple St. Bridges, north of Riverside Ave., Spokane

Before the white man erected the first dwellings along this stretch of the Spokane River, it was an Indian campground and a good area for salmon fishing. In 1891, Franz Pietsch built the valley's brick house in this neighborhood at the corner of Main and Ontario streets. Other homes constructed in this blue-collar residential district were small, two-bedroom rentals. Peaceful Valley is listed on the National Register of Historic Places.

Occident School
Grove and Greenwood Sts., Spokane

One of the first Spokane structures listed on the State Register of Historic Places was this "little red schoolhouse." Built in 1902, it was typical of the wood frame, one-room schools where children of every age were taught in the same room.

Review Building
Monroe and Riverside Sts., Spokane

The unusual style of this brick and terra cotta building has made it one of the city's most recognized landmarks. Constructed in 1890, a year after the city's disastrous fire, it reigned for a decade as the city's tallest structure. Although tours can no longer be made to the tower a visit to the building is worth the stop. The ground floor's enchanting interior design remains virtually unchanged from the original design.

Four Corners
Spokane Falls and Howard Sts., Spokane

James N. Glover arrived at Spokan Falls in May 1873, and purchased a 160-acre squatter's claim from Seth Scranton and John Downing. Although Scranton and Downing were the first to build in Spokane Falls (they constructed a saw mill downstream in 1871), Glover is considered the first permanent resident and is called the "Father of Spokane." In November 1873, Glover opened his first store at this intersection. Three years later he constructed a two-story building on the southwest corner that housed a post office, bank, city hall, theatre, and meeting hall. On February 13, 1878, Glover filed the plat of Spokan Falls, and the city was officially born. This intersection, the hub of the new community, is listed on the State Register of Historic Places.

Spokane Club
1002 Riverside Ave., Spokane

Construction of this dark red brick, Georgian Revival-style building, with its white glazed terra cotta trim was completed in 1910 for members of the Spokane Club. The club decor includes period furnishings that complement the purpose of each room. Inside the paneled library is the second-largest fireplace in the state. Outside the club is a statue honoring Ensign John Monaghan, the young Navy hero from Chewelah who gave his life in the line of duty during the Spanish-American War.

Next door, at 1020 Riverside Avenue, in the 1921 Italian Renaissance-style building is Spokane's Chamber of Commerce. An interesting decorative feature is the design of Indian faces at the top of the building's columns.

Our Lady of Lourdes Cathedral
1115 West Riverside Ave., Spokane

One of the most impressive church buildings in the city is this late Romanesque revival-style Roman Catholic Church. Built between 1902-08, it is the oldest existing Roman Catholic Church in the Inland Empire. The church's striking granite and brick exterior, with its two square towers, is matched by an equally magnificent interior.

Davenport Hotel
West 807 Sprague Ave., Spokane

Louie Davenport's 1902 restaurant and adjoining 1914 hotel were known for more than just its imposing Mission-style architecture and lavishly appointed rooms. The amenities and service were "five-star." It was considered by many to be the grandest hotel in the Pacific Northwest. Former guests of the hotel included several U.S. Presidents and foreign heads-of-state. The Davenport is no longer an operating hotel, but remains an important landmark in Spokane's history. The hotel and restaurant are listed on the National Register of Historic Places.

James N. Glover House
West 321 Eighth Ave., Spokane

Kirtland Cutter, the well-known architect of many of the city's finest homes, designed his first mansion for Spokane's founding father, James Glover. The English-style home was built for Glover in 1888, but he lost it in the financial Panic of 1893. Today, it houses the administrative offices of the Unitarian Church of Spokane. None of the original furnishings remain, but the home, which is listed on the National Register of Historic Places, is open to the public.

Browne's Addition Historic District
Bordered by Maple, Sunset, Couer d'Alene and Riverside Sts., west of downtown Spokane

Many of Spokane's finest homes built during the period from the 1880s to 1930s were constructed in this upper-class residential section of Spokane. A wide variety of architectural styles can be viewed in this well-preserved neighborhood. In addition to the district's listing on the National Register of Historic Places, several homes within the district are also listed individually.

Daniel Dwight House, 1887 Queen Anne, West 1905 Pacific Ave.
Dwight was successful in real estate and banking. He donated his summer home "Brookside" for the Finch Arboretum, and the tower chimes to Westminister Congregational Church.

Edward Roberts Home, c.1886, West 2027 First Ave.
A well-known civil engineer, Roberts constructed the Canadian Pacific Railroad through the Selkirk Mountains from Winnipeg to Vancouver.

Jay Graves House, 1900 Georgian Revival, West 2123 First Ave.
Real estate and mining brought fortune to Graves. He donated the land and brought Whitwood College to Spokane from Tacoma. After Graves sold this home to Aubrey White, he moved to a 1000-acre estate in the Selheim Springs area on the Little Spokane River.

Campbell House, 1898 Tudor Revival, West 2316 First Ave.
Listed on the National Register of Historic Places and part of the Cheney Cowles Museum. Amasa Campbell's wealth came from the gold mines of the Coeur d'Alene. (See listing that follows for the Cheney Cowles Memorial Museum.)

Campbell House

John Finch Mansion, 1898 Colonial Revival, West 2340 First Ave.
Finch made his money in mining, hardware, fruit and lumber. He was also a business associate of Amasa Campbell. Finch's home is listed on the National Register of Historic Places.

Patsy Clark Mansion (Patrick Clark Mansion), 1898, West 2208 Second Ave.
The Clark family also made their fortune in the mining business. Their architect, Kirtland Cutter, toured Europe for the Clarks and incorporated several architectural styles in his design for their mansion. The glamorous interior was decorated with Tiffany chandeliers, stained glass windows, Onyx fireplaces, and Turkish rugs. In 1981, the new owners converted the Clark's 3½-story home into a restaurant. It still retains its turn-of-the-century appearance and atmosphere.

Fortheringham House, 1891
West 2124 Second Ave.

In the early 1890s, while their mansion was being built across the street, the Clark family lived in this Victorian home. Today, the owners once again provide a place for others to eat and stay. They operate the home as a bed-and-breakfast inn.

Couer d'Alene Park
Bounded by West Fourth, South Spruce. South Chestnut and West Second.

Spokane's first park was established here in 1891. J. J. Browne and A.M. Cannon donated this parcel of land to the city from Browne's original homestead tract. Other Browne's Addition residents were also generous contributors. Patrick "Patsy" Clark donated the exquisite altar and altar rail to Our Lady of Lourdes Cathedral in Spokane. His brother's widow, Mrs. James Clark, donated one of the church's stained glass windows.

Cheney Cowles Memorial Museum
West 2316 First Ave., Spokane (509) 456-3931

The Eastern Washington State Historical Society administers both this museum and the adjacent Campbell House. The main museum building was given to the city of Spokane by the Cowles family as a memorial to their son, Maj. Cheney Cowles, who lost his life in World War II. Development of the region's culture and economy from early Indian times to the Twentieth Century is exhibited in several theme areas in the main gallery. Archaeological artifacts, pioneer relics, Native American arts

77

and crafts, and an extensive photographic collection are included in the society's changing history displays.

Original furnishings and family heirlooms are preserved in the adjoining 1898 home of Amasa Campbell. A grand example of Spokane's "age of elegance" can be seen in every room of this elegantly restored mansion.

A guide to the other homes in this historic district is available at the museum.

Cheney Cowles Memorial Museum

Cowley Park
South Division St., between Sixth and Seventh Aves., Spokane

Reverend Cowley, a Presbyterian minister, was one of the first to settle in this region with his family. He founded Spokan Falls first public school and the city's first school district in 1875. In the beginning, classes were conducted in his home for Indian students and children from the town. Rev. Cowley's influence on the early development of Spokane is memorialized by this monument in the City Park that bears his name. The site of Rev. Cowley's first school is a National Registered Historic Landmark.

The Cathedral of St. John the Evangelist
East 127 12th Ave., Spokane (509) 838-4277

Lemuel Henry Wells, Spokane's first Episcopal Bishop, laid this Cathedral's foundation stone on June 10, 1928. Stones from the All Saints Cathedral, which once stood in downtown Spokane, are part of this foundation stone. In December

1969, 44 years after construction began on the Cathedral, the final structure, the carillon, was dedicated. Within the Cathedral visitors can see: a memorial to those who gave their lives "for freedom and Christ;" an archives room with artifacts and displays featuring the history of Spokane and the Cathedral; and beautiful stained glass windows and carvings depicting prominent events in the life of Christ, figures from the Old and New Testaments, the Holy Trinity, and the history of the church. Tours of the Cathedral are conducted throughout the week and after the main service on Sunday.

Spokane County Courthouse
West 1116 Broadway Ave., Spokane

It was considered one of the most beautiful county courthouse buildings in the West when constructed in 1895. Willis A. Ritchie, chose a French Renaissance style for his design, an unusual style for this part of the Pacific Northwest. Ritchie, who learned his profession through a correspondence course from the superintendent of architecture in the U.S. Treasury Department, also designed the Jefferson County Courthouse in Port Townsend and the State Capitol Building in Olympia.

Jay P. Graves Estate
Waikiki Retreat House, North 12415 Fairwood Dr., Spokane

Graves moved from his mansion in the exclusive Browne's Addition area of Spokane to the former estate of William E. Hall. He hired Spokane's well-known residential architect, Kirtland Cutter, and the country's most famous civic landscape architects, the Olmstead brothers, to design the "finest country estate" in the Pacific Northwest. When completed, his 1000-acre "farm" included a formal garden, wildlife sanctuary, observatory and an English Tudor country manor. The home, which in more recent times served as a retreat for Gonzaga University, is listed on the National Register of Historic Places.

Gonzaga University
Bing Crosby Library, East 502 Boone, Spokane (509) 328-4220

Father Joseph Cataldo, a Jesuit missionary, who established St. Michael's Mission east of Spokane Falls in 1877, began building Gonzaga University in 1881. The original mission of the university was to bring higher education opportunities to the region's Native Americans. First classes began in 1887. The university's library contains a large collection of early books and historic Northwest Territory documents.

The school's Crosby Library was a gift from Bing Crosby, the school's most famous alumnus. A museum of Crosby memorabilia includes his Oscar for "Going My Way," gold and platinum records, photographs, awards and trophies, and some of the entertainer's personal items. Crosby's boyhood home at East 508 Sharp is home to the Gonzaga Alumni Association.

James Monaghan's 1902, 14-room home at East 217 Boone Avenue is home to Gonzaga University's Music Conservatory. Monaghan was involved in Spokane's early mining and railroads, and planted the first apple trees in the county. His son, John, was one of the first students to attend the university.

Museum of Native American Culture
East 200 Cataldo, Spokane

History of Native Americans of the Western Hemisphere, from Alaska to Peru is preserved in the collections of this world-famous museum. Pre-Columbian ceramics and textiles, goldworks from Latin America, Northwest Indian cedar carvings, copper drums, and ceremonial masks, are but a small sample of the many types of artifacts on display. The museum houses the nation's largest collection of North American trade beads, war bonnets as well as fine nineteenth and twentieth century western art.

Corbin Park
Waverly and Park Place at the foot of North Hill, Spokane

Citizens of Spokane Falls raised $5,000 in 1887 to build the city's first horse race track and stables at this site. They added grandstands and other buildings and established the city's first fair grounds. When the city moved the track and fairgrounds, D.C. Corbin purchased the property for a housing development, but left the old race tract as Corbin Park. The site is listed on the State Register of Historic Places.

The Carousel
Riverfront Park, Spokane

At the turn-of-the-century, Natatorium Park, affectionately called "The Nat," was a popular amusement park with rides, municipal pool, and "big band" entertainment at the Pavilion. In 1909, this $20,000, handcrafted carousel was opened to the public. Charles I.D. Looff, who built Coney Island's first carousel in 1876, designed and hand-carved the giraffe, tiger, two Chinese dragon chairs and the 54 horses that would ride on the carousel. Looff's carousel also featured a 300-pipe organ, imported German cut glass, over 330 mirrors and a ring arm with steel and brass rings. Natatorium Park has since closed, but the fully-restored merry-go-round, one of the last remaining Looff carousels in the world, can still be enjoyed here at Riverfront Park where it was relocated in 1975. The only noticeable difference is that the price of a ride is no longer a nickel.

Fire of 1889 Historical Marker
South end of the suspension bridge, Spokane

A plaque at this site describes the disastrous fire that began the evening of August 4, 1889 in a restaurant on Railroad Avenue and consumed 32 blocks of the city's business district by the next morning. No lives were lost, but property damage was estimated at $6,000,000. Businesses established a tent city and immediately began rebuilding. Within a year, the city had nearly 100 new business buildings and a 50% increase in population.

Monroe Street Bridge
Spanning the Spokane River, Spokane

The present concrete bridge was the third to cross the river at this site. When constructed in 1911, it was the longest concrete arch bridge in the United States, and the third longest in the world. Its single center span measures 281 feet long and is 136 feet high. The arches over the sidewalks feature a buffalo head motif.

City Hall
West 808 Spokane Falls Blvd., Spokane

Spokan Falls pioneer sites are identified on a relief map displayed west of the city hall on Spokane Falls Blvd. Another plaque, on the Post and Spokane Falls corner of the city hall building identifies those who lived at this site before the present building was constructed as a department store in 1929.

Flour Mill
West 621 Mallon, Spokane

This brick building was one of the first flourmills built west of the Mississippi. Constructed in 1895-96, it originally used water from the Spokane River for power. It was converted to electric power in the mid-1930s. In 1973, the mill's machinery was removed and the seven-story building remodeled into restaurants, retail shops and offices. Some remnants from the original mill's interior were left intact and can be seen today in this National Registered Historic Place.

Great Northern Depot Clock Tower
Havermale Island, Stevens and Washington Sts., Spokane

James Hill, king of the "empire builders," acquired a right-of-way into Spokane for his Great Northern Railroad in 1893. When construction of the Great Northern's depot was completed at this site in 1902, it was considered the "finest railroad station west of Chicago." The landmark, 155-foot clock tower was left standing after the depot closed in 1972 to serve as a reminder of the contribution railroads made to the development of the Inland Empire. The tower is listed on the State Register of Historic Places.

Indian Rock Paintings Historical Marker
North of the Rutter Parkway Bridge over the Little Spokane River

"Such paintings are found in all parts of western North America. Present-day tribes usually deny knowledge of their origin, but they must be the works of Indians, for prior to Europeans, no other peoples are known to have inhabited this region. Their meanings are obscure but they are considered to be hunting records; notes of inter-tribe meetings; or expressions of religious experiences. Area was given to the State Park Commission by Professor and Mrs. H.M. Hart, Jr. Mrs. Hunt was the daughter of Aubrey White, founder of the Spokane park system." These early Indian petroglyphs are listed on the National Register of Historic places.

The Hutton Settlement Children's Home
East 9907 Wellesley, Spokane (administrative offices at West 422 Riverside, Suite 901, Spokane)

Neither Levi or May Hutton came from well-to-do families. Levi was an orphan; May was raised in a fatherless home. Levi became a narrow-gauge railroad engineer and May a cook in a Coeur d'Alene mining town. They "grubstaked" the miner who discovered the richest silver ore in the Coeur d'Alene region. With their new wealth they built the 1907 Hutton Building in Spokane, supported labor union causes, and programs to help unwed mothers and homeless children. May campaigned successfully for the women's right to vote in Washington State. In 1918, Levi and May Hutton financed the construction of the Hutton Settlement, a private orphanage, on this 364-acre site in the Spokane Valley. An endowment from the Hutton estate enables this home to operate today without federal funding. Both this settlement and the Hutton Building are listed on the National Register of Historic Places.

Royal Riblet Mansion
Arbor Crest Winery, 4505 Fruithill, Spokane (509) 489-0588

When constructed in 1924-25, this grand residence featured the latest, most up-to-date electrical luxuries, including an electric tramway that spanned the Spokane River. For more than 30 years, the tram was the only way to reach the estate, which is perched atop a 425-foot cliff. The Riblet brothers, Royal and Byron, were both inventors. Byron invented the mechanism used for ski lifts. The restored mansion and well-maintained grounds is listed on the National Register of Historic Places and is now home to the Arbor Crest Winery.

Plante's Ferry
Plante's Ferry County Park, 12308 Upriver Dr., Spokane

Antoine Plant settled here in 1851 and established a ferry to provide passage across the Spokane River. Plante's Ferry was an important link along the Mullan Road that connected Walla Walla with the gold mines of the Coeur d'Alenes and Bitterroot Mountains, and Fort Benson on the Missouri River. A section of the old Mullan Road can be followed along the ravine up to the cement post that marks the location of the original wooden ferry post. In 1864 a permanent bridge was built to cross the river at Spokane Bridge, which took most of the business away from Plant. Plante's Ferry is listed on the State Register of Historic Places.

Fort George Wright
Fort George Wright Historic District
Government Way and Ft. George Wright Dr., Spokane

Fort George Wright was established in 1894 on the site of the Spokane Plains Battlefield where Col. George Wright's army troops fought and defeated a large band of Indians in 1858. When the Spanish-American War broke out in 1898, Fort Spokane closed and its troops relocated here. The fort was home to the Army's Fourth Infantry until 1941, when it was converted to an Air Force base. After the base closed in 1958, Fort Wright College was established on the grounds. Today, Mukogawa Fort Wright Institute, the U.S. branch of Mukogawa Women's University in Nishinomyia, Japan, owns the property. Nineteen of the fort's original brick and Victorian buildings are preserved in this historic district and are listed on the National Register of Historic Places.

Spokane Plains Battlefield
Monument located on north side of U.S. 2 at Brooks Rd., west of the main entrance to Fairchild Air Force Base

In May, 1858, a thousand Coeur d'Alene, Yakima, Nez Perce, Palouse and Spokane Indians attacked and defeated Col. Edward Steptoe and 150 soldiers under his command in a battle near the present town of Rosalia, about 35 miles south of this site. Seven Americans and an unknown number of Indians were killed. On August 7th, Col. George Wright was dispatched from Walla Walla with 700 troops to locate and punish the Indians responsible for this unprovoked attack.

The decisive battle between Indians from these tribes and the U.S. Army troops commanded by Col. Wright took place near this marker on September 5, 1858. Col. Wright's well-trained troops, with their superior weapons and artillery, defeated the Indians after a four-day running battle that began at Four Lakes. Spokane Plains Battlefield is listed on the State Register of Historic Places.

SPOKANE BRIDGE

Spokane Bridge Monument
Washington State Information Center and Rest Area, north side of I-90, west of the Idaho State line.

The town of Spokane Bridge gained prominence in the early 1860s with the construction of a bridge that spanned the Spokane River near this site. When the bridge was opened in 1864, it became part of the Mullan Road, the main route of travel between Walla Walla and western Idaho. In 1867, the first post office in what is now Spokane County was opened in a log building at the southern approach to the bridge. A monument commemorates the importance of Spokane Bridge, one of Washington's registered places of historic interest.

Horse Slaughter Camp Monument
West side of the I-90 truck scales, near the Idaho State line.

Col. George Wright's ultimate defeat of the hostile Coeur d'Alene, Palouse, and Spokane Indians came, not from the annihilation of their braves on a battleground, but from destruction of their horses, the Indians' most prized possession and vehicle of war. On September 9, 1858, as the Indians were driving 800 horses away from the Spokane Plains Battlefield, Col. Wright's forces captured the herd about a mile northwest of this monument. Except for 100, all were destroyed. Two days later, the Indians, whose spirit was broken, met with Col. Wright at the Cataldo Mission in Idaho to surrender. The site of this infamous slaughter is listed on the State Register of Historic Places.

Stevens County

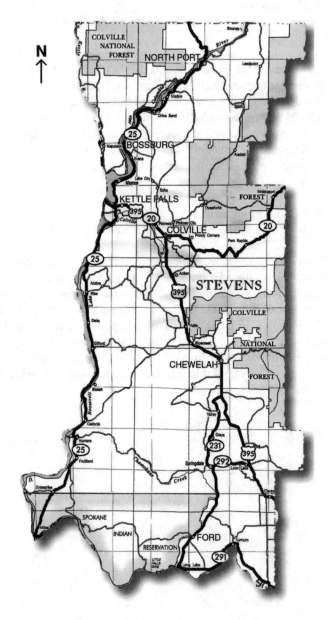

STEVENS COUNTY

BOSSBURG

Bossburg Ghost Town
Hwy. 25, north of Kettle Falls, near present town of Bossburg

During the early 1890s Bossburg's Young America and Bonanza silver mines flourished. The town boomed. A stamp mill was built in town, businesses opened, and a school and church was established. Then the depression of 1893-97 hit the country and the demand for silver was sharply reduced. Falling prices forced the Young America Mine to close. Some remnants of the old townsite of Bossburg are all that remain today.

CHEWELAH (chuh-WEE-luh)

Chewelah Historical Museum
East Second St., Chewelah (509) 935-6091, or (509) 935-6302

The history of Chewelah, from military post to agricultural center to industrial town, is presented in the museum's exhibits. Important events that took place here: the first Protestant religious services in the Colville Valley and publication of the county's first newspaper, the *Stevens County Sun*, are displayed. Pioneer and Indian artifacts, photographs, and periodicals describing the history of Stevens County are also displayed here.

Chewelah Historical Museum

McPherson Cabin
309 Third St., Chewelah

Native Americans of this region who took up farming received their seeds, farm machinery and training at the Indian agency that operated from this log cabin between 1873 and 1885. In 1902, Dr. S. P. McPherson purchased the cabin and converted it into a home for his family by adding a granary building. Some years after the family moved, Dr. McPherson's daughter, Alice Salisbury restored the cabin to its original state.

Congregational Church
Chewelah

The 100th anniversary of the first Protestant religious service held in the Colville Valley was commemorated at this church in September 1938. Reverends Cushing Eells and Elkanah Walker, missionaries from the Tshimakain Mission north of Spokane, conducted the first service.

COLVILLE (KAWL-vil)

Keller Historical Park
700 North Wynne, Colville (509) 684-5968

Several historic buildings and displays from the Colville area are exhibited on this seven-acre city park.

Keller House (509) 684-6324. In 1910, Louis Keller, an affluent Canadian miner, built this beautiful, three-story Craftsman-style bungalow for himself and his wife, Anna. The elegant interior features beveled glass windows, birch beams, and oak inlaid floors. Period furnishings grace the interior. The home, carriage house and garden are listed on the National Register of Historic Places.

Keller House

Historical Society Machinery Building. Early twentieth century horse-drawn and steam-powered farm, mining and lumber industry equipment from the Stevens County area is exhibited. Relics include: a horse-drawn ice cutter, side plow, covered wagon, and a rare 1925 grain separator.

Colville's Schoolhouse. This c.1885 log building, the city's first schoolhouse, is furnished with period desks, benches and a wood-burning potbelly stove.

Farmstead Cabin (Alphonse Snook Cabin, c.1916). Early settlers and miners built cabins such as this throughout the county using locally harvested trees. Housewares, furnishings and objects from pioneer days are exhibited in a realistic setting within this well-constructed miner's cabin.

Graves Mountain Lookout Tower c.1930s.

For nearly 50 years, forest rangers manned this lookout tower from the top of Graves Mountain in the Colville National Forest. As more sophisticated fire detection methods were adopted, these stations were closed. In 1985, the tower was relocated here, restored and authentically furnished.

An original **trapper's cabin** and **sawmill**, a building containing **antique blacksmith equipment** and a **stone sculpture garden** complete this park's impressive historic collection.

Stevens County Historical Society Museum
On the grounds of Keller Historical Park, 700 N. Wynne, Colville

Nothing remains today of Fort Colvile, Hudson's Bay fur-trading post, or Fort Colville, the U.S. Army post built 14 miles to the east. But the iron and silver mines, and the gold mines that brought prospectors to this area in 1854, continue to be a major industry. More than 3,000 items of historic interest including: artifacts, period clothing, antique dolls, housewares and other memorabilia from Stevens County's past is preserved, and its history recorded in this county museum.

Stevens County Historical Society Museum

Arden Flour Mill Grindstones
County Courthouse, Colville

On the courthouse grounds is a lawn sculpture comprised of original grindstones from the Arden Mill, the first American grist mill built north of the Snake River. Two of the mill's grindstones were shipped around the Horn to Tumwater, and then, in 1858-59, across the territory to the original mill site.

Arden Flour Mill Grindstones

Fort Colville Monument
Aladdin Rd, 1 1/2 miles south of Hwy. 20, 1 mile west of the junction of U.S. 395 and Hwy. 20, Colville

The U.S. Army established Fort Colville at this site in 1859 to maintain peace between the region's settlers and local Indian tribes. Nothing remains today of the old fort's log buildings, but the legacy of the men who served here for more than two decades can be found throughout the Colville Valley.

FORD

Tshimakain Mission Site
Marker on East Side of Hwy. 231 near the north boundary of Ford

Two Congregational missionaries, Rev. Cushing Eells and Rev. Elkanah Walker, and their wives Myra Eells and Mary Walker established the first mission in the Spokane River Valley at this site in 1838. Their ten-year effort to convert nomadic Indians to farmers was, for the most part, unsuccessful. In 1848, following the massacre of the Whitmans at the Waiilatpu Mission, the Eells and Walker families abandoned the mission. The site of their mission is listed on the State Register of Historic Places.

KETTLE FALLS

St. Paul's Mission
Three miles west of Kettle Falls on U.S. 395

For more than a thousand years before the white man set foot on this land, Indians spent their summers here and fished for salmon at the nearby Columbia River. In 1845, 900 Colville Indians received mass at this site from Father Jean Pierre De Smet, the first missionary to attempt to convert this area's Indians. Later that year, Father Anthony Ravalli and the Kettle Indians built the first St. Paul's Mission. Two years later, this larger French-Canadian style log church was constructed. Restoration began in 1939. Today, the completely restored St. Paul's Mission, one of the oldest churches still standing in the state, is managed by the National Park Service. A trail with historical exhibits is nearby.

On the Mission grounds is a monument to Fort Colville. Fort Colville was established at this site in 1826 by the Hudson Bay Company, which operated the post until 1871. It was here that trade, farming, milling and stock raising began in Stevens County.

St. Paul's Mission

Log Flume Heritage Site
Along Hwy. 20 in the Colville National Forest, west of Kettle Falls

A half-mile interpretive trail tells the history of logging along the banks of Sherman Creek and the two methods used here in the early part of the twentieth century to bring the region's ancient forests of Ponderosa Pine to an expanding nation. A

92

replica of a log chute accompanies the story of the flumewalkers who guided logs along their journey to the creek below for water transport. Remnants of the railroad that used steam locomotives to bring timber out of the area to railheads can be seen along the interpretative trail.

Log Flume Heritage Site

NORTHPORT

In the summer of 1892, the town of Northport had it all: railroad service, a newspaper, mining operations and a booming business district. A series of fires, and the flood of 1894, didn't dampen the town spirit. After every disaster the town rebuilt for the better. Wood-frame buildings were replaced with brick. New structures were erected above the high water mark. But a 9-month labor strike in 1901, by the men who worked at the Northport Smelting and Refining Company, was the final blow. The company never fully recovered. When it closed in 1921, most of the townsfolk left. One stack remains from the smelter along with some of the old business district's turn-of-the-century brick stores.

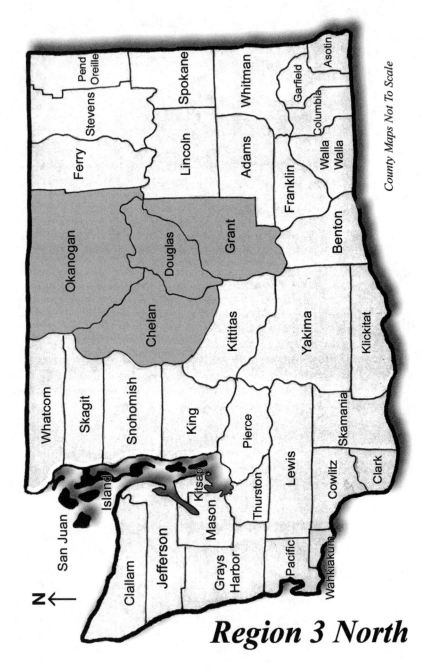

County Maps Not To Scale

Region 3 North

REGION 3 NORTH

CHELAN COUNTY

AZWELL

Wells Dam
One mile north of Azwell on U.S. 97 (509) 923-2226

Wells Dam has more to offer visitors than just a tour of its whirling hydroelectric generators. Exhibits also include Native American and pioneer history, the story of the old fur trading post at Fort Okanogan, and the dam's hatchery where millions of salmon and trout are raised annually. One display shows the life cycle of salmon and includes a viewing window where salmon can be seen ascending a fish ladder. The dam, and nearby town of Azwell, were named for Alfred Z. Wells, a successful orchardist in this fertile region of the Columbia River.

CASHMERE

Old Mission Historical Marker
One mile east of Cashmere on the south side of Hwy. 2/97

"Near this site, in the summer of 1872, Father Urban Grassi, S.J., visited the Simpesquensi Indians. Winning over their Chief, Patoi, he soon baptized many of the band. In 1873 he erected a log mission church named St. Francis Xavier near the present town of Cashmere. By diverting the small stream, Mission Creek, over a garden patch, Father Grassi taught these Indians irrigation and elementary agriculture. A replica of his mission may be seen on the museum grounds south of this marker."

Chelan County Historical Museum
600 Cottage Ave., Cashmere (509) 782-3230

For many years this museum was known as the Willis Carey Museum, for it was the donation of his outstanding collection of Indian artifacts and pioneer relics to the Chelan County Historical Society that formed the foundation for their museum. The addition of a reconstructed pioneer village, and the Society's on-going acquisition of historic material has earned the museum national recognition. More than 9000 years of Native American culture is exhibited in the form of arrowheads, pottery, stone tools, and other relics. The village includes: a replica of the St. Francis Xavier Mission; fifteen original Chelan County log homes and buildings from the period between 1872 and 1910, including Wenatchee's first business, the Miller-Freer Trading Post; an 1891 Stoffel water wheel; and a Great Northern Railroad exhibit. All the buildings have been restored and contain period furnishings and antiques in realistic settings.

The community's pioneer spirit is reflected in the Early American theme of the city's downtown district.

Liberty Orchards
Aplets and Cotlets Candy Factory, 117 Mission St., Cashmere (509) 782-2191

In the early 1900s, Cashmere valley was blanketed with acres of bountiful fruit orchards. It was in this valley that two Armenian immigrants, Mark Balaban and Armen Tertsagian, settled and purchased this apple orchard, which they named "Liberty." In 1918, when faced with an abundant harvest, and a small market for their apples, the men created "Aplets," the combination of an Old World candy recipe mixed with apple juice and walnuts. Demand for this new fruit and nut confection soon spread from Cashmere to surrounding towns and then throughout the Pacific Northwest. "Cotlets," made with apricot puree, became just as successful.

Visitors can tour this world-famous candy factory during regular business hours seven days a week from May to December, and Monday through Friday from January through April.

CHELAN

Lake Chelan Historical Museum
204 E. Woodin Ave., Chelan (509) 682-5644

The 1903 Miners & Merchants Bank building is home to this fine museum of local history. Its acclaimed collection of apple labels from local growers and packers range from the stone lithographs of the early 1900s to the classic commercial labels of the 1950s. Other displays include: the history of the apple industry; a scene from the Whaley store; a doctor and dentist office, pioneer kitchen, and parlor; family scrapbooks; newspaper clippings and photographs from early town residents; Indian artifacts; and a history of the development of Lake Chelan Valley.

Museum staff can provide visitors with information about Chelan's other landmarks: the 1901 **Campbell House**; the "old" 1890 **Whaley house**; 1879-80 **Camp Chelan**; and the **Lucas Homestead** that was destroyed by fire in 1994 (was listed on the National Register of Historic Places)

Lake Chelan Historical Museum

St. Andrew's Episcopal Church
120 E. Woodin Ave., Chelan (509) 682-2851

The centerpiece of downtown Chelan is this 1898 brown log church. It was built for the members of the congregation who first held services in this region as early as 1889. This impressive structure, with its stained glass windows, is a symbol of the

faith of Chelan's early settlers and their belief that this church could be built. St. Andrew's, one of the oldest churches in the Northwest, is listed on the National Register of Historic Places.

Whaley Mansion

Mary Kay's Romantic Whaley Mansion, 415 S. 3rd, Chelan (509) 682-5735

Charles E. Whaley, one of Chelan's founding fathers and a leading town merchant, lived in this elegant mansion with his family in the early 1900s. The restored mansion is now operated as a Bed & Breakfast complete with antique furnishings, old silver and fine china. The "old" Whaley home, built in 1890, can be seen in downtown Chelan.

Whaley Mansion

Ruby Theatre

Downtown Chelan

A visit to this well-preserved 1913 theatre is like a trip back in time. It's not unlike the other one-screen theatres of its era; the kind that were centerpieces of many downtown districts across the Nation. The inside features an authentic tin ceiling, horseshoe-shaped balcony, velvet curtains, and a plaster arch that surrounds the

stage. The only noticeable change is the larger screen that's been tastefully added to accommodate today's feature films. The Ruby has earned the distinction of being placed on the National Register of Historic places.

ENTIAT (EN-tee-at)

Earthquake Point Historic Marker
Two miles north of Entiat on U.S. 97

"This site on Ribbon Cliff, called Broken Mountain by the Indians, experienced a violent earthquake in December, 1872. The shock split the mountain, forming the cliff to the west and causing a huge rockslide which stopped the flow of the Columbia River for several hours. The black ribbons of the cliff are lava-filled fissures. Plateau lavas of the region later covered this rock mass. The white volcanic ash in road excavation is so recent as to have buried undecayed logs. It was blown from Glacier Peak, a volcanic cone, 50 miles to the northwest."

LEAVENWORTH

Leavenworth Nutcracker Museum
735 Front St., Leavenworth (509) 548-4708 or (800) 892-3989

One of the world's largest collections of nutcrackers is exhibited in this unusual museum. Over 2,000 different types of antique and modern nutcrackers, from life-size to miniature models are on display. The museum, and its collection, complements the surrounding Bavarian-style village of Leavenworth.

After Leavenworth was founded in 1892, it became a major railroad and lumbering town. A roundhouse, rail yard, and sawmill were the town's major employers. When the railroad moved out and the sawmill closed in the 1930s Leavenworth's economy was seriously impacted. With advice from the University of Washington, the style of the town architecture was changed to look like a Bavarian village in the German Alps. Tourists were attracted to the Alps-like setting and the local economy was revitalized. Today, Leavenworth's restaurants feature authentic German food, beverages and music. Employees in the village's theme shops and restaurants wear old world costumes. And seasonal events, such as the annual Christmas festival, feature a Bavarian theme.

Old Mining Arrastre Historical Marker, 11 miles south of US 2, between Liberty and Peshastin on Hwy. 97

"One of few remnants of water-powered ore-grinding machines, numerous in the west before the 1840s through the 1880s. Chunks of gold-bearing ore were ground to powder on this stone base by heavy 'dragstones' geared to a water wheel. Gold was recovered by amalgamation with mercury. The Blewett Arrastre was built in 1861 when some 260 miners worked here, and was active until 1880. An arrastra near Liberty, about 10 miles south, was used until 1932."

Blewett Arrastre, on the west side of Hwy. 97 across from this historic marker, is listed on the National Register of Historic Places.

STEHEKIN (steh-HEE-kin)

Golden West Visitor Center, Golden West Lodge
Behind the North Cascades Stehekin Lodge at the Stehekin Landing, Stehekin
For boat schedule and other information call (509) 682-2224 (recorded message)

Half the adventure of discovering Stehekin is getting there. The 55-mile boat trip from Chelan to Stehekin, at the northwestern end of Lake Chelan, cuts through national forests and wilderness areas, giving travelers a commanding view of cascading waterfalls, unspoiled landscape, and wildlife in their natural environment. A number of historic sites in Stehekin and the surrounding area can be toured from Stehekin Landing:

Golden West Lodge Historic District, Stehekin Landing. For more than 40 years it was operated as a hotel; today its the National Park Service visitor center. This former hotel is listed on the National Register of Historic Places and features exhibits on the history of Stehekin.

Buckner Cabin and the Buckner Homestead Historic District, Lake Chelan National Recreation Area. William Buzzard built this log cabin on land he homesteaded around 1890. In 1910, William Buckner purchased the cabin and 149 acres of surrounding land and planted a fifty-acre apple orchard. The cabin, which is listed on the National Register of Historic Places, and many of Buckner's original outbuildings, can be seen at this historic homestead.

Stehekin School and Museum, two miles up the valley from Stehekin Landing. Students attended classes in this one-room schoolhouse from 1921 until 1988, making this the last one-room school to operate in the State of Washington. The building is listed on the National Register of Historic Places and is now operated as a museum of local history.

Stehekin School, Courtesy of Judy Menish

Another mile up the valley from the Stehekin School is the inspiring, 312-foot **Rainbow Falls**. Among the other places of historic interest in and around Stehekin are: **McKellar Cabin Trail**, featuring a Pelton water wheel; the c.1880-90 **Courtney cabin**; and the **Black Warrior Mine** which began producing lead and silver in 1891.

TELMA

Trinity Camp
6 miles south of Telma on Hwy. 207, and then 24 miles north from the junction of the Chiwawa River Road #311 and Chiwawa Loop Road. Guide is available from the Lake Wenatchee Ranger District, 22976 State Hwy. 207, Leavenworth

It was a desolate lifestyle for the 300 men who worked and lived in this copper mining camp between 1918 and 1936. Not only was the work hard, but little activity existed outside the mines. For six months every winter, the miners were snowed-in. While very little of the original camp remains to be seen, other sites are worth the trek. The 24-mile road to Trinity follows pioneer and ancient Indian trails, transverses an old Indian encampment and ends at the boundary of the half-million-acre Glacier Peak Wilderness.

102

White River Self-guided Tour
Two miles west of the Lake Wenatchee Ranger Station at the junction of the White
River and Little Wenatchee Rds. Guide is available from Lake Wenatchee Ranger
District, 22976 State Hwy. 207, Leavenworth

Five points of scenic or historical interest are identified in this 24-mile round-trip
road guide. The gravesite of one of the first settlers in the White River Valley, the
site of her cabin where she lived until 1913, and the wagon trail that followed the
river up the valley can be seen at the first stop. Old logging roads, Indian trails, the
site of a clash between Wenatchee Indians and the Calvary, remnants of old homestead
cabins, a 1904 schoolhouse, White River Falls, and the natural beauty of the area
make the trip worthwhile.

STEVENS PASS

Cascade Tunnel

The longest railroad tunnel still in use in North America was cut through the Cascade
Range just south of this pass in 1929. It was built to replace the original 2.7-mile
Cascade Tunnel, built in 1897-1900 on the north side of the pass. A tragic avalanche
in 1910, that took the lives of ninety-six passengers and crew, prompted construction
of this newer tunnel at a lower elevation where the slopes were more stable. More
than two thousand men worked on the 7.79-mile tunnel, which was completed in a
record 3 years and 47 days. The headframe of the east portal at Scenic and the west
portal by the old construction camp at Berne are visible from U.S. 2. A model of
the switchbacks, trestles and tunnels of the three Stevens Pass rail routes can be
seen at the North Central Washington Museum in Wenatchee.

WENATCHEE (wuh-NACH-ee)

North Central Washington Museum, 127 S. Mission St., (509) 664-3340

The history of Washington State's famous apple industry, and Wenatchee's role as
the "Apple Capitol of the World, " is featured in the museum's extensive apple
industry exhibit. Rare apple box labels, vintage equipment, and an operating antique
apple processing assembly line are among the interesting exhibits. Other galleries
contain: an HO gauge model of the three historic railroad passes through Stevens

103

Pass, with switchbacks, trestles and tunnels; Indian artifacts and petroglyphs of the Rock Island Rapids; settings depicting rooms from a pioneer home, farm shop, the Miller-Freer trading post, a print shop and general store; and the Clyde E. Pangborn Exhibit commemorating the first nonstop transpacific flight from Misawa, Japan to Wenatchee. The museum is housed in the former 1937 Post Office building and contains murals and other reminders of the WPA era.

North Central Washington Museum

Old Wenatchee Walking Tour
Guide available from the North Central Washington Museum, 127 S. Mission St., Wenatchee (509) 664-3340

The history of thirty-four of Wenatchee's historic commercial buildings is detailed in this guide. Some of the listed buildings are original structures; others have been remodeled or razed. This interesting guide includes sketches of each building and the story of the owners, or tenants, the type of business they operated and renovations made to the original structure.

John Horan House
2 Horan Rd., Wenatchee

One of the town's first merchants was John Horan, a butcher who moved here from Roslyn in 1889. At the turn-of-the century, Horan built this riverbank home for his family who first lived in a small log cabin. The log cabin, where he and his family lived has been reconstructed at the Cashmere Pioneer Village. Today, Horan's home is operated as a restaurant, where many original furnishings and family memorabilia is showcased.

A. Z. Wells House
1300 Fifth Street, Wenatchee Valley Community College, 1300 Fifth St., Wenatchee

Turning Wenatchee into the "world's apple capitol" hinged on irrigating a large number of acres of land in near desert-like conditions. W. T. Clark is credited with that accomplishment by developing the Highline Irrigation Canal in 1903. The site where the Highline Canal crosses the Wenatchee River can be seen at the north end of town from Wenatchee Avenue. Clark's wife designed this 10-room home, which was built in 1909 from native stone and river rocks. A. Z. Wells, a prosperous orchardist and hardware businessman, bought the home in 1919 and later donated it and the surrounding property for use as a college. The home is listed on the National Register of Historic Places.

Ohme Gardens
3327 Ohme Rd., near junction of U.S. 2 and U.S. 97, Wenatchee (509) 662-5785

In 1929, Herman Ohme began transforming the arid land around the family's private retreat into an alpine garden. Ohme planted thousands of evergreen trees, lush gardens, and alpine plants. Walkways and pool settings were created with tons of rock set by hand. In 1939, the gardens were opened to the public. These critically acclaimed gardens were purchased by the State of Washington in 1991 and are operated today as a Chelan County Park.

Rocky Reach Dam
On the Columbia River, US 97A, 7 miles north of Wenatchee (509) 663-8121

Although the history of the dam is fairly recent (dedicated in 1963), its powerhouse galleries house exhibits on the development of electricity, early life along the Columbia River, and the outstanding Nez Perce Indian Portrait Collection. The Gallery of Electricity is a chronological look at the development of electricity from Ben Franklin's kite to today's advanced electronics. Electric antiques, including Thomas Edison artifacts are featured. The Galley of the Columbia includes the Columbia River Indian Exhibit, a 10,000-year history of the Native Americans who lived here. Artifacts found during excavation of the dam and Indian arts and crafts are exhibited. Models of Columbia River steamships, history of local railroading, a fish viewing window and 18 acres of parkland make this a favorite stop with something of interest for every family member.

Lincoln Rock Historic Marker,
Lincoln Rock State Park, 8 miles north of East Wenatchee on the east side of U.S. 2

"On the rocky mountainside to the west there has been sculptured by the hand of nature a profile which bears a remarkable likeness to that of the sixteenth president of the United States, the beloved Abraham Lincoln. May this monument of nature and the memory of Lincoln alike endure as an admonition of our great obligation of citizenship to preserve inviolate the American institutions and secure the blessings of liberty to ourselves and our posterity, "that government of the people, by the people, and for the people, shall not perish from the earth.""

Lincoln Rock is listed on the State Register of Historic Places.

Rock Island Railroad Bridge
Spanning the Columbia River, 7 miles south of Wenatchee

The final link in Great Northern Railroad's transcontinental railroad between the Mississippi River and Puget Sound was erected across the Columbia River at this point in 1893. The bridge was fabricated in Wilmington, Delaware by the Edge Moor Bridge Works and shipped here. Use of counterweights enabled the bridge to be erected without a center span support. In 1925, the bridge was rebuilt using the existing truss. Rock Island Bridge is listed on the National Register of Historic Places.

Rock Island Dam
On the Columbia River, 11 miles southeast of Wenatchee, on the west side of U.S. 2

The first hydroelectric dam to span the Columbia River was constructed at this site between 1930 and 1931 to fill the growing need for low cost electricity. Each of the four turbines in the original powerhouse is rated at 32,000 horsepower and is connected to generators that produce a total of 77,100 kilowatts of power. Additional powerhouses were completed in 1953 and 1979. The Rock Island Dam Project is listed on the State Register of Historic Places.

Douglas County

DOUGLAS COUNTY

BRIDGEPORT

Berryman Memorial Park
2000 block of Fisk St., Bridgeport   Contact City Hall for key (509) 686-4041

Military history, so much a part of Eastern Washington's past, can be seen in this city park. But its not stockades, sabers, or rifles on display here. Instead, weapons of the mid-twentieth century: an Ajax and Sparrow Missile, F-87 Saber Jet, anti-aircraft guns, the only Nike Hercules Missile prototype in the world, and the Chance Vought Cutlass aircraft that broke the sound barrier for the Navy. Most of what's on display can be seen by walking around the ten-acre city park, or get the key from the City Hall for a better view.

MANSFIELD

Gallaher House
12 miles northwest of Mansfield on Deyer Rd.

With the arrival of the Great Northern Railway in 1909, Mansfield became an important shipping point for the area's wheat farmers. The combination of bountiful harvests, and rail transportation to distant markets brought prosperity to Manfield's business owners and local farmers. Evidence of that success can be seen in the construction of this octagonal house, one of the few examples of this type of architecture in the Pacific Northwest. James Kinney built the eight-sided home in 1914 as a gift for his daughter and her husband, Clyde Gallaher.

WATERVILLE

Douglas County Historical Museum
Walnut and Central (Hwy. 2), Waterville (509) 745-8435

After this section of the Moses-Columbia Indian Reservation was opened to settlement in 1886, A. T. Green filed his plan for the town that would eventually be called Waterville. Native American and pioneer artifacts from this region and one of the state's most extensive rock collections, including meteorites found in the local area, are among the museum's featured exhibits. Early family picture albums, musical instruments, typewriters and radios are also displayed. Across the street, at 102 South Central is the town's original two-story hotel, which is listed on the National Register of Historic Places.

Downtown Waterville Historic District
Locust and Chelan Sts., Waterville

Locally fired brick was used in the construction of many of the buildings that still stand in Waterville's turn-of-the-century downtown district.   Nearby clay pits provided the raw material that would be used by the town's first brickyard, established here in 1889. The impressive Douglas County Bank, the town's first brick building and the frame home of the city's pioneer banker are among the structures preserved in this historic district.

Grant County

GRANT COUNTY

BEVERLY

Wanapum Dam Heritage Center,
Hwy. 243 on the east side of the Columbia River, 6 miles south of where the I-90 bridge crosses the Columbia River, Beverly (509) 754-3541 Ext. 2571

It wasn't that many years ago that the Wanapum Indians lived off what this land along the Columbia provided: Salmon in the late spring; Sockeye in the fall; with roots and berries, and deer and elk in-between. The culture of these resourceful and self-reliant people is told in the Center's archaeological and ethnographic exhibits. Other displays recall the region's mining and agriculture history and the development of hydropower on the Columbia.

COULEE CITY (KOO-lee)

McEntee's Crossing, as it was called after Philip McEntee settled here in 1881, was an important point on the military road that brought explorers, miners and settlers through this region of the state. In 1885, Grant County's oldest road was surveyed here. With the arrival of stage lines and the Northern Pacific Railroad in 1890, the town was renamed Coulee City and became the first platted town in Grant County. The seven-year drought that began in 1917, which nearly destroyed the town, underscored the need for a dependable source for irrigation for the entire Columbia Basin. In December 1933, 30 miles to the north, the Grand Coulee Dam was begun.

Dry Falls Historical Marker
Two miles southwest of Coulee City on Hwy. 17, near Sun Lakes State Park

"In the towering walls of Grand Coulee may be read the history of a torrential river which, flowing from immense glaciers, carved this picturesque canyon and then retired, upon recession of the glaciers, to become the Columbia River of today. To the south, at the head of lower Grand Coulee, is Dry Falls, one of the geological wonders of the world. Three and one-quarter miles across the crest and four hundred feet high the Ghost Falls now stands bearing mute evidence of a prehistoric cataract forty times mightier than Niagara."

111

Dry Falls Interpretive Center
Sun Lakes State Park, 7 miles southwest of Coulee City on Hwy. 17 (509) 632-5583

A commanding view of one of the great wonders of the ancient world is afforded visitors to this Interpretive Center. Large picture windows in the Center's observation area overlook Dry Falls' giant precipice where, in ancient times, tremendous torrents of water cascaded into the river below. The history of the formation of Dry Falls and the surrounding coulees is displayed in a number of exhibits at this Center.

Diorama of Lake Lenore Caves exhibit at Dry Falls Interpretive Center

Lake Lenore Caves
17 miles southwest of Coulee City on Hwy. 17

Floods that followed the Ice Age created these caves by eroding volcanic rock out of the walls of the coulees. In prehistoric times nomadic families used the caves for temporary shelter as they roamed this region in search of food. A trail at the north end of Lake Lenore leads to some of the caves.

Summer Falls State Park
10 miles south of Coulee City on the Stratford Rd.

During the spring and summer irrigation season, water from Banks Lake flows through the main canal of the Columbia Basin Reclamation Project and cascades over Summer Falls 165 feet to Billy Clapp Lake. More than 2,000 miles of canals and laterals then distribute the water to irrigate over 500,000 acres of farmland.

EPHRATA (e-FRAY-tuh)

Grant County Historical Museum
742 N. Basin St., Ephrata (509) 754-3334

Every period of time in the history and pre-history of Grant County is exhibited in this museum's galleries. Displays are arranged chronologically, beginning with pre-historic petrified trees and fossils, through the periods of Indians, stockmen and homesteaders, to the building of the Grand Coulee Dam. Period rooms depict scenes from pioneer life with great attention to historical accuracy.

This museum's pioneer village is more than just an assemblage of old buildings. It's a recreated village, reminiscent of life in Grant County during the early part of the twentieth Century. At the center of the village is the original St. Rose of Lima Catholic Church and a restored one-room, furnished schoolhouse. Among the village's other 27 original and replica buildings are: a blacksmith shop with a working forge, Wilson Creek State Bank, print shop featuring antique printing equipment, Line Cabin, a camera shop with more than 300 vintage cameras, Grant County Fire Hall, and a compete 1902 pioneer homestead. Buildings contain period furnishings, vintage clothing, antiques or memorabilia in realistic settings. Wooden sidewalks, a sod-roofed log cabin, and an assemblage of antique farm machinery and steam-powered equipment add to the authentic-looking village setting.

113

Street scene at Grant County Museum Pioneer Village

Justice of the Peace Office

Line Cabin

Grant County Courthouse
First NW and "C" Sts., Ephrata

The important role government played in the development of Ephrata's economy is reflected in the quality construction of its courthouse. Built in 1917, the neo-classical revival-style building is one of the largest, best-designed and most beautiful government buildings in Grant County. The architect, George H. Keith, designed the building with a geothermal heating system by utilizing water from a local hot spring. Its significance as the county's first permanent courthouse earned it a listing on the National Register of Historic Places. The original frame courthouse, which stands across the street, has been converted to use as a church.

114

Grant County Courthouse

GRAND COULEE DAM

COULEE DAM

Just about everybody's heard of it, thousands worked to build it, and millions have seen it: Grand Coulee Dam, the eighth wonder of the world.

Grand Coulee Dam, one of the largest concrete structures in the world; is taller than the Washington Monument and nearly a mile across. It's the nation's largest hydroelectric plant, producing almost 6.5 million kilowatts of energy. The Dam controls flooding and provides irrigation to more than 500,000 acres of farmland. And, more than a million people a year enjoy a wide variety of recreational activities in the 100,000-acre Coulee Dam National Recreational Area.

Billy Clapp proposed the idea for a concrete dam across the Columbia to Grant County citizens in 1917, the first year of a severe, 7-year drought in the Columbia Basin. Rufus Woods, editor of the "Wenatchee World" took-up the cause, but it would be sixteen years before the first concrete would be poured. The first power was produced eight years later in September 1941, three months before the outbreak of World War II. It would be 1952, 35 years after Billy Clapp's proposal, before the first water was pumped to farms in the Basin. Lake Billy Clapp at Summer Falls, and Lake Rufus Woods, north of the dam, were named as a tribute to these two visionaries.

115

Grand Coulee Dam, Courtesy of U.S. Department of the Interior,
Bureau of Reclamation

Coulee Dam Historical Walk
U.S. Bureau of Reclamation's Visitor Arrival Center, Hwy. 155, 2 miles north of
the city of Coulee Dam (509) 633-9265

Entire towns were built virtually overnight when construction of Coulee Dam began
in 1933. Government offices, a school, dormitories, homes and recreational facilities
were needed to support the community of workers it would take to build the dam.
A guide to the buildings that remain from that era can be obtained at this Center.
Among the places listed are: the Post Office, designed to resemble Franklin D.
Roosevelt's summer home; Columbia School (now used for credit union offices);
Federal Administration Building (presently houses the city hall); Douglas Park,
constructed by the Civilian Conservation Corps in 1936; and temporary housing
remaining from the old town of Mason City. The Center also provides information
about tours of the dam, the summer laser light show, community events and visitor
services.

116

Grand Coulee Laser Light Show
Visitor Arrival Center, Coulee Dam

A spectacular laser light show, the largest show of its kind in the world, can be viewed nightly during the summer from various sites around the Dam. From Memorial Day through September 30th, laser images, some nearly 300 feet high, are beamed to the surface of the dam where they tell the story of the Dam and how it was built to harness the mighty Columbia River. Synchronized stereo sound effects can be best enjoyed at the Visitor Center or the nearby park during the light show.

Four Winds Guest House
301 Lincoln St., Coulee Dam (800) 786-3146

Single male engineers, who designed Grand Coulee Dam, as well as inspectors and clerks who worked on this massive project, lived here during the nine-year period it took to construct the dam. It's been said that President Franklin D. Roosevelt met with engineers at this site during the dam's early construction days to review progress of the project. One of the President's wheelchair is displayed in this former dormitory that is now operated as a Bed & Breakfast Inn. This 1935 Guest House was the last of the Government Camp houses at Coulee Dam.

Colville Confederated Tribes' Museum and Gift Shop
512 Mead Way, Coulee Dam (509) 633-0751

Centuries before white men first explored Eastern Washington this region was home to the Wenatchee, Entiat, Chelan, Methow, Okanogan, Nespelem, San Poil, Lakes, Moses, Palouse and Nez Perce Indians. Today, more than 7,000 Native Americans from these eleven tribes live on the 2,300-square-mile Colville Reservation as members of the Colville Confederated Tribes. The history of their Nation is displayed in this museum. Tribal artifacts, some 5,000 years old; original Indian art; a replica sweatlodge; large tule mat tipi (teepee); cedar root and bear grass baskets; fishing gear; two Books of Matthew which were translated into the Nez Perce language by Reverend Spalding in 1871; and a rare 1801 Thomas Jefferson Medal are some of the items exhibited. Among the hundreds of photographs preserved here is one of Chief Moses, who lived from 1829 to 1899, hunted buffalo on the Great Plains as a young boy, and rode into battles against the Blackfeet with Salish allies.

117

MOSES LAKE

Adam East Museum Art Center
122 W. Third, Moses Lake (509) 766-9395

Sinkiuse (Columbia) Indian relics collected by the late Adam East were bequeathed to the city of Moses Lake in order that they would remain in their native area after his death. These artifacts formed the nucleus of the museum's collection. The museum, named in his honor, also features exhibits depicting the history of Moses Lake, photographs and works by Northwest artists.

Schniffer Military & Police Museum
4840 Westshore Dr., Moses Lake (509) 765-6374

It all started with George and Margaret Schniffer's large gun collection. In 1977 they added a reference and research library; then a showroom displaying more than 100 military uniforms from all branches of the service covering the period from 1912 to present. Unique and rare military artifacts are exhibited including: the 41-foot wooden flag pole from the former Larson Air Force Base, a 1904 Navy anchor, World War I field command desk, cavalry saddle, and a sword designed by General George S. Patton. In 1986, the Schniffers began adding police memorabilia to their museum. Their collection of police badges represents almost every city and town in the state.

Moses Lake Chamber of Commerce is located at 324 S. Pioneer Way (509) 765-7888 or (800) 992-6234

SOAP LAKE

Soap Lake Historic Sites
Soap Lake Chamber of Commerce, East 300 Beech, Soap Lake (509) 246-1821

The lure of the lake's medicinal powers has drawn people to Soap Lake for generations. Before white men learned of the lake, Indians were here. They called the lake "Smokiam" which means, "healing water." A "Treasure Map," a guide to Soap Lake's natural and historic sites is available from the Chamber of Commerce. The guide lists 17 sites including: the town's first homestead, the 1904 home of Lucy Gray, its first salt mine and an old Indian trail.

Smokiam "Healing Waters" water fountain at Soap Lake

WILSON CREEK

Wilson Creek State Bank
One mile north of Hwy. 28, Wilson Creek

Years before the Great Northern Railroad began bringing settlers to Wilson Creek, this was a favorite stop for cattlemen, sheepherders, and Native Americas. The brick Wilson Creek Bank, built in 1906, is a fine example of the types of buildings erected by independent banks in small Washington State towns. Although now closed, the bank played an important role in the development of the town, and is listed on the National Register of Historic Places.

119

Okanogan County

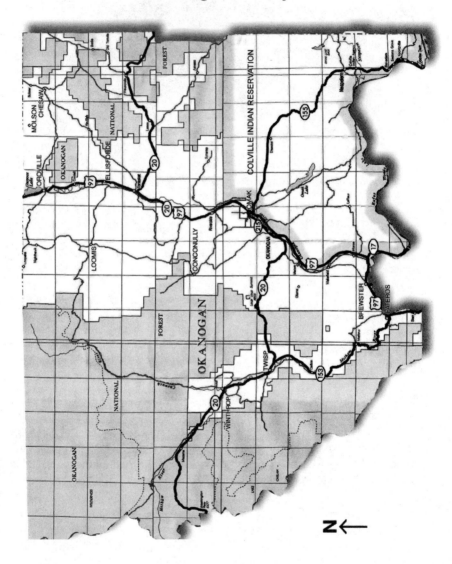

OKANOGAN COUNTY

BREWSTER

Fort Okanogan Historic Marker,
South side of U.S. 97, at the confluence of the Okanogan and Columbia rivers, 5 miles east of Brewster

"John Jacob Astor's fur traders built Fort Okanogan in September, 1811. The British North West Company took possession in the War of 1812. The Hudson's Bay Company owned the fort from 1821 to 1860. It was moved in the 1830s to the Columbia River. A flagpole in the distance marks the second site. Here, at the mouth of the Okanogan River, the Fort served as a trading center. The United States won authority over the region in 1846. The Hudson's Bay Company abandoned Fort Okanogan 14 years later."

Fort Okanogan Interpretive Center
Fort Okanogan State Park, Hwy. 17, east of U.S. 97, 5 miles northeast of Brewster
(509) 943-2473 or (509) 689-2798

Driftwood collected from the Columbia River was used by men from the Pacific Fur Company to build Fort Okanogan at this site in 1811. During the next 50 years, this important fur trading post would be moved and expanded, and would see new owners. It would be the site where the first American Flag to fly over what is now Washington State was raised. This Center overlooks the sites where Fort Okanogan once stood. The history of the fort, its people, and the Indians who lived here for generations before the white man arrived is exhibited. Among the interesting Indian artifacts on display is Long Jim's dugout canoe.

121

CHESAW (CHEE-saw)

Chesaw
Toroda Creek Rd., east of Oroville

The opening of this part of the Colville Indian Reservation to homesteaders, and the 1896 discovery of gold in the Myers and Mary Ann creeks brought a boom, and 500 residents to the town of Chesaw. Today, the town, with its few inhabitants, contains the remains of a few turn-of-the-century buildings. Some restored; others abandoned.

CONCONULLY (kahn-kuh-NEL-ee)

Conconully Dam
One mile south of Conconully

One of the first federal irrigation projects undertaken by the Bureau of Reclamation was begun in 1907 with the construction of Conconully Dam. It was the first hydraulic earth-fill dam built by the Bureau.

Conconully, a gold mining town in the late 1800s, was once the county seat of Okanogan County. A replica of the log cabin once used for county commissioner meetings was erected in nearby Conconully State Park. Floods, a major fire in 1892, and the Panic of 1893 led to the loss of the county seat to Okanogan in 1914.

ELLISFORD

Old Okanogan Mission Site
Brethren Church, Ellisford

Jesuit missionary, Father Urban Grassi began constructing a mission chapel at this site in 1885 to serve the region's Indians and early settlers. Father Etienne de Rouge finished the project after Father Grassi was called to supervise construction of Gonzaga University in Spokane. Father de Rouge planted French flower seeds and raised the region's first garden flowers. The mission's original church bell and Indian cemetery is all that remain to be seen from the early mission site. Both are preserved behind the Brethren Church.

LOOMIS

A scattering of historic sites in and around the Loomis area preserve the history of this region's ranching, agriculture and mining activities in the 1800s. A pioneer apple orchard, gold mines cut into Palmer Mountain, and an original stone store are a few of the remnants of once-thriving ventures. Loomis today is but a shadow of the once-bustling mining town that stood here in the 1880s.

MOLSON

Molson School Museum
11 miles east of Oroville on Toroda-Chesaw Rd., then north 4 miles at Molson sign, Molson (509) 485-3292

Disputes over squatter's rights and homestead claims literally divided the town of Molson in the early 1900s. In 1914, a three-story, brick school building was constructed on "neutral" ground between the "old" and "new" towns of Molson. When train service was discontinued in 1935, the town's population dwindled, but many of its historic buildings, including this school, have been preserved. The school building is listed on the National Register of Historic Places and has been converted into a museum of local history. It contains the original school library, a restored classroom and pioneer post office fixtures. The school's old classrooms contain exhibits of antique tools, vintage clothing, period furniture and household items.

Old Molson Outdoor Museum
Molson

The town of Molson wasn't the typical "boom & bust" gold mining town. It was a well-laid-out town financed by George Molson, a member of the famous Canadian brewing family. It boasted a 34-room, three-story hotel, newspaper, bank and a number of retail stores and professional services. When one of its citizens filed a homestead claim on the entire town, a number of residents moved a quarter-mile north and formed "New Molson." Even the bank was put on skids and moved block-by-block out of the old town. Today, Old Molson is a registered State Historic Landmark. An outdoor museum contains a number of the town's original buildings, including the "traveling" bank. Mining equipment and one of the largest collections of horse-drawn farm machinery in the state are also exhibited.

NESPELEM (nez-PEE-luhm)

Chief Joseph Historical Marker
Hwy. 155, Nespelem

"Chief Joseph (1840-1904) war leader of the Nez Perce Indians in the 1870s, was a military genius. In 1877, when his tribe was driven from its homeland by forces of white settlers, Chief Joseph led men, women and children more than 1500 miles through the Montana wilderness for escape to Canada. Captured near the border by the U.S. Army, exiled with his people to the bitter country of Indian Territory, Chief Joseph worked tirelessly for peace. He won a return to the Northwest for his Nez Perce in 1885. They were confined on the Colville Reservation in Northeast Washington. Chief Joseph forgave his enemies and was a peacemaker to the day of his death. He is buried at Nespelem."

Chief Joseph Memorial
Nez Perce Cemetery, near junction of WA 10A and Cache Creek Rd., northeast edge of Nespelem

For years, Chief Joseph, leader of the Nez Perce Indians, fought for the right to return his people to their homeland, the Wallowa Valley in northeastern Oregon. His battles were often fought with words, but neither his eloquent speeches or the bravery of his young warriors would win their return. In 1904, Chief Joseph died in exile on the Colville Indian Reservation. The marker at his grave faces southwest towards the Wallowa Valley of his ancestors, the land he loved so deeply.

"Let me be a free man, free to travel, free to stop, free to work, free to trade where I choose, free to choose my own brothers, free to follow the religion of my fathers, free to think and talk and act for myself." Chief Joseph

OKANOGAN (oh-kuh-NAH-guhn)

Okanogan County Historical Museum
Legion Park, 1410 2nd North, Okanogan (509) 422-4272

The forces of nature that shaped the Okanogan valley, and the history of the people who lived here: the Native Americans who first inhabited this region, traders, miners and settlers unfolds in the museum's exhibits. Thousands of photographs that capture the history of Okanogan County are included in the historical society's Frank Matsura photography collection. Among the interesting Indian artifacts on display is a rifle that once belonged to Chief Joseph, leader of the Nez Perce from the 1870s to 1904. Several vintage buildings, including the county's oldest standing structure, an 1879 sod roof log cabin, are included in an Old West town that's been reconstructed behind the museum.

Sod roof log cabin, Okanogan County Historical Museum

Curtis Sheep Massacre Site
4 miles southwest of Okanogan on Hwy. 20

Range wars between cattlemen and sheep ranchers over grazing rights are a part of the history of the Old West. If intimidation didn't discourage sheepmen, violence drove them away. In 1901, A. A. Curtis stood his ground against cattlemen's threats and brought in a flock of 1,200 sheep. One morning, Curtis found all 1,200 had been clubbed to death. The site of that massacre is marked by a plaque at this site.

OMAK (OH-mak)

St. Mary's Mission
5 miles east of Omak via Hwy. 155 (509) 826-2097

Father Etienne de Rouge, a French Roman Catholic missionary, founded a mission at this site in 1886 to minister to Indians of the Okanogan Valley. Father de Rouge was highly respected by both Indians and settlers, an attribute that enabled him to intervene and prevent violence. Chief Joseph and Chief Moses attended services

here. The original mission building burned in 1938. The remaining mission buildings and church stand along side the Paschal Sherman Indian School, the only Indian boarding school in the state.

St. Mary's Mission

OROVILLE

Oroville Depot
1204 Ironwood, Oroville (509) 476-3693

Great Northern Railway's original depot at Oroville now houses the city's museum of local history. Changing exhibits feature the history of the region from: the region's first explorers and fur trappers; to the state's first apple orchards, planted here in 1856-57; mining in the late 1880s; lumbering; and the area's oldest continuously operating sawmill, built in 1920. An old caboose and a fine collection of railroad memorabilia are on permanent display.

Log Custom House,
On 14th St. between Ironwood and Juniper, Oroville

Oroville's first customhouse, a single-story log cabin, was built in the 1870s north of here near the ranch of "Okanogan Smith". This present log house, c.1890, replaced the original customhouse and served as the inspector's residence. Canadian custom's officials on the opposite side of the border at Osoyoos, British Columbia also lived in log cabins around the turn-of-the-century.

Oroville Chamber of Commerce and Visitor Information Center is located at 1730 Main St. (509) 476-2739

Hiram F. "Okanogan" Smith Apple Orchard,
East shore of Osoyoos Lake, 2 miles north of Oroville on Hwy. 97

This region's first white settler, Hiram Smith, initially traveled to the Okanogan Valley in the early 1850s as a mail carrier out of Hope, British Columbia. He returned in 1856-57 and planted 1,200 apple trees at this site, beginning what many believe to be Washington's famous apple industry. Smith's original log cabin is preserved inside a wooden shed at this Nationally Registered Historic Site, where some of his original apple trees still bear fruit.

Smith served as a member of the 1865-66 territorial legislature and was elected to the Washington State Legislature in 1892.

Hee Hee Stone Historical Marker
17 miles east of Oroville on the Toroda-Chesaw Rd.

"Native American legends told of an Indian princess who turned to stone at this well-known spot along an ancient Indian trail. The object of their tale, a large boulder from the ice age, was deliberately dynamited by white prospectors in 1905. Pieces of the boulder, and monument and plaque are all that remain."

PATEROS (puh-TAIR-uhs)

Methow Rapids U-Bolt Historic Marker
At the junction of the Methow and Columbia Rivers, Pateros

The challenge: get sternwheelers through the Methow rapids to Pateros' asbestos mines and farming regions. The solution: anchor an iron u-bolt in a rock and use it to pull ships through the rapids. A highway road sign placed by the Okanogan County Historical Society marks the site.

TWISP

North Cascade Smokejumper Base
Methow Valley State Airport, East County Rd. 9129, 4 miles north of Twisp
(509) 997-2031

Studies were made above this 50-acre valley in 1939 to test the feasibility of parachuting fire fighters into remote areas. Today this site is the base for the airborne fire-fighting unit responsible for five nearby national forests. Summer tours can be arranged by calling in advance.

WINTHROP

Old Town Winthrop
Riverside Ave. at Hwy. 20, Winthrop

Wooden sidewalks and false-front buildings add to the atmosphere of this reconstructed 1890s pioneer town. Among the original buildings are: the 1891 Duck Brand Saloon, now used as the City Hall; the c.1909 Winthrop Hotel, renamed the Winthrop Palace with authentically furnished rooms; the Last Trading Post, the town's original trading post and post office; and the "Castle," the log cabin home of Guy Waring, one of the city's first settlers. Guy Waring's Harvard roommate, Owen Wister, wrote America's first western novel, "The Virginian," while honeymooning in Winthrop. Three Finger Jack's Saloon at 176 Riverside Ave., has the distinction of being Washington State's first legal saloon.

Winthrop Visitor Information Center
Riverside Ave. and Hwy. 20 (509) 996-2125

Guides to historic sites and interesting places to visit in the Winthrop area are available at this Center in the hub of the town's historic area.

White Buck Museum
241 Riverside Ave., Winthrop (509) 996-3505

In the heart of downtown Winthrop is the White Buck Museum, a privately owned and operated museum containing one of the largest antique collections in the state.

Local and regional artifacts comprise the bulk of the 10,000-piece collection. Just about every type of collectible is displayed: three vintage autos, a 1924 Studebaker, 1926 Model T and a 1938 Dodge; an early drug store with turn-of-the-century cure-alls; general store; 1900s kitchen; blacksmith shop; railroad lanterns and memorabilia; one of the largest displays of World War I bond posters; graphophone with twenty-five original wax cylinders to teach Spanish; office equipment; fishing and hunting supplies; Coastal Indian artifacts; World War I and II memorabilia; antique toys; and Morninglory Phonographs, are just a sampling of what visitors can see here.

Interior view, White Buck Museum

Shafer Museum
285 Castle Ave., Winthrop (509) 442-4272

Guy Waring's 1897 log cabin, "the Castle," which is listed on the National Register of Historic Places, is the centerpiece of this large indoor and outdoor museum. Period furnishings, authentic antiques, and relics from the early days of Winthrop are displayed in original buildings that have been relocated here from the surrounding

area. Mining and farm equipment, old horse-drawn wagons, an 1880 sleigh, stagecoach and a Rickenbacher automobile can be seen outside the museum buildings. A furnished replica of an early print shop, church and pioneer home are among the featured exhibits.

129

Reconstructed Schoolroom

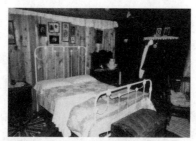

Pioneer Bedroom

Farm Implements

Early Winters Interpretive Site
14 miles northwest of Winthrop on Hwy. 20 (509) 996-2534

History of the 1.7 million-acre Okanogan National Forest, and the geological history of the Early Winters Spires is exhibited along with information about the nearby North Cascades National Park and National Recreation Areas.

130

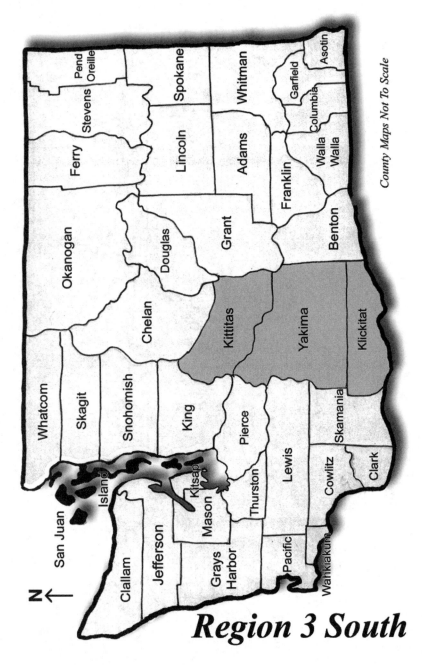

County Maps Not To Scale

Region 3 South

Kittitas County

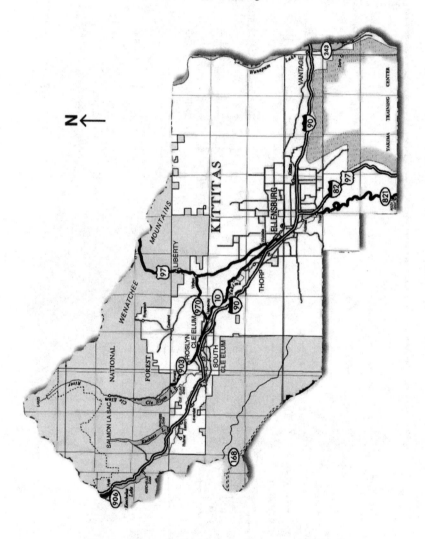

132

REGION 3 SOUTH

KITTITAS COUNTY

CLE ELUM (klee-EL-uhm)

Cle Elum Bakery
501 E. 1st St., Cle Elum (509) 674-2233

Two major fires before the turn-of-the-century almost destroyed the town. When the town rebuilt brick was used in the construction of many of its new buildings. Today, a number of those brick buildings from the early 1900s line the city's main streets, including the Cle Elum Bakery. The bakery still produces hearth-baked French bread and other bakery products in the original brick oven that's been in continuous operation in this building since opening day in 1906.

Historic Photo, Courtesy of Cle Elum Bakery

Cle Elum State Bank
Key Bank, 1st and Harris Sts., Cle Elum

The importance of coal mining to this region's economy brought about the construction of this bank in 1906. The original safe, and many of the bank's antique fixtures have been preserved in this brick building, which continues to serve the community's banking needs.

133

Cle Elum Historical Museum

Cle Elum Historical Museum and Chamber of Commerce, 221 E. First St., Cle Elum (509) 674-5702

Cle Elum was the last city in the Pacific Northwest Bell Telephone Company's service area to be automated. On September 18, 1966, service changed from a manual switchboard to automatic dialing and the first dial telephone call was made. That same year, this former telephone company office building became the historical society's museum. A fine collection of old switchboards, antique telephone equipment and just about every type of telephone ever used are featured exhibits. The museum's telecommunications collection is one of the most complete in the United States. Not to be overlooked are the society's displays that tell the history of this former coal mining town.

Cle Elum Historical Museum

Carpenter Memorial House

302 W. Third St., Cle Elum (509) 674-2268

Visitors who tour this magnificently restored and authentically furnished 1914 Victorian mansion are given an opportunity to glimpse into the world of Cle Elum's upper-class as it existed in the early 1900s. By the time your visit takes you to the grand ballroom on the mansion's third floor, you will have already seen an outstanding collection of Tiffany lamps, marble-topped tables, a mahogany Chippendale desk, an upright rosewood piano, family heirlooms, antiques and furnishings of the period.

Carpenter House Museum

The Moore House
526 Marie Ave., South Cle Elum, (509) 674-5939

Railroad buffs won't want to miss seeing this former railroad boarding house; turned bed & breakfast and museum. Originally constructed in 1909 by the Chicago, Milwaukee, St. Paul and Pacific Railroad, it provided lodging for the men who operated trains through some of America's roughest terrain: the Cascade Range. An outstanding collection of railroad memorabilia and artifacts is displayed throughout the inn's common areas and in each of the refurbished guest rooms. Vintage photographs, schedules and timetables, posters, old matchbooks, switch lights and train signals, a scissor phone, and signal lanterns are just a few of the treasures on display. Breakfast is served on authentic Olympian Hiawatha dining car china. The old tracks that once ran behind the inn have been removed and the railbed is now the Iron Horse State Park, a part of the 25-mile John Wayne Pioneer Trail. The old depot, substation, company houses, and train yard with remnants of the turntable can still be seen.

The Moore House Logo, Courtesy of The Moore House Bed and Breakfast Inn

135

Hidden Valley Guest Ranch
Hidden Valley Road, south of Hwy. 970, northeast of Cle Elum (509) 674-5990

In 1895, the Evans family settled here and homesteaded this valley of open range and gently rolling hills. Fifty years later the 700-acre Hidden Valley Ranch became one of the state's first working guest ranches. Original log buildings built by the Evans family have been preserved and renovated into guest quarters.

ELLENSBURG

Ellensburg Historic District
Between 3rd and 6th Sts. and Main and Ruby Sts., Downtown Ellensburg Guides available from Ellensburg Chamber of Commerce, 436 N. Sprague (509) 925-3137 or the Kittitas County Museum (509) 925-3778.

The year "1889" engraved on many of Ellensburg's brick buildings gives the impression that the city's downtown was established that year. It was actually laid-out fourteen years earlier. Ellensburg was rebuilt in 1889 following a fire that destroyed two hundred Victorian homes and ten business blocks. Before the fire, Ellensburg, the geographic center of the state, was being considered as the site for the state capitol. Although the city lost its bid to be capitol, a normal school would be opened here two years later. The Chamber of Commerce publishes a walking tour guide listing 33 buildings of interest in Ellensburg's Historic District.

Kittitas County Museum
114 E. 3rd, Ellensburg (509) 925-3778

The history of Ellensburg from the days when the town was named "Robber's Roost" to its distinction as the county seat and educational center of Central Washington, is exhibited in the county's museum of history. The story of hostile Indian tribes who camped here in peace, the evolution of Central Washington University, the city's hosting of the 1889 Admissions Convention, arrival of the Northern Pacific Railroad, and the pioneers who settled here is preserved in this unusually-designed 1889 brick building. The museum's Rollinger Gem and Mineral Collection includes petrified wood from the Ginkgo Petrified Forest in Vantage, a six-pound blue agate from the gem fields in northwest Ellensburg, and a large collection of other stones and gems from the region.

Kittitas County Museum

Clymer Museum and Gallery
416 N. Pearl St., Ellensburg (509) 962-6416

The town's historic Ramsay Hardware Building has been converted into a gallery featuring the art of Ellensburg native, John Ford Clymer. Clymer, who passed away in 1989, was a well-known illustrator with more than eighty Saturday Evening Post covers to his credit. Historical art was his passion. Clymer and his wife, Doris,

would travel to historic sites to research the subject he planned to paint. His paintings of the Old West were historically accurate depictions of life and events of the period. Clymer earned many awards and honors including the inclusion of his work in a permanent display at the Cowboy Hall of Fame.

Potbellied stove inside entrance to
Clymer Museum and Gallery

137

Barge Hall

Central Washington University, 8th and "D" Sts., Ellensburg (509) 963-1211

The state's first legislature established Washington State Normal School on this 350-acre site in 1890. First classes were conducted the next year. The oldest building on campus today is the Romanesque-style Barge Hall, built in 1893-94. CWU features several interesting buildings to visit while on campus: the Sarah Spurgeon Art Gallery in Randall Hall; the anthropology museum in the Instructional Building; and the university's library, with more than a million books, maps, government publications and a large microfilm department where historic documents, old newspapers and other material can be viewed.

Olmstead Place State Park

921 N. Ferguson Rd., 4 miles east of Ellensburg off the Kittitas Hwy. (509) 925-1943

Samuel Olmstead, a former Union soldier during the Civil War, came west in 1875 with his wife and children and homesteaded this 217-acre plot of land. He raised beef cattle at first and then converted to a dairy operation. Butter from his highly successful dairy was shipped to markets as distant as Seattle. Today, Olmstead Place is listed on the National Register of Historic Places and is managed by the Washington State Parks and Recreation Department as a heritage site. The original squared-log cabin, built by Olmstead in 1875 from cottonwood logs, an 1892 dairy barn and granary, an 1894 wagon shed, and the 1908, five-bedroom family farmhouse and hay barn are preserved on this living history farm. Original and period furnishings, farm implements, antiques and family possessions help convey the impression of what a working farm was like at the turn-of-the-century. The renovated c.1870s

Seaton Cabin schoolhouse, where the Olmstead children attended class, has been relocated to this site to show visitors an example of pioneer education.

Olmstead Cabin, Courtesy of Olmstead Place State Park

LIBERTY

Liberty Historic District
Two miles east of U.S. 97, 3 miles north of the junction of U.S. 97 and Hwy. 970, Liberty

A big gold strike at Swauk Creek in 1873 brought a steady number of miners into this region. In 1880, the town of Williams Creek was established. It was renamed Meaghersville in 1897, and Liberty in 1916. A dozen of the town's original buildings remain in this part of the Swauk Mining District and can be seen along Williams Creek Wagon Road.

ROSLYN

Roslyn Historic District
Hwy. 903, Roslyn

Its been called the town that time forgot; almost unchanged from the turn-of-the-century. Rustic wood and brick buildings with corrugated metal roofs line the town's main street. Modern street lights and names on some of the business establishments are the only reminders that you are in the present. Roslyn was built on top of one of the largest coalfields in the west. Within ten years after its mines

opened, half the coal in the state was produced here. Roslyn was a company town. The Northern Pacific Railroad, and its subsidiaries, owned the mines, the town and the company store. The last mine closed in 1963, but evidence of the town's major industry can be seen everywhere.

The town's rustic buildings made it the perfect backdrop for the television series, "Northern Exposure," which was filmed here.

139

Roslyn Historical Museum
28 Pennsylvania Ave., Roslyn (509) 649-2776

Samples of coal mined from the region's vast coal fields, mining equipment, historical documents and old photographs portray the history of Roslyn's mines; from the pick-and-shovel days of 1884, to 1963, when the last mine closed. Other exhibits include pioneer furnishings, tools and mementos from the town's early families.

Log cabin on grounds of the Roslyn Museum

Northwestern Improvement Company Store
First St. and Pennsylvania Ave., Roslyn

This "company" store, a vestige from the past, was built by the Northern Pacific Railroad in 1889 to sell tools and provisions to the men working their coal mines. Charges made at the company store, as well as rent, utilities and health care, were deducted from the well-paid miners' earnings. The original brick building was remodeled in 1916 and is listed on the National Register of Historic Places.

Northwestern Improvement Co.

Other vintage Roslyn buildings worth visiting are:

The Brick Tavern, built in 1898 of locally fired brick is one of the state's oldest operating taverns. It features an ornate bar that was shipped around the Horn and a 20-foot spittoon with running water.

Roslyn Bank was built in 1910. The vault is original, as are many of the bank's fixtures.

City Hall and Library. Erected in 1902 by the Northwest Improvement Company as a YWCA.

Roslyn Theatre, 101 W. Dakota. This large, two-story frame building off the town's main street is the state's oldest operating theatre.

Washington State's Oldest Operating Theatre

Roslyn Log Cabin
North Second St. and Utah Ave., Roslyn

This fine example of an early 1880s log cabin was built by Nez Jensen on the 160-acre plot he homesteaded at this site. A trapper, John Stone, who lived with Jensen, was the first to discover coal in this region. Jensen dug the coal out with pick and shovel and hauled it to Ellensburg where he sold it to blacksmiths. Within two years of Stone's discovery, Northern Pacific Railroad miners were underground and Roslyn was being established as a company town.

141

Roslyn Cemetery
Southwest of Roslyn

Experienced miners, many from European countries, migrated to Roslyn to work the area's extensive coal fields. This cemetery reflects the diversity of those who settled here. Roslyn Cemetery is actually a combination of 26 separate ethnic, religious and fraternal burial areas. Each section has its own identity. Elaborate headstones are found in some; others have above ground graves. And some plots are identified with only simple wooden markers.

SALMON LA SAC (SA-muhn-lah-SAK)

Salmon la Sac Guard Station
26 miles north of Ronald in Wenatchee National Forest, Salmon le Sac

The lack of rail transportation to haul minerals that were being mined in this region during the early 1900s prompted a French investment firm to form the Kittitas Railway and Power Company with the intent of constructing an electric railroad. They built this two-story log depot in 1912, but the possibility of war in Europe forced them to abandon their plans. The U.S. Forest Service acquired the depot in 1914 and used it as a guard station until the 1980s. In 1974 the station was added to the National Register of Historic Places.

THORP

Thorp Mill
Exit I-90 north at milepost 101 (Thorp exit). Continue through Thorp (west) three miles to the millstream and mill (509) 964-9640

Visitors to this historic mill get a good feel for what it took to turn grain into flour before the turn-of-the-century. Oren Hutchinson built the mill in 1883, which helped the town of Thorp develop into a major crossroads community. Steam from the mill powered a generator that provided electricity to the town of Thorp. Because of the mill, Thorp became one of the first towns in the state to get electricity. A major restoration project has preserved the mill, all of its original water-powered machinery and the maze of chutes and elevators that crisscross from floor-to-floor. Members of the Thorp Mill Town Historical Preservation Society conduct tours and give first-hand information about the history of the mill and adjacent 23-acre ice pond. Thorp Mill is listed on the National Register of Historic Places.

Thorp Mill

Flour Bagging Machine, Thorp Mill

VANTAGE

Ginkgo Petrified Forest Historic Marker
At the entrance to Ginkgo State Park, Exit 136 north off I-90, Vantage

"Millions of years ago this area was a low-lying tree-covered, swampy land, bordered on the north by mountains. Eventually, after completion of their life spans, trees of both the mountains and lowlands mingled as logs in the swamps. In following ages successive flows of lava covered the area deeply burying the accumulated vegetation. The elements have persistently eroded the strata of lava, exposing the petrified remains of over 200 species of trees, including the sacred Ginkgo, now growing naturally only in the orient. No other fossil forest approaches this in number of species."

Ginkgo Interpretive Center
Wanapum Forest State Park, Heritage Area, on the Columbia River by Vantage
Bridge, Vantage exit off I-90 (509) 856-2700

Thousands of petrified trees have been uncovered at this 7,100-acre state park
since the 1930s when Professor George Beck discovered this forest of rare petrified
Ginkgo trees. Most of the 200 species of trees that have been identified are no
longer native to Washington including the Ginkgo. The Ginkgo last grew wild in
Eastern Asia; today it can be found in Chinese Buddhist Temples where it's cultivated
as an ornamental tree. Displays of petrified wood and exhibits at this Center describe
the events that created this fossilized forest. One of the Center's interpretive trails
leads to an area where ancient petroglyphs have been carved in the cliffs over the
Columbia River.

Wanapum Dam Tour Center and Museum
Wanapum Dam, 3 miles south of I-90 on Hwy. 243 (509) 754-3541

Artifacts uncovered during construction of the Priest Rapids Project are included in
exhibits that depict the life of the region's Indians, fur traders, miners and pioneers.
An underwater fish-viewing room and dam overview can also be toured.

Klickitat County

KLICKITAT COUNTY

BICKLETON

Herschell-Spillman Carrousel
Cleveland Park, Bickleton

The end of Spring is a special time in Bickleton. That's when the town celebrates its annual Pioneer Picnic and operates its vintage carrousel. The carrousel, built in the early 1900s, was purchased from a Portland amusement park in 1928 and relocated here. Unlike many carrousels built with a floor that radiates from a central hub, this model runs on a track. An antique motor drives the carrousel and its original horses.

Bickleton National Bluebird Trail

In the mid-1960s, Jess and Elva Brinkerhoff began developing the Bickleton Bluebird Trail in eastern Klickitat County. They built and placed more than 1,500 birdhouses for the thousands of bluebirds that migrate to this region every spring. Fence posts along more than 300 miles of roads around the Bickleton area are topped with these blue-roofed birdhouses, which are now maintained by a large number of volunteers.

Whoop-N-Holler Ranch and Museum
12 miles south of Bickleton on East Rd. and 13 miles north of Roosevelt and the Columbia River (509) 896-2344

First-hand knowledge of a homesteader's lifestyle in the early 1900s can be gained by visiting with this rural museum's owners, Ada Ruth and Lawrence Whitmore. Both were raised in families who settled in the Bickleton area before the turn-of-the-century. Their large collection of family heirlooms and artifacts fill one of the large buildings on their property. Hand-carved doll furniture, Coca-Cola cans gathered from around the world, home remedies purchased from traveling salesmen and many one-of-a-kind items can be seen in this interesting museum. A second building houses one of the state's largest antique and classic auto collections; including a 1927 Studebaker, Model T Ford, Maxwell, and a horse-drawn hearse on sled runners. A 1900 Fairview school house, where Lawrence Whitmore's great-aunt once taught, and a local Grange Hall are also on the grounds.

Bull Tractor, Courtesy of Whoop-N-Holler Ranch and Museum

BINGEN (BIN-jin) – WHITE SALMON
Highway 14

Water from the nearby Columbia River has made farming and ranching profitable for both of these neighboring cities. But they have much more in common. Germans settled both cities, and both have adopted a German architectural theme. Bingen was named for Bingen-on-the-Rhine because of its resemblance to that city; while White Salmon has the distinction of having the only authentic Glockenspiel bell tower west of the Mississippi. Many older buildings in both cities have been remodeled to reflect the Rhineland style, matching new structures that are now being built.

The Gorge Heritage Museum
202 E. Humbolt, Bingen (509) 493-3573 or (509) 493-3228

Pictures of American Indians fishing at the once popular Celilo Falls are part of the exceptional photograph collection displayed in the 1912 Congregational Church building that now serves as the West Klickitat County Historical Society's museum. The museum's wide-ranging exhibits feature artifacts and memorabilia from the Native Americans, explorers, trappers, ranchers, miners, loggers and early settlers who came to this scenic region of the state. A replica country store containing original containers of foodstuffs, antique toys, medical and surgical equipment and a fine collection of household implements and tools are among the museum's interesting exhibits.

147

The Gorge Heritage Museum

GOLDENDALE

Presby Mansion
Klickitat County Historical Society Museum
127 W. Broadway, Goldendale (509) 773-4303

One of the most beautiful museum buildings in the state is the striking Presby Mansion. Winthrop Presby was mayor of Goldendale, a U.S. Land Commissioner, and member of the State Senate. While studying law in Goldendale, he assisted with the drafting of the Washington State Constitution. In 1902, Presby built this 20-room Victorian home. Today it's managed and preserved by the Klickitat County Historical Society as a historic landmark and museum. The elaborately designed mansion contains displays of furniture, clothing, utensils and personal effects depicting home life and family customs of the 1880-1930 era. Special exhibits include antique camera equipment, coffee mills, and Indian crafts and tools.

Goldendale Observatory
Brooks Memorial State Park, 1602 Observatory Dr., Goldendale (509) 773-3141

The nation's largest amateur-built Cassegrain telescope that's available for public use was dedicated at this site in 1973. The world-class, 24 1/2-inch reflecting telescope was originally built for Vancouver's Clark College. In 1980 it was acquired by the Washington State Parks and Recreation Commission and opened to the general public. This interpretive center contains a wealth of resources for the amateur astronomer, but, more important, it provides an opportunity for all to view celestial objects firsthand.

MARYHILL

Maryhill Museum of Art
35 Maryhill Museum Dr., off Hwy. 14, 3 miles west of U.S. 97, south of Goldendale in Maryhill (509) 773-3733

Seattle attorney, Samuel Hill, built this European-style palace in 1914 and named it for his daughter, Mary. After Hill's death, his "castle" was turned into a museum of fine arts. Its galleries house: North American Indian artifacts, including more than 1,000 baskets and rare petroglyphs; a large collection of Rodin sculpture; Russian icons; art glass by Galle; more than 100 chess sets; and American and European art. Queen Marie of Romania, who participated in the dedication of Maryhill, contributed Romanian furniture and personal memorabilia to Hill. Her gifts are displayed in a large memorial exhibit on the museum's main floor. Maryhill is listed on the National Register of Historic Places.

Maryhill Museum

Maryhill Community Church
At the junction of Maryhill Hwy. and Stonehenge Ave., off Hwy. 14 by Maryhill State Park, Maryhill

Amos Stark, the first white man to settle in Klickitat County, and Dr. William Chapman, an Iowa preacher, were chiefly responsible for establishing Maryhill's Advent Christian Church in 1888. Amos Stark donated the land and Dr. Chapman organized the townsfolk who built the church. Restoration of the church began in 1970 after the church building and pioneer cemetery was donated to the Maryhill Women's Club. The church's original pews, which were built by Amos' brother, Benjamin, have been refurbished and are once again being used by parishioners who attend services in this historic church. In 1991 the church was added to the National Register of Historic Places.

Maryhill Community Church

Stonehenge at Maryhill
One mile east of the junction of U.S. 97 and Hwy. 14, Maryhill

Samuel Hill, the wealthy attorney and son-in-law of railroad "Empire Builder" James J. Hill, built a life-size replica of England's famous Stonehenge in 1918, five miles east of his Maryhill estate. "Stonehenge at Maryhill" was dedicated on Decoration (Memorial) Day in 1930. It was the nation's first monument to honor those who died in World War I. Inscribed on its concrete pillars are the names of Klickitat County's young men who gave their lives in the "War to End All Wars." A plaque on the 18-foot-high altar stone reads: "To the memory of the soldiers of Klickitat County who gave their lives in defense of their country. This monument is erected in the hope that others inspired by the example of their valor and their heroism may share in that love of liberty and burn with that fire of patriotism which death alone can quench." Sam Hill died a year after this memorial was dedicated. His final resting-place is 200 feet below the bluff, south of Stonehenge.

Stonehenge World War I Memorial

WISHRAM

Spearfish Historic Marker
Hwy. 14 north of Wishram

"Among the rocks and rapids of the nearby Columbia River, early day Indians secured an annual supply of salmon, using crude spears and nets. The salmon were smoked on racks over a heavy bed of coals; then packed in leaf lined baskets for winter use. Remains of underground "pit houses" and many Indian artifacts have been discovered in this area by archaeologists. The Lewis and Clark expedition found several hundred Indians fishing here in 1805 as they had done for centuries."

Wishram Indian Village Site
Horsethief Lake State Park, Hwy. 14, 6 miles east of Lyle

For centuries this was a popular meeting place where Indians of several cultures would gather in the summer to fish, trade and socialize. Archaeologists consider this to be one of the richest ancient Indian sites in the nation. Clams and seashells from the Pacific Coast and artifacts that originated as far east as Minnesota have been uncovered from the ancient debris mounds that formed here. Indian petroglyphs can also be found at this National Historic Site.

Celilo Falls Historic Marker
Along Hwy. 14 overlooking the town of Wishram

"A historic waterfall, fishing ground and annual gathering point for untold generations of Northwest Indians and always an obstruction to water travel on the Columbia was buried deep beneath the waters of the Dalles Dam in 1957. The railroad town immediately below originally called Fall-bridge later was named Wishram for the Wish-com or Wish-ham Indians found here by early travelers. The area seen from here has been a center of life in the Mid-Columbia through the ages."

Celilo Falls Historic Marker

152

Yakima County

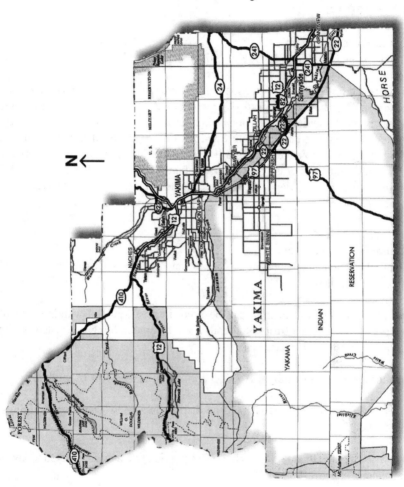

YAKIMA COUNTY

GRANDVIEW

Ray E. Powell Museum
313 Division, Grandview (509) 882-2070

The railroad brought settlers; the men and women who farmed the land and built the town. Their history is recorded in a number of exhibits at the city's museum. Antiques, memorabilia, toys and dolls, old rifles and guns, Indian artifacts, lapidary, and rooms containing period furniture and clothing vividly recall life of the pioneer community. A photo gallery of Grandview's high school graduates dating back to 1910 is a vivid record of the generations of families who lived here. A rare 1907 Kiblinger horseless carriage, maybe the last one in existence, is preserved in this museum of history.

Grandview Historic Tour
Grandville Chamber of Commerce, Division and 5th streets, Grandview
(509) 882-2100

Ten places of historic interest can be seen on a self-guided walking tour of Grandview's business district. Several of the town's buildings are listed on the National Register of Historic Places.

Grandview Herald Building, 107 Division, a well-preserved 1922 building.

Iowa Building, 125-133 Division, one of the town's few two-story buildings, constructed in 1911.

Dykstra-Howay House, 114 Birch, c.1923 prairie-style house, operated today as a restaurant and gift shop.

Burlington Northern Depot, Division and 5th, home of the Chamber of Commerce.

Chateau Ste. Michelle Winery, 5th and Ave. "B", the state's oldest bonded winery.

Grandview Rose Garden, 2nd and Ave. "G", a 40-year project with over 1,000 rose bushes.

Grandview City Hall, 201 W. 2nd, built in 1937.

Grandview State Bank, 100 W. 2nd, 1918 sandstone building containing original bank vault.

Keck Building, 138 Division, the town's oldest two-story building, erected in 1910.

Cornell Farmstead
Pleasant and Old Prosser Rds., south of Grandview

S.D. Cornell, a local dairy farmer erected one of the few round barns in the state here, in 1912-16. It was patterned after similar barns in the Midwest. The "round-style" structure was thought to be more efficient for sheltering, feeding and milking cows. Cornell sold the barn to John Marble whose name appears on the building's tower today. The farmstead is listed on the National Register of Historic Places.

NACHES (na-CHEEZ)

Naches Bandstand, Naches-Tieton Rd. and Main St., Naches

A gazebo or bandstand was a fixture in most early American town parks. It provided a stage for community bands, a central point for civic events, and a forum for public speeches. Naches' bandstand was funded by the community and built in 1919 by the Naches Commercial Club. It has been well maintained through the years and is listed on the National Register of Historic Places.

SAWYER

Mattoon Cabin
South of Sawyer on U.S. 12

When J.P. Mattoon was appointed farm instructor for the Indians at Fort Simcoe in 1884 he built this two-room log cabin. It was one of the first cabins constructed in this region and the first house in the county to be placed on the National Register of Historic Places.

W. P. Sawyer House and Orchard
On U.S. 12, Sawyer

Successful Toppenish orchardist, W. P. Sawyer, built this impressive Colonial Revival-style, three-story home in 1910. It addition to the home's ample living quarters, it also served as his office. The house featured its own chapel, library, and theater. Sawyer's home and orchard are listed on the National Register of Historic Places.

SUNNYSIDE

Sunnyside Historical Museum,
704 S. 4th St., Sunnyside (509) 837-6010

A mammoth pioneer irrigation project and the establishment of a religious colony brought life to this community in the late 1800s. The history of those events is on exhibit, along with a fine collection of Indian artifacts including baskets, beadwork and clothing. The museum building, the former Ball Funeral Home, features three

period rooms that depict pioneer life in Sunnyside. Across the street from the museum is the historic Ben Snipes log cabin.

Sunnyside Historical Museum

Ben Snipes Log Cabin
321 Grant Ave., Sunnyside (509) 837-6010

Ben Snipes built the first white man's cabin erected in Yakima Valley in 1859, seven miles south of Sunnyside's present town limits. It was relocated to this site in 1953 for preservation. Snipes, and his brother-in-law, H. H. Allen drove tens of thousands of head of cattle on central Washington's vast open range between 1859 and 1893. Ben Snipes was one of Washington's greatest cowboys; an accomplishment that earned him an election to the Cowboy Hall of Fame in Oklahoma City.

Ben Snipes 1859 Log Cabin

TOPPENISH (TAH-puhn-ish)

Yakima Indian Nation Cultural Center and Museum
280 Buster Road, off U.S. 97, one mile west of Toppenish (509) 865-2800

Rising from the ancestral grounds of the Yakima Indian, this 76-foot high Winter lodge beckons visitors to this Cultural Center, one of the finest in the state. The "Challenge of Spilyay" guides Indian and non-Indian guests through the Yakima Nation Museum where the evolution of the Yakima people from prehistoric times to the present is displayed. Through a series of dioramas and exhibits Spilyay challenges visitors "to increase understanding within a culture and among cultures," and "to draw strength and richness from the differences between individuals and cultures." The Center's library contains 10,000 books and artifacts collected by Nipo Strongheart during his career as a Hollywood movie consultant. It's the country's only library specializing in the American Indian. The Center also features a theatre, restaurant and gift shop. Guests who choose to stay in the Center's RV park can enjoy all the luxuries of full hook-ups, or experience what the "Old West" was like by staying in a tent or an authentic teepee.

157

Yakima Indian Nation Cultural Center and Museum

Yakima Valley Rail & Steam Museum
Toppenish Depot, 10 Asotin Ave., 1/2-block south of Toppenish Ave., Toppenish
(509) 865-1911

This restored 1911 Northern Pacific Railway Depot serves a dual purpose today. It's home to the Yakima Valley Rail & Steam Museum and a working railroad. Inside the depot is an authentic telegraph office and antique oak showcases filled with railroad memorabilia. The 1929 Northern Pacific Freight building has been renovated into an engine house and is being used for the restoration of a 1902 Baldwin steam locomotive. A number of pieces of rolling stock in various stages of reconstruction can be seen in the yard adjacent to the depot. Excursions on the Toppenish Simcoe & Western Railroad to White Swan in vintage 1920s passenger cars originate at the depot.

Antique Steam-powered Tractor, Yakima Valley Rail & Steam Museum

American Hop Museum
22 South "B" St., Toppenish (509) 865-4677

The old Hop Growers Supply building has been converted into a one-of-a-kind museum: the country's only hop museum. History of hop farming in the United States, from its start in New York state in the late 1700s, the westward movement of hop farms in the 1850s, and Yakima Valley's domination in the 1940s is exhibited. Cast iron ring stoves from New York, antique hop presses, a horse-drawn crop duster, and a portable picking machine from California are among the interesting pieces of equipment on display. Old photos, publications and memorabilia from across the country fill the museum. Seeing the exterior of the museum building by itself is worth the visit. Artist Eric Allen Grohe transformed a plain stucco building into a work of art by painting false architectural features and beautiful murals framed by replicated archways.

American Hop Museum

Toppenish Murals
Toppenish Mural Society, 11-A South Toppenish Ave., Toppenish

Murals decorate the walls of buildings in many Washington communities, but Toppenish ranks as the mural capitol of the state. Historically accurate, bigger-than-life works by famous Western artists from across the Northwest appear on dozens of building walls throughout the city. Murals depict events and scenes from the city's past as well as its pioneering residents including: Maud Bolin, a rodeo star and one of the country's first female pilots; L. S. Shattuck, an expert in 6-horse events and one of the original Toppenish Pow Wow Rodeo boosters; and

159

Ruth Parton, an inductee into the Cowgirl Hall of Fame and the first woman in the United States licensed to train race horses. A guide to the town's murals, and the history behind each work of art is available from the Society.

Mural Depicting an Artist Painting a Mural on one of Toppenish's Buildings

Toppenish Museum
1 S. Elm St., Toppenish (509) 865-4510

Estelle Reel Meyer amassed an extensive collection of Indian arts and crafts from Indian schools across the country while serving as Superintendent of Indian Affairs under President McKinley from 1898 to 1910. She donated her collection to the museum in 1952 where it remains on permanent exhibit. The museum also features a Depression glass and antique glass bottle collection, historical photographs and rotating exhibits from private collectors.

Liberty Theatre
211 S. Toppenish Ave., Toppenish (509) 865-7573

The city's first theatre was built and operated by Dr. H. M. Johnson in 1915. Originally called the Lois Theatre, it is the only one of thirty Vaudeville theatres built during this period still standing in the United States.

UNION GAP

Central Washington Agricultural Museum
Fullbright Park, 4508 Main St. Union Gap (509) 457-8735

The agricultural history of the Yakima Valley and Central Washington is vividly displayed in this 15-acre museum complex. Eighteen large display buildings house an extensive collection of more than 1,000 antique and early twentieth century farm implements, machinery and tools. Some of the pieces are horse-drawn or steam-powered; many are restored and fully operational. The museum features other interesting exhibits including: a steam engine that once powered the Old Naches sawmill, a 1917 log cabin containing period furnishings, and a Burlington-Northern boxcar housing an exhibit of railroad memorabilia (the car sits on rails from the old Yakima Interurban Electric Railroad). One of the more recent additions is a U.S. Army tank that's perched on a hill overlooking the museum.

Central Washington Agricultural Museum

Union Gap Pioneer Graveyard
200 E. Antanum Rd., Union Gap

This final resting-place for many of the region's early inhabitants serves as a reminder of the diversity of cultures and backgrounds of those who once lived here. In one corner, among the simple headstones and monuments, is the Kingsbury family plot. Anna Adams Kingsbury, lineal descendant of John and Priscilla Alden and the ancestor of two American presidents, is buried here along with other members of the Kingsbury family who played important roles in the region's history. The archway at the entrance of this well-maintained pioneer cemetery was built by the Works Progress Administration (WPA) during the Great Depression.

Entrance to Union Gap Pioneer Graveyard

Old Town Mill
Main St., south end of town, Union Gap

In 1869, the year "Yakima City" became the first city in Yakima County, the old town mill was established. It continues to grind wheat into flour using water power; the same as it did the year it opened.

Ah-Wah-Tum (Deep Water) Historical Marker
At Sunnyside Diversion Dam, off Hwy. 12, two miles south of Union Gap

"A natural fishery, a fishery old when the Sunnyside Canal intake was built at the turn of the century, the site of prehistoric 'pit houses' and present day Indian activities. This area was the home of the Saluskin family, whose chiefs descended from We-Ou-Wicht, head chief of the entire region. One of the few remaining sites from which the Indians can dip-net steelhead in the early spring and salmon during the early summer and fall runs."

WHITE SWAN

Fort Simcoe Interpretive Center
Fort Simcoe State Park, 5150 Fort Simcoe Rd., at the end of Hwy. 220, 7 miles southwest of White Swan (509) 874-2372

In 1856, Fort Walla Walla and Fort Simcoe were both constructed to quell an uprising by the Yakima Indians against white settlers. For three years officers and men of the 9th Regiment of the U.S. Army were stationed here. At the end of the Indian Wars, the Army's duties turned to protecting treaty lands against white intruders and guarding military roads. Five of the fort's original buildings remain intact: the Commandant's house, three captain's dwellings and a log blockhouse. They are among the best preserved and least altered frontier buildings in the state. The Bureau of Indian Affairs used the fort's buildings as an agency office and Indian school from 1859 until 1923. An adjacent brick museum houses interpretive exhibits with Indian crafts and relics.

YAKIMA (YAK-i-maw)

Yakima Valley Museum and Historical Association
2105 Tieton Dr., Yakima (509) 248-0747

Indian resistance to the intrusion of the white man on their ancestral lands delayed settlement of the Yakima Valley until the early 1860s. A few skirmishes between the Indians and settlers developed into the Yakima Indian War of 1855-57. The U.S. Army established Fort Simcoe in 1856. Two years later a treaty was signed. Irrigation transformed the valley from an open cattle range to a major farming and fruit-growing region. An extensive Native American collection, pioneer household furnishings and artifacts, a comprehensive agriculture exhibit, and 72 horse-drawn vehicles are among the museum's featured exhibitions. Memorabilia from the Washington D.C. office of Supreme Court Justice and Yakima native William O. Douglas is also displayed. A hands-on children's museum brings history down-to-earth for the museum's young visitors.

H. M. Gilbert Homeplace
2109 West Yakima, Yakima (509) 248-0747

Yakima Valley Museum maintains the 1898 Victorian home of Yakima pioneer farmer and orchardist, Horace M. Gilbert. Gilbert was active in the development of land in the lower Yakima Valley and was instrumental in bringing an ample supply of irrigation water to the valley. The Gilbert's well preserved home is furnished with Victorian antiques and is listed on the National Register of Historic Places. Yakima Valley Museum staff conducts tours.

Gilbert House, Courtesy of Yakima Valley Museum

Ahtanum Mission
Ahtanum Mission Park, 17740 Ahtanum Rd., Yakima (509) 966-0865

Jesuit Missionaries built a mission church at this site in 1847, well before the arrival of the region's first white settlers. It was burned during the Yakima Indian War of 1855-57, and rebuilt in 1868. Religious services have been continuously conducted here since reconstruction.

Yakima's North Front Street Historical District
North Front St., Yakima

In the winter of 1884 Yakima City was literally a "city on the move." When the Northern Pacific Railroad selected this site for its station, it was four miles to the north of the town of Yakima City. The railroad called the town North Yakima, offered free lots and paid 100 businesses to move, "lot, stock and barrel" to the new town. Buildings were put on rollers, or pulled on skids, and conducted "business as usual" as they were being relocated to the new city. A city hall was built the following year and is now preserved in this historic district as a retail store center. The 1909 Mission Revival-style Depot has been fully restored and houses Grant's Brewery Pub, America's oldest brewpub. North Yakima was renamed Yakima in 1918, and that same year, the former Yakima City took the name Union Gap.

Yakima's 1909 Depot

Capitol Theatre
19 S. 3rd St., Yakima

When this building was constructed in 1920, it was one of the West's largest and most elegant theaters. Its imposing Renaissance Revival-style exterior is matched

by an equally impressive interior that features murals and ceiling paintings. Originally the theater presented Lowe and Pantages Vaudeville acts, motion pictures and stage shows. Today the restored theater, a National Historic Site, is home to the Yakima Symphony Orchestra as well as other community cultural programs and presentations of performing arts.

The **Federal Building** next door was named for Yakima's famous son, and former U.S. Supreme Count Justice, William O. Douglas.

St. Michael's Episcopal Church
5 S. Naches Ave., Yakima

Clustered along several blocks of East Yakima Avenue in the center of town are six well-preserved historic buildings. The oldest is the 1888 St. Michael's Episcopal Church. The church was designed by the son of Bishop Alonzo Potter of Pennsylvania and is constructed of native lava rock and was the first stone building erected in Yakima. A wood portico was added to the structure in 1923. St. Michael's is listed on the National Register of Historic Places.

Yakima Interurban Trolley Lines
3rd Avenue and Pine St., Yakima (509) 575-1700

The 41 miles of rails of this interurban line connected Yakima to orchards and farms on the outskirts of the city from 1907 until the end of World War II. During the first 25 years of operation, these electric trolleys carried both passengers and freight and were a major force in the growth and development of the city. Public rides in the historic single-truck wooden streetcars are conducted on summer weekends.

Indian Painted Rocks Historical Marker
Hwy. 12, 4 miles northwest of Yakima

"Origin of these paintings is unknown to present-day Indian tribes of this region. They are similar to many others found in western North America and are often interpreted as depicting religious experiences, as well as records of hunts or meetings with other tribes. This location was the old Indian trail which ran from the Wenas Mountains to the Ahtanum band of the Yakimas. In the 1850s, miners en route to British Columbia gold fields used the same trail. Later, as Americans settled Yakima Valley, a stage coach route passed these cliffs."

Fred G. Redmon Memorial Bridge
6 miles north of Yakima on I-82

The largest concrete single span bridge on the North American continent was dedicated at this site in 1971. The supporting bridge lanes that span the 549-foot wide canyon are 1,336 feet long and 335 feet above the canyon floor. An observation deck at the rest stop that borders the south end of the canyon offers impressive views of the canyon and this engineering masterpiece.

Fred G. Redmon Memorial Bridge

ZILLAH (ZIL-uh)

Teapot Dome Service Station
Old State Hwy. 12 parallel to the south side of U.S. 12 , 1/4 mile east of Zillah

The Teapot Dome oil reserve scandal of 1921 that involved President Harding's Secretary of the Interior inspired construction of this teapot-style service station. Most of the country's novel roadside businesses have disappeared, but this station continues to serve customers the same as when it was built in 1922.

1922 Teapot Dome Service Station

167

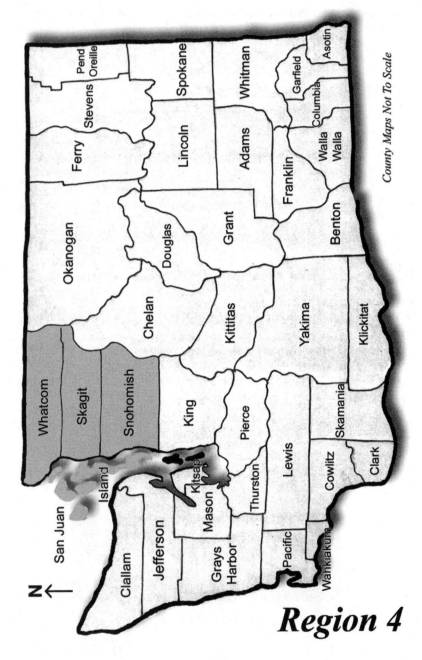

County Maps Not To Scale

Region 4

Island County

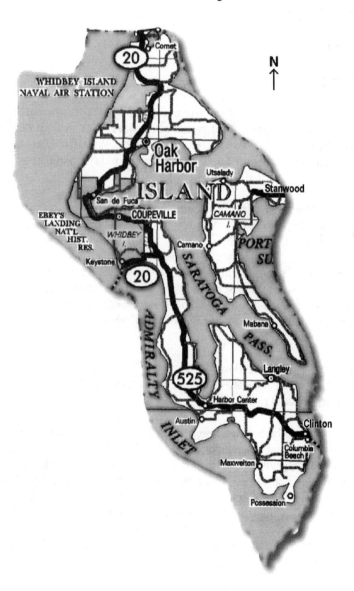

REGION 4

ISLAND COUNTY

WHIDBEY ISLAND

OAK HARBOR

The heritage of the Dutch who settled here in the late 1890s is celebrated in the city's annual "Holland Happening" celebration. Full-size replica windmills can be seen year-around at City Beach Park and Holland Gardens. A stand of Garry Oaks, the tree for which Oak Harbor is named, has been preserved at Smith Park.

Orren and Ruth Ward Memorial Museum
James Andrew Neil Farm, Neil Park, Whidbey Ave. at State Hwy. 20, Oak Harbor
(360) 675-5464 or (360) 675-2552

Two structures from the pioneer farm of James Neil have been preserved at this city park: the 1912 barn, once the largest on the West Coast (now a roller skating rink), and the restored western cedar water tower that was originally constructed in 1910. The water tower building houses a collection of Oak Harbor memorabilia.

Whidbey Island Naval Air Station,
West shore of the Strait of Juan de Fuca, north of Oak Harbor (360) 257-2211 or the Public Affairs Office at (360) 257-2286

Although the city had its beginnings before the turn-of-the-century, Oak Harbor is best-known today as the home of Whidbey Island Naval Air Station. NAS Whidbey Island was built at the beginning of World War II as a base for seaplanes that patrolled the west coast. More recently, seven A-6E Intruder medium attack bomber squadrons were based here along with fourteen tactical electonic warfare squadrons. (A retired A-6 jet can be seen at City Beach Park in Oak Harbor) Today, most of the squadrons based here fly the Grumman EA-6B Prowler, the newest generation of carrier-based tactical jamming aircraft. Group tours of the station for 10 to 40 visitors can be arranged in advance.

Navy Jet displayed outside NAS Whidbey Island's Main Gate

Ebey's Landing National Historic Reserve
Guide available from the Island County Historical Society Museum, Coupeville
(360) 678-3310

Near the center of Whidbey Island, 17,400 acres were designated the nation's first
National Historical Reserve by an Act of Congress in 1978 to "preserve and protect
a rural community which provides an unbroken historic record from the nineteenth
century exploration and settlement in Puget Sound to the present time." The
boundaries of this Reserve are the same as those filed by the original settlers in the
1850s. Although the Reserve is part of the National Park Service, most of the land
is privately owned. The trust that administers the Reserve is composed of
representatives of federal, state and local governments, and nearly every local
landowner. They work together to "preserve the scenic, natural and cultural resources
of the area, without disturbing the community's way of life."

Dense forests, pastoral prairies, the historic seaport town of Coupeville, desert-like
beaches, a pioneer cemetery, an underwater park, Fort Casey, a natural bird sanctuary,
Admiralty Head Lighthouse, log blockhouses, old orchards, Victorian homes, and
Indian village sites can all be seen within this historic Reserve.

171

COUPEVILLE

Island County Historical Museum
902 NW Alexander St., Coupeville (360) 678-3310

In the early to mid-1800s, sea captains, who encountered bad weather or rough seas off the Strait of Juan de Fuca, would often seek protection for their ships in the

calm waters along Whidbey Island's eastern shore. Some were so impressed with the island that they retired here on the shore of Penn Cove and called their town the "Port of Captains," in honor of the many seamen who took up residence here. In 1853, the town of Coupeville, was officially named for Captain Thomas Coupe, its first settler. This museum's "Bow to Plow" exhibit chronicles the lives of pioneers who "debarked from the bow of their ships to get behind a plow and farm." Photographs, relics of pioneer life from as early as 1852, Skagit Indian artifacts, the Cora Cook doll collection, and the Wayland Northwest and Alaska Indian basket collection are displayed. For more information about Coupeville's Victorian homes and historic buildings, ask museum staff for a copy of their self-guided walking tour brochure, "A walk Through History." Guided weekend tours are also offered.

Island County Historical Museum

Alexander's Blockhouse
Alexander and Coveland Sts., Coupeville

Well-founded fear of Indian attack prompted this area's early settlers to join together in the mid-1850s to build a series of blockhouses and palisades. Three are open to the public: John Alexander's two-story blockhouse, which was constructed on his homestead in 1855 and relocated here in later years for preservation; the Davis

(Cook) Blockhouse, at the edge of Coupeville's Sunnyside Cemetery, one of the largest on the island; and the Crockett Blockhouse, near Eagle and Fort Casey roads, just south of Coupeville.

Jacob Ebey's Blockhouse, where Issac Ebey's family and houseguests fled the day Issac was killed by Haida Indians, is on private property about 1 1/2 miles from Sunnyside Cemetery and is not open to the public. The Ebey family plot, and those of other island settlers, can be viewed at the pioneer Sunnyside Cemetery.

Next to the Alexander Blockhouse is a canoe shed housing Indian racing canoes from the 1920s and Chief Snakelum's canoe that was used to transport pioneers around Puget Sound.

Alexander's Blockhouse

Central Whidbey Island Historic District
Approximately 6 miles either side of Coupeville Guide available from the Island County Historical Society Museum, Coupeville Chamber of Commerce, and Front Street merchants in Coupeville

Scores of historic structures are preserved within this nationally registered historic district. In the city of Coupeville alone are 38, pre-1900 homes, businesses, civic buildings, churches, and historic sites. Coupeville, the state's second oldest town, is a historic treasure chest. Residential streets are lined with restored Victorian homes from the 1850s, including one of the oldest in the state, the 1853 home of

173

the city's founder, Captain Thomas Coupe. Plaques identify when these old homes were built and the names of the original owners. The pioneer spirit of the period can also be seen in the city's business district; from the town's early-1900s wharf to the quaint turn-of-the-century frame stores that face each other along Front Street. Coupeville is also included in Ebey's Landing National Historic Reserve, the first reserve of its type in the nation.

Colonel Crockett Farm Bed and Breakfast Inn
1012 S. Fort Casey Rd., Coupeville (360) 678-3711

The Crocketts built this five bedroom, two-story Victorian farm house in 1855, along with two blockhouses for protection from possible Indian attack. One of the blockhouses was removed in 1909 and reconstructed in Seattle for the Alaska-Yukon-Pacific Exposition. When the Exposition closed, the blockhouse was moved to Point Defiance Park in Tacoma. The second blockhouse was restored at its original site on the edge of the Crockett Farm by the Works Progress Administration in 1938. Colonel Crockett's renovated farmhouse is listed on the National Register of Historic Places and is decorated with Victorian furnishings and turn-of-the-century antiques.

*Original Crockett Blockhouse, Courtesy of The Colonel Crockett
Farm Bed and Breakfast Inn*

Captain Whidbey Inn
2072 W. Captain Whidbey Inn Rd., Coupeville (360) 678-4097 or (800) 366-4097

Unlike many historic B & B's, the Captain Whidbey Inn was never a residence. It was built in 1907 from nearby madrona trees as a summer resort for guests from the mainland. Its location on the shore of Penn Cove is not only picturesque, but in the early days it was also functional. The Inn had a private pier where steamers docked and guests to the Inn could embark. The warm and cozy inn features all the amenities that makes the stay comfortable and views of the cove and forest that make it memorable.

Other historic inns in the Coupeville area include: the **1889 Victorian Bed & Breakfast**, filled with family keepsakes, and the **1890 Compass Rose Bed & Breakfast**.

Captain Whidbey Inn, Courtesy of Captain Whidbey Inn

Fort Casey Interpretive Center
Fort Casey State Park, 1280 S. Fort Casey Rd., Coupeville (360) 678-4519

Three coastal defense forts were built in the late 1890s to guard the entrance to Puget Sound: Fort Worden, near Port Townsend; Fort Flager on Marrowstone Island east of the Quimper Peninsula; and here at Fort Casey. Together they formed a "triangle of fire" that effectively protected the waterway to Seattle and surrounding ports. The firepower at Fort Casey was impressive. Two, 10-inch "disappearing guns" could each fire 600-pound projectiles more than 9 miles. All the fort's original cannons have been dismantled and removed, but two World War II guns from Fort

Winton in the Phillippines were brought here and mounted in the original batteries to bring back a historical perspective to this part of the fort. Some of the original military buildings and parade grounds remain in this 137-acre state park. And, the old fort's large concrete bunkers, with their series of interconnecting tunnels, bridges and walkways, can be explored.

10-inch disappearing gun, William Worth Battery, Fort Casey

Admiralty Head Lighthouse
Fort Casey State Park, 1280 S. Fort Casey Rd., Coupeville (360) 678-4519

In 1861, before Fort Casey was erected on this site, one of the West's first lighthouses was constructed near here to guide ships into Puget Sound. When Fort Casey was built in the 1890s, the first lighthouse was demolished. It was replaced by the picturesque Admiralty Head Lighthouse that stands here today. The restored lighthouse now serves as an interpretive center and museum for Fort Casey and is home to Washington State University/Island County Extension Beach Watchers. Historical exhibits and examples of the types of ammunition once fired by the fort's guns is displayed in the first floor museum. Although visitors who climb the stairs to the top of the tower won't see the original lighthouse lens (it was relocated to the New Dungeness Lighthouse), they will be treated to a commanding view.

Admiralty Head Lighthouse, Fort Casey State Park

Fort Casey Inn
1124 S. Engle Rd., Coupeville (360) 678-8792

Officers' housing at Fort Casey in 1909 included ten Georgian Revival-style homes that are now operated as a bed and breakfast inn. The authentically restored quarters, which even include a basement bomb shelter, are furnished in early 1900s period antiques. Patriotic Americana memorabilia: china, throw pillows, quilts, paintings, wall decorations, and collectibles accent every room. In restoring these houses, the owners have done more than just preserve a piece of American military history, they've given others an opportunity to live it.

Fort Ebey State Park
395 N. Fort Edey Rd. Coupeville (360) 678-4636

At the beginning of World War II, Fort Ebey was established at this site and equipped with rapid-fire 6-inch guns designed to back-up the larger guns installed at points along the Strait of Juan de Fuca. In designing this coast artillery fort, the Japanese air attacks on Pearl Harbor and the Aleutian Islands was given major consideration. When completed, the entire military complex would be invisible from the air. An underground concrete fire-control center and the emplacements where the fort's guns once stood is all that remains of this former military installation. Its buildings were dismantled at the end of the war and the grounds donated to the state for use as a park.

LANGLEY

South Whidbey Historical Society Museum
312 Second St., Langley

Jacob Anthes, Langley's first homesteader and the city's founder, along with several investors, logged the dense forests of southern Whidbey Island for cordwood they could sell to the many steamers that sailed the waters around the island. In 1898, when lumber was needed to build shipping docks to handle the supply demands of the Alaskan Gold Rush, Langley boomed. Original Anthes' family furniture, vintage farm tools, an old-time kitchen, photographs, native American artifacts, bones of pre-historic animals discovered in the region, and pioneer family memorabilia are among the featured exhibits on display in the bunkhouse that Anthes constructed before the turn-of-the-century.

Dog House Tavern
Backdoor Restaurant, 230 First St., Langley (360) 221-9825

Among the rustic buildings in Langley's downtown district is the turn-of-the-century Dog House Tavern, where the sound of punches being thrown weren't from the club's patrons, but from the boxing matches that used to be held here. In the 1920s, the first floor was converted into a pool hall, and the upstairs used for a theater. The building was placed on the National Register of Historic Places in 1991.

Several fine bed and breakfast inns are located in the Langley area including the Country Cottage of Langley, a 1927, two-story farmhouse. One of the farm's outbuildings, the former creamery, has been converted into a small cottage.

San Juan County

SAN JUAN COUNTY

SAN JUAN ISLANDS

The 400 islands that comprise the San Juan Islands archipelago were first claimed for the United States by an American expedition that landed here in 1841. Great Britain disputed the claim and, for 31 years, both country's flags were flown over the islands. The boundary dispute came to a head in the "Pig War" of 1859 when an English pig uprooted an American potato patch and was shot. When British authorities threatened to arrest the farmer, American citizens asked for military protection. What followed was a sizable military build-up by both sides that nearly led to war. A joint occupation of the islands was agreed upon and, for 12 years, a small garrison from each country was stationed on San Juan Island (at American Camp and English Camp). In 1872, Emperor William I of Germany, an international arbitrator, established the present boundary and British forces left the island.

Only 172 of the 400 islands are named, and fewer than three dozen are inhabited. The four largest islands: Lopez, Shaw, Orcas and San Juan, can be reached by regular ferry service from Anacortes. For schedules phone (800) 843-3779 (within the state only). For San Juan Islands visitor information phone (360) 468-3663

LOPEZ ISLAND

Lopez Island Historical Museum
Weeks Rd. and Washburn, Lopez Village (360) 468-2049 or (360) 468-3447

Lopez Island was mapped by Spanish explorers, occupied by the British and settled by the Americans who sailed here in the late eighteenth century. It's not unlike other agricultural communities in the Pacific Northwest; with roots that go back to Indian and pioneer times, and the era of the Hudson Bay Company. The museum is a good place to start a visit to the island's historic places. It contains artifacts, old photos, a cedar Indian dugout canoe, models of historic steam boats, a 100-year-old captain's gig and other local maritime exhibits.

Nearby places of historic interest include: a 1904 pioneer church at Lopez Village and a World War II cannon at Odlin County Park.

Spencer Spit Park
Southeast of Swifts Bay, Lopez Island

Evidence of prehistoric Indian habitation was uncovered at this state marine park by the University of Washington Archaeology Department. Ancient Native American fire pits, spear points, tools and refuse mounds were identified during excavation. Logs from an 1886 log cabin, constructed by the Spencer family who homesteaded here, were used to build the park's log shelter that's located at the end of the spit. Visitors can hike in to the park or dock their boat here, but cars are not permitted.

Richardson General Store and Warehouse
On the wharf at Richardson

The port at Richardson was once the busiest in the San Juans. A large fishing fleet was based here and millions of pounds of all varieties of fish were processed annually at the town's large cannery. When regular steamer service was started between Seattle and the islands Richardson was the first port of call. The first Richardson general store was opened in 1889 when the wharf was constructed. The present store, which is listed on the National Register of Historic Places, replaced the original building in 1918.

SHAW ISLAND

Little Portion Store
Shaw Ferry Landing, Shaw Island

First-time visitors to Shaw Island are usually surprised to find Franciscan nuns, in their brown habits, operating the ferry slip and the old-time general store, the only commercial enterprise on the island. Locally grown and dried herbs and spices packaged by nuns from Our Lady of the Rock Benedictine monastery near the center of the island can be purchased here.

Little Red Schoolhouse
Hoffman Cove Rd. and Neck Point Rd., Shaw Island

Since 1890 this frame, one-room schoolhouse has been the island's only school building for its 100 year-around residents. Children, from kindergarten through the eighth grade attend classes in this building, which is listed on the National Register of Historic Places.

Shaw Island Library and Historical Society
Blind Bay Rd. and Broken Point Rd., Shaw Island (360) 468-4068

Timbers from the island's 1870 log cabin post office were used to construct this library and historical society museum. The rustic museum building contains relics from Shaw Island's past, memorabilia from some of the area's first settlers and old documents.

ORCAS ISLAND

Orcas Hotel
Overlooking the Orcas Island Ferry Landing, Orcas

Canadian landowner William E. Sutherland erected this three-story Victorian inn between 1900 and 1904 to serve tourists who traveled here on island-hopping steamships. A complete restoration of the building and grounds was completed in 1985, three years after the hotel was placed on the National Register of Historic Places. Overnight guests have access to a private parlor replete with Queen Anne-style furnishings. The dining room, which is open to the public, overlooks the ferry landing and part of the hotel's flower garden.

Orcas Hotel, Photo by Judy Menish

Orcas Island Historical Museum
5 North Beach Rd., Eastsound   (360) 376-4849

Six, one-room log cabins, constructed between 1885 and 1902 on Orcas Island homesteads, were disassembled, moved here and reassembled in the late 1950s to house the collections of the Orcas Historical Museum.   Exhibits on early pioneer life, household and farming equipment, early resorts, the island's fruit farming industry (Orcas Island is said to be the originator of the Red Gravenstein apple), and Indian artifacts collected by Ethan Allen. Allen was superintendent of the county schools during the 1900s and a descendant of the Revolutionary War hero. His 3,000-item collection includes: arrowheads, spearheads, Indian baskets, pottery, stone dishes, grinding implements, paint pots, ornaments and ceremonial pieces.

In the surrounding community of Eastsound are several buildings erected before the turn-of-the-century. Two are particularly noteworthy: the 1883 Victorian-style Outlook Inn, furnished with American and English antiques; and the 1886 Emmanuel Episcopal Church, on the National Register of Historic Places.

Orcas Island Historical Museum,
Courtesy of the Orcas Island Historical Museum

Crow Valley School Museum
Crow Valley Rd., three miles southwest of Eastsound (360) 376-4260

Before Washington was granted statehood, children from this region were educated in this 1888 territorial school. Authentic period furnishings and an outstanding photographic collection of historical images from the San Juan Islands now fill the building. Museum staff can give information about other places of historic interest to visit on Orcas Island such as Deer Harbor with its clapboard buildings dating from the 1890s.

Moran Mansion
Rosario Island Resort and Spa, Cascade Bay, south of Eastsound (800) 562-8820 (in WA) or (360) 376-2222

In 1904, when Robert Moran, former mayor of Seattle and millionaire shipbuilder, was told he had but one year to live, he moved here and poured his assets and energy into construction of this elegant mansion. The interior was finished using the finest hardwood paneling, intricate parquet floors and solid mahogany doors. Moran survived well-beyond the year doctors had given him and, in 1921, donated 3,000 acres from his 5,000-acre estate to the state for a park (Moran State Park). Today, Moran's mansion is a highly rated resort and is listed on the National Register of Historic Places.

Fire Lookout and Observation Tower
Summit of Mount Constitution in Moran State Park, on Horseshoe Hwy., 13 miles from the ferry landing.

Five lakes, large stands of old-growth trees, the 100-foot Cascade Falls, and the panoramic view from the top of Mount Constitution attracts thousands of visitors to Moran State Park every year. Before 1921, this park was part of the estate of Robert Moran. That year he donated more than 60% of his land to the state for use as a park. Moran Park comprises one-tenth of the island, making this the largest state park in Western Washington, and the fourth-largest in the state

At the summit of Mount Constitution, the highest peak in the San Juans, is a 52-foot, twelfth century-style, granite **observation tower**, built by the Civilian Conservation Corps in 1936. The CCC also constructed the archway at the park entrance and other facilities in the park using massive timbers and hand-cut stone.

South of the park is the community of Olga where visitors will find the island's oldest general store and a converted strawberry plant that's now home to the **Orcas Island Artworks**, an artists' cooperative.

SAN JUAN ISLAND

San Juan Historical Museum
405 Price St. Friday Harbor (360) 378-3949

James King's restored, two-story, turn-of-the-century farmhouse is headquarters for the San Juan Historical Society and a repository for their collections. Featured exhibits emphasize San Juan Island history and include: artifacts, old photographs of pioneers and historic scenes, the city's old fire bell, a 45-star American flag, and relics from the Pig War incident. Also on the grounds is the original county jail, the Scribner family log cabin, carriage house, root cellar and milk house.

Friday Harbor Historic Landmark Tour
Guide available from the San Juan Historical Museum, 405 Price St., Friday Harbor (360) 378-3949

Streets lined with preserved homes, churches, and business establishments from the turn-of-the-century add to the charm of this island community. A guide to 32 places of historic interest in Friday Harbor is published by the Historical Society and is available from their museum. Included in the guide is: the 1876 Bowman House, the oldest residence in the city; Tourists' Hotel that's been in business since 1891; the Perry house, a maternity hospital in the 1920s and 30s where many of the island's oldest residents were born; and a 1904 dry goods store that "carried everything and no one paid cash." For more places to see contact Friday Harbor Chamber of Commerce at (360) 378-5240, or Tourist Information Services, East St. next to the ferry lanes (360) 378-6977.

Whale Museum
62 1st St., Friday Harbor (360) 378-4710

Within the walls of the 1892 Odd Fellows Hall is the world's only museum devoted to whale biology. Early island settlers established the Mt. Dallas International Order of the Odd Fellows in this building. In 1978-79, the building was converted to house the Whale Museum where today, exhibits showcase natural history in the form of life-size skeletons, sculptures, models, photographs, and paintings. Through art, touch, science and sound, these exhibits reveal insights to the physiology, growth, migration, communication and intelligence of whales.

Friday Harbor is an appropriate location for the Whale Museum for it was on the west shore of the island that the county's first whale-watching park was founded, Lime Kiln Point State Park. It's the only park in the state devoted to marine life. The natural environment of this region of the San Juans, where orcas, porpoises and seals live openly, brought film makers here to shoot footage for the popular Free Willy movies.

Pig War Museum
620 Guard St., Friday Harbor (360) 378-6495 or (360) 378-4151

In 1859, three British warships with a force of more than 2,100 Royal Marines were preparing to battle American troops for control of the San Juan Islands. The outnumbered Americans, under the command of Captain George A. Pickett, held their position at the south end of the island; determined to resist any attempt by the British to land. It was a local dispute over the shooting of an English Pig by an American farmer that brought these two great nations to the brink of war. The story of the Pig War, the boundary dispute over ownership of the San Juans, and how the United States won the war in 1872 is told in this unique museum.

University of Washington Oceanographic Laboratories
Friday Harbor (360) 378-2165

The depth of the waters off the San Juans and the abundance and diversity of plants and marine life in this area attracted scientists from the University of Washington to Friday Harbor in 1903. That year, they established their first marine biology research center in a Friday Harbor fish cannery. Today, the marine research and teaching laboratory is one of the finest in the country. Visitors should call ahead for tour schedules before planning a visit to this facility.

San Juan Island National Historical Park
Friday Harbor, San Juan Island NHP Information Center, 125 Spring, Friday Harbor. Two separate locations comprise this National Park: American Camp, 6 miles southeast of Friday Harbor on the southern tip of the island (360) 378-2902; and English Camp, 10 miles northwest of Friday Harbor overlooking Garrison Bay (360) 378-2240.

The park was founded to commemorate settlement of the San Juan Islands border dispute between Great Britain and the United States, and to protect and preserve the sites where troops from these two nations were stationed during the 1859-72 Pig War. At American Camp, where 461 soldiers defended the United States' claim to these islands, the original officers' and laundress' quarters remain. Along the self-guiding interpretive trail is the remnants of a redoubt an earthen gun emplacement, and the Hudson's Bay Company farm site. Remains at English Camp, which was established by British Royal Marines, include the restored hospital, barracks, commissary, and guardhouse buildings and a small formal garden. Near the barracks is a 300-year-old, large-leaf maple tree with a trunk that's 24-feet in circumference, one of the largest in the world. Graves of several British soldiers can be seen along the trail near the summit of Mount Young.

Blockhouse at the American Camp, San Juan Island National Historic Park
Photo by Judy Menish

Re-enactment at American Camp, San Juan National Historic Park, Courtesy of
San Juan National Historic Park

187

Cattle Point Lighthouse
At the southern tip of San Juan Island, east of American Camp

One of the first navigation aids in the San Juan Islands was installed at this site in 1888. The white concrete tower that now stands here was built in 1935. It soars 80-feet above the island's only sand dunes.

English Camp Historic Marker
Northwest section of San Juan Island near Garrison Bay, at the top of Officers' Hill above the garden

"In 1859 the killing of a pig on San Juan Island brought England and the United States to the brink of war over the issue of territorial rights here. By agreement, both nations' troops were permitted to occupy this area while the problem was being studied. British soldiers established camp at Garrison Bay, just west of here, while American troops camped at the southern end of the island. Peaceful arbitration of the dispute in 1872 placed the San Juan Islands within the territorial United States. In October of that year the British garrison was abandoned."

Roche Harbor Resort
North end of San Juan Island, Roche Harbor (360) 378-2155 or (800) 451-8910

Before this resort and marina opened in the 1950s, Roche Harbor was a company town for John McMillin's Roche Harbor Lime Plant, the largest lime producer in the West. Employees lived in company-owned cottages and were paid in script that could only be redeemed at the company store. McMillin erected a combination schoolhouse and chapel for his employees and their families, built the Hotel de Haro for the growing tourist trade and designed an elaborate family mausoleum. The original company store at this nationally registered historic place is still in operation and the former employee's cottages now accommodate some of the resort's guests.

The rich heritage of Roche Harbor's inhabitants is celebrated at day's end with an impressive flag ceremony. Flags of the United States, Canada, England, Washington State and the resort are lowered as the anthems of each country fill the air.

Roche Harbor Resort, Photo by Judy Menish

Afterglow Vista, Site of McMillin Family Mausoleum, Roach Harbor Resort
Photo by Judy Menish

Hotel de Haro
Roche Harbor (360) 378-2155

John McMillin began construction of this ornate hotel in 1886 to accommodate customers who were purchasing lime from his company. Steamers that hauled freight and supplies to the island began bringing tourists to McMillin's hotel. One

 of the hotel's best-known guests was President Teddy Roosevelt who stayed here in 1906 (his signature appears on the guest register that's displayed in the lobby). A free guide to places of historic interest in Roche Harbor is available at the hotel.

189

Our Lady of Good Voyage Catholic Church
Roche Harbor

When new owners purchased the Roche Harbor Resort, they converted McMillin's 1892 combination schoolhouse and chapel into a Catholic church, making it the only privately-owned Catholic church north of Mexico.

Lime Kiln Lighthouse
Lime Kiln Pt. State Park, West Side Rd., just south of San Juan County Park
(360) 378-2044

One of Washington State's last light stations was installed at this point in 1914. The present building, with its octagonal tower, was completed in 1919. Its remote location made it one of the last lighthouses in the United States to convert to electricity. It would be 1969 before the station was fully automated. Lime Kiln Light Station is listed on the National Register of Historic Places.

The surrounding Lime Kiln State Park was established as the first whale-watching park in the United States. It is the only state park devoted to marine life. From its rocky shoreline, visitors can get great close-up views of passing orca whales during the whale-watching season.

Skagit County

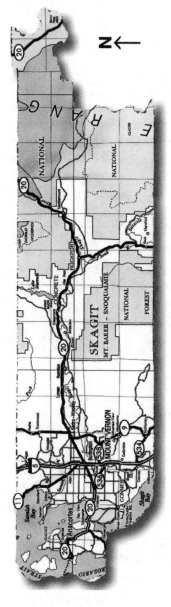

SKAGIT COUNTY

ANACORTES (an-uh-KOR-tis)

Anacortes Museum
1305 8th St., Anacortes (360) 293-1915

Amos Bowman founded Anacortes in 1876; established the first general store, post office, newspaper, wharf, and planned for the day when the city would be connected to the transcontinental railroad. Artifacts that trace the city's maritime and industrial growth and the cultural heritage of Fidalgo and Guemes Islands are exhibited in the city's former 1909 Carnegie Library building. A Victorian Parlor, doctor's and dentist's office, salmon cannery office and a large photo exhibit are among the museum's permanent displays.

Anacortes Museum

Anacortes Historical Tour
Anacortes Chamber of Commerce, 819 Commercial Ave., (360) 293-7911 or Anacortes Visitor Information Center (360) 293-3832

For 11 blocks, Commercial Avenue runs through the heart of the city's historic district. Within just a few blocks of this main street, from the Port of Anacortes, through the city's "old town," are 65 places of historic interest. Marine Supply and Hardware, the oldest continuously operating marine store on the West Coast, with its oiled, wood plank floors and turn-of-the-century fixtures; and the site of Curtis Wharf, where early twentieth century steamships once docked, are among the city's points of interest that are listed on the National Register of Historic Places.

Dozens of life-size murals, depicting scenes and residents from Anacortes' last 100 years, can also be seen on a tour of the buildings in this historic district.

Mural at 6th and Commercial Sts. depicting the city's first auto accident

Causland Memorial Park
8th St. and "N" Ave., Anacortes

The multi-colored rock walls and stone band shell in this park were constructed in 1921 by a Frenchman as a tribute to those who lost their lives in World War I. In later years, memorials were also dedicated at this site to the memory of those who made the supreme sacrifice in service to their country during World War II, Korea and Vietnam.

Stone Band Shell at Causland Memorial Park

Samish Coastal Salish Cultural Interpretive Center
803 31st St., Anacortes (360) 293-6404

Anacortes' cultural ties to the Samish Indians who lived here long before the arrival of the white man can be found at this Center, in Washington Park and at other sites in and around Fidalgo Island. Through a series of hands-on exhibits, visitors can experience the rich history of these first Americans.

W.T. *Preston* Sternwheel Snagboat
703 "R" Ave., Anacortes (360) 293-1915 (Anacortes Museum)

The U.S. Army Corps of Engineers, operated the *W.T. Preston* on Puget Sound and its tributaries until 1981, clearing log jams and keeping Puget Sound's waterways clear for navigation. When the 90-year-old *W.T. Preston* was decommissioned in 1983 it was the Northwest's last operating stern-wheeler. Today, the restored, 163-foot vessel serves as an interpretive museum where visitors can get a sense of what it was like to work on board this unusual type of ship. The *W.T. Preston* is listed on the National Register of Historic Places.

The Depot
7th and "R" Aves., Anacortes

Next door to the W.T. Preston is the restored 1911 Burlington Northern Railroad Depot. The depot, which is listed on the National Register of Historic Places, is now used as a cultural arts and community center.   Hour-long excursions aboard the Lake Whatcom Railway depart from the depot twice a week during July and August.

Anacortes Steam Railway
7th and "R" Aves., Anacortes

Anacortes resident, Tommy Thompson, reconstructed this authentically scaled 0-4-4 Forney-type coal/wood burning steam locomotive as a 20-year "backyard" project. His 1909 narrow-gauge steam engine, a former mine locomotive, departs from the old depot during the Summer months for tours of the historic Commercial Avenue district and Downtown Anacortes. The train's three passenger cars are elegantly appointed with: red velvet upholstery, crystal lamps, cherry-wood paneling and Italian marble fireplaces.

Paul Lavera, Sr. Totem Poles
2102 – 9th St., Anacortes

Outside the home of former State Senator, Paul Lavra, are examples of some of the 2600 story poles he's carved. His work has been shipped to cities around the world.

BURLINGTON

Historic Burlington

Dense forests once stood where Burlington's strawberry fields and dairy farms now dot the landscape. Logging began in 1882. Ten years later east-west and north-south railway lines met here and Burlington began to develop as a transportation hub. Many buildings constructed around the turn-of-the-century can be seen throughout the city. Of particular interest: the Carnegie Library at 901 Fairhaven St., which is listed on the National Register of Historic Places; the restored 1907 Moody home at 531 N. Garl St.; the George McMillan home at 980 Green Rd., built in 1907 from the "Carpenter's Pattern Books;" the old Burlington Telephone office at 600 Cherry; and the Washington Hotel at Fairhaven and Cherry Streets, built by W.T. McKay who platted the town site in 1891.

Former Carnegie Library Building at Fairhaven and Holly, Burlington

1926 Burlington City Hall Building at Fairhaven and Oak, Burlington

CONCRETE

Historic Downtown Concrete Walking Tour
Concrete Chamber of Commerce and Visitor Information Center, Hwy. 20 at the train depot between Dillard and "E" Sts., Concrete

Forty percent of the cement used in the construction of Grand Coulee Dam, the largest concrete dam in the world, was shipped from the Superior cement plant in Concrete during the 1930s. Concrete's portland cement was also used to build dams on Diablo and Ross Lakes and the Baker River Dam, then the highest hydroelectric dam in the world. In 1916, the longest single-span cement bridge in

the world was built across the Baker River in northeast Concrete. Throughout the town are buildings that were reconstructed using concrete following the disastrous fire of 1921 that destroyed many of the city's original wooden structures. A guide to fifteen of the city's historic sites and buildings is available at the Visitor Center.

Cement City Theatre
Concrete Theatre, 128 Main St., Concrete

Among the concrete buildings nestled in the compact historic downtown district is the 1924 Concrete Theatre. It was the town's primary source of entertainment during the pre-World War II boom and is listed on the Washington Heritage Register.

Concrete Theatre

Baker River Bridge
Henry Thompson Bridge, East Main St. and Dillard Ave. across the Baker River, Concrete

At the time this concrete bridge was constructed in 1916, reinforced concrete was just emerging as a viable construction material. This method of building bridges gained wider recognition when this bridge was completed two years later as the world's longest single-span concrete bridge. The Baker River Bridge, which is still in use today, is listed on the National Register of Historic Places.

Baker River Bridge

Camp 7 Museum
119 Railroad Ave., Concrete (360) 853-7185 on weekends

Bridges, dams and roadways, all built from the town's concrete, are visual reminders of the important role played by the city of Concrete and its residents. But the city's history goes deeper than the obvious influence Concrete's resources had on the development and growth of the state. There was logging, too. At Camp 7 Museum there's exhibits of logging tools, wood and talc carvings, a logging camp kitchen, Indian dugout canoe and historic photos.

Visitors to the museum can also catch a ride on the *Sockeye Express*, a tram that tours 30 points of interest in the area. The 45-minute narrated trip lasts 45 minutes and takes weekend guests on a journey from "Cement City to Superior Heights."

DECEPTION PASS

Deception Pass Historic Marker
On Hwy. 20 near the south end of Deception Pass Bridge, 9 miles north of Oak Harbor

"To the north of this narrow passage is Fidalgo Island, so named for the Spanish explorer, Lieutenant Salvador Fidalgo. To the south is Whidbey Island, second largest insular area in the continental United States, which Captain George Vancouver, while exploring in this region in 1792, at first thought to be a peninsula. Further exploration conducted by him disclosed the existence of this intricate channel. Upon the realization that he had been deceived as the character of the large island, Vancouver gave to this channel the name of Deception Passage and in naming the island he honored his trusted officer, Joseph Whidbey."

Deception Pass State Park
5175 N. State Hwy. 20, at the south end of Fidalgo Island, the north end of Whidbey Island and six smaller islands in-between (800) 562-0990 (in Washington)

Thousands of tourists visit Deception Pass Park every year, making it one of the state's most popular parks. Many stop to enjoy the magnificent natural beauty of the Pass, others stay for the excellent recreational facilities, and some come to explore the rich history of the region. Little evidence remains of the coastal Indians who made Deception Pass their home centuries before Captain George Vancouver sailed here in 1792, but events of the nineteenth and twentieth centuries are easier to identify: remnants of the old ferry landing on Hoypus Point; the 182-foot high Deception Pass Bridge which replaced the ferry in 1935; the Civilian Conservation Corps Interpretive Center at the Bowman Bay campsite that pays tribute to the young Depression-era men who constructed many of our nations' park facilities; and gun emplacements, where cannons guarded the Pass during WWI and WWII.

Civilian Conservation Corps Interpretive Center

Maiden of Deception Pass
Deception Pass State Park, State Hwy. 20 at the north end of Whidbey Island.

At Rosario Beach, a cedar story pole, known as the Maiden of Deception Pass, stands at the site of an ancient Samish Indian village. The 24-foot pole depicts Ko-

kwal-alwoot, a mythical sea spirit who lives in the waters near the Pass. An intrepretive display tells the legend of the Maiden and how she sacrificed her life in the village to prevent starvation of her people.

Maiden of Deception Pass Story Pole
Photo by Judy Menish

199

LA CONNER

Skagit County Historical Museum
501 South 4th St., La Conner (360) 466-3365

The evolution of the city of La Conner, from trading post to commercial waterfront, and the development of Skagit County's diverse agriculture is displayed in this county museum. Permanent exhibits include: a fully equipped turn-of-the-century farmhouse kitchen, blacksmith shop, and general store. Pioneer clothing, household items and relics from early fishing, logging, transportation, mining and farming activities are displayed in period settings. The museum features an outstanding collection of old photographs and a fine exhibit on the area's first inhabitants, the Northwest Coastal Indians. A guide to the city's historic buildings, "Self-guided Walking Tour of La Conner," is available at the museum.

La Conner Historic District
Swinomish Channel waterfront, La Conner

Totem Pole Park, which marks the site of Alonzo Low's 1867 trading post, where La Conner got its start, is just one of 160 pioneer places found in this Nationally Registered Historic district. Also included are most of the downtown's original frame and brick buildings, with their old-time, false store fronts, and neighborhoods filled with ninteenth century homes. The district also boasts the oldest operating seed store in the West, and a waterfront village reminiscent of those found along the New England coast. Information about the town's historic places is available from many of the town's merchants and from the Skagit County Historical Museum.

Magnus Anderson Cabin
Next to City Hall, 2nd and Douglas, La Conner

In 1869, Magnus Anderson built this log cabin on a hill overlooking the North Fork of the Skagit River. It was constructed in a style that was popular in the Scandinavian countries, instead of the split cedar and shakes generally used by this region's pioneers. Anderson's cabin was relocated here for preservation by the Daughters of the Pioneers. The neighboring City Hall building was erected around 1886 as the Skagit County Bank (a.k.a. Schricker's Bank), and once housed the city's early fire department. Across from the City Hall is the 1878 George Calhoun Home. Dr. Calhoun was founder of the Washington Children's Home and was instrumental in bringing the first of Washington's World's Fairs to Seattle, the 1909 Alaska-Yukon Pacific Exposition.

Magnus Anderson Cabin

Tillinghast Seed Co.
623 Morris St., La Conner (360) 466-3329

The West's oldest operating seed store began as a home business by Alvinza Tillinghast and his wife, Emma, who emigrated here from Pennsylvania. They began growing cabbage seed on their Indian Slough farmstead in 1873. Turnip, cauliflower and mustard seed followed. In 1886 they published their first seed catalog and started a mail order business, distributing seeds throughout the West. About four years later, Tillinghast opened a retail seed store in this white clapboard building. Today, more than 1000 varieties of vegetable, flower and grass seed fill

 the 750 original wooden bins that line the store's walls. On one wall of this large store is a collection of Tillinghast's seed catalog covers that span more than a century. Relics from the store's early years can be seen in the aisles and on the shelves of this pioneer business establishment.

201

Gaches Mansion
703 S. 2nd, La Conner (360) 466-4288

English immigrants, George and James Gaches purchased the dry goods store formerly owned by John and Louisa Conner and became very successful La Conner merchants and grain dealers in the late nineteenth century. George Gaches, who wanted the "finest house in La Conner," built this 3-story, 22-room Victorian mansion in the early 1890s. In later years, the home was used as a hospital, and then converted into apartments. An extensive restoration of the building was undertaken in 1976. Today, this well-known local landmark is a house museum filled with period furnishings. James Gaches' c.1890 home is also located in La Conner at 211 E. Douglas.

La Conner Civic Garden Club
622 S. 2nd, La Conner

Like many other La Conner structures, this building has been used for many purposes since its construction in 1875. Among its many uses its been an Episcopal church, school, library, lodge hall and the first courthouse in Skagit County. In the early

1920s, the Civic Improvement Club, forerunner of the La Conner Civic Garden Club, restored the building. It was the first building in La Conner recognized for its historical significance by being listed on the Washington Heritage Register.

New Brunswick Hotel
103 E. Morris, La Conner

La Conner's last surviving nineteenth century hotel building, the c.1890 New Brunswick Hotel, is now home to Nasty Jacks's Antiques one of the city's numerous antique dealers. Before the turn-of-the-century, hotel guests stayed in rooms on the upper floor of the building, while, on the first floor, customers shopped at the Fair Department Store.

La Conner Volunteer Firemen's Museum
First St., La Conner

The city's 1884 horse-drawn, hand-operated fire fighting pumper and hose cart is proudly displayed in a storefront along La Conner's historic main street. This antique fire-fighting device was built in New York City and shipped around the Horn to San Francisco where it was used to fight the devastating fire that followed that city's major earthquake in 1906.

Sacred Heart Church
410 E. Douglas St., La Conner (360) 466-3967

Louisa Conner's efforts brought about construction of the first Sacred Heart Church at this site in 1872. That first Catholic church, which was built to serve the white residents of La Conner, was rebuilt in 1899 with an interior closely resembling the original. At that time, Indians attended services at the 1868 St. Paul's Roman Catholic Church on the neighboring Swinomish Indian Reservation (Reservation Road, facing Swinomish Channel). St. Paul's, the oldest church in Skagit County, is now part of the same parish as Sacred Heart and is used for special services.

Hotel Planter
715 S. First, La Conner (360) 466-4710 or (800) 488-5409

The city's oldest hotel that's still standing was constructed in 1907 using solid concrete blocks made on site. During the early 1900s, when La Conner was a hub for the steamers that brought passengers and freight north from Seattle, the hotel's "modern" 22 rooms accommodated travelers as well as workers from nearby lumber mills and canneries. To preserve the historic atmosphere of the old hotel, its doors, window moldings, trim and many original light fixtures were restored when the building was renovated into a 12-room hotel in the late 60s.

John Peck Home
503 S. 3rd St., La Conner (360) 466-3366

Sea Captain, John Peck, built this two-story Victorian home in 1876. He then sent for his wife and four daughters who made the voyage to La Conner by sailing around the Horn from their New Brunswick home. The Peck's four daughters were all married in this home, that has been restored and is now operated as Katy's Inn, a bed and breakfast.

MOUNT VERNON

Historic Mount Vernon Walking Tour
Mount Vernon Chamber of Commerce, 325 E. College Way, Mount Vernon
(360) 428-8547

It was along the shores of this stretch of the Skagit River that the region's first pioneer, Jasper Gates, homesteaded in 1870. The site where he built his cabin, and 27 other places of local historic significance are identified in a walking tour guide available from the Chamber of Commerce. Among the other interesting places listed in this guide is: the Fire Department Office with its collection of antique fire-fighting equipment; the 1893 Matheson Building, the first building erected specifically for use as the county courthouse; the 1892 Down's Opera House, now the Lido Theater; the Skagit River Bakery that still operates pioneer wood-fired ovens; the town's grainery that's been converted into Scotts Bookstore, and the 1906 Carnation plant that's now Condensery Mall. A number of pioneer homes remain around present-day Mount Vernon, including the c.1890s home of Jasper Gates.

Skagit County Courthouse
Kincaid St., Mount Vernon

A display case in the lobby of this building contains an American flag pieced together by the pioneer women of Mount Vernon in 1877 for the community's first

Independence Day celebration. The 24-foot by 36-foot flag was made from red, white and blue bunting and was flown from the top of a trimmed, 147-foot-tall living cedar tree twelve years before Washington became a state. The natural cedar flagpole stood along the city's waterfront until 1891.

Skagit County Courthouse

Old Safe displayed inside Skagit County Courthouse

Lincoln Theater and Commercial Block
301-329 Kincaid St., Mount Vernon

Within the walls of this historic theater stands a now-silent Wurlitzer organ, one of the few remaining on the West Coast. When the theater opened in the 1920s, the Wurlitzer played for Vaudeville acts who performed on stage and accompanied silent movies that played here. This early twentieth century theater and surrounding business structures are listed on the National Register of Historic Places.

205

REXVILLE

Rexville Grange
1929 Rexville Grange Rd., east of La Conner (360) 466-3202 or 466-5151

The nationwide organization of the Grange (officially called the "Patrons of Husbandry") began in 1867 to give farmers a voice in politics. In communities where granges were established they soon became centers for social and community activities. Although the town of Rexville, which was platted in 1883, never became the community it was planned to be, the Rexville Grange has survived. In 1925, the grange's founders first met in the city's one-room schoolhouse. Two years later they erected this wood-frame building at a site just east of the grange's present location. In 1929, the original building was relocated over a newly constructed basement where it stands today as one of the largest remaining granges in the state.

Rexville Grange

ROCKPORT

David Douglas Historic Marker
Near the entrance to Rockport State Park, 2 miles west of Rockport on Hwy. 20.

"A famous botanist at the age of 27, David Douglas voyaged from the Thames to the Columbia in 1825, on a mission for the British Royal Horticultural Society. Among his many botanical discoveries from this and a second trip in 1830 were the Douglas fir and the sugar pine. He was the founder of forestry in the Pacific Northwest."

Three-hundred-foot high, old growth Douglas fir trees, named for David Douglas, line the five miles of trails that wind through this state park.

Seattle City Light Depot (Site)
Porter Cabin
Sah-ku-meh-hu Dugout Canoe
Rockport Ferry
Howard Miller Steelhead Park, Rockport (360) 853-8808

Between 1924 and 1954, visitors taking the Seattle City Light tour to Ross, Diablo and Gorge Dams would board trains here for the first leg of their tour, a 29-mile rail trip to Newhalem along the scenic Skagit River.   After Hwy. 20 was completed between Rockport and Newhalem in 1953, the tour center at Diablo became the starting point for tours of the three dams. Tours are conducted from mid-June until early September. Call (206) 233-2709 for schedules and reservations. The site of the former Rockport depot is now a 24-acre park where three treasures from the region's past are showcased:

Porter Cabin. One of the first families to homestead this area were the Porters who built a split cedar log cabin in the early 1880s. This cabin, which was home to the Porters and their six children, was donated to the county and relocated here in 1967 for preservation.

Sah-ku-meh-hu Canoe. This original cedar log dugout canoe, built by a member of the Sah-ku-meh-hu tribe of the Upper Skagit Indians, is a fine example of the type of canoes used by Native Americans for transportation on the Skagit River. This type of canoe was also used to guide bolts of cedar (4-foot sections of cedar logs) down the Skagit River to lumber mills.

Sah-ku-meh-hu Canoe

Rockport Ferry. Before bridges were constructed to span the Skagit River, ferry boats provided the only access across the river. This ferry, one of the last to see service on the Skagit, was retired in October, 1961.

SEDRO WOOLLEY (SEE-droh-WOO-lee)

Sedro Woolley Museum
In the old Murdock Mall building in downtown Sedro Woolley

When two nearby towns, Sedro (a variation of the Spanish word for cedar) and Woolley (named for the developer Phillip Woolley), merged in 1898 they retained the heritage of each community by naming the new city Sedro Woolley. Sedro was known for the thick groves of western red cedar that once covered this region of the Skagit River valley. Woolley was the area's transportation center with three rail lines serving the city. The early history of the two towns, Sedro and Woolley;

208

events that brought the two cities together; relics from the past; and a recreated main street replete with period artifacts can be found in this interesting museum of local history.

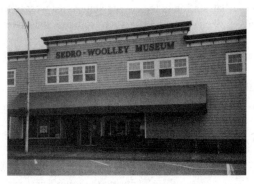

Sedro Woolley Museum

Historic Sedro Woolley
Sedro Woolley Chamber of Commerce, State Hwy. 20, north of Sedro Woolley

From this former Great Northern caboose visitors can get information about the places of historic interest to visit in the region and at points along Hwy. 20, the North Cascades Highway. In addition to a number of turn-of-the-century homes and buildings that can be seen in and around town, two important community landmarks remain: the last interurban station and bandstand.

Puget Sound & Baker River Railway Engine and Coal Tender at Visitor Center

209

Interurban Station
Hwy. 20, west of Sedro Woolley

The last intact interurban station in the county stands just west of town on Hwy. 20. Between 1912 and 1929 electric street cars ran from this station to Burlington with connections to points north and south.

Sedro Woolley Bandstand
724 Ferry St., Sedro Woolley

A 1900, 2-story bandstand, now on private property behind the house at 724 Ferry St., was the center of all town celebrations during the town's early years.

North Cascades National Park Service Complex
2105 Hwy. 20, Sedro Woolley

It took nearly 80 years, from the state legislature's approval in 1893 to its opening in 1972, for Hwy. 20, the North Cascades Highway, to be completed. Named one of the nation's most scenic highways, Highway 20 takes travelers from Sedro Woolley to one of our newest National Parks, North Cascades National Park. The visitor center at this gateway to the North Cascades includes exhibits on the natural history of the 1,053-square mile park.

Snohomish County

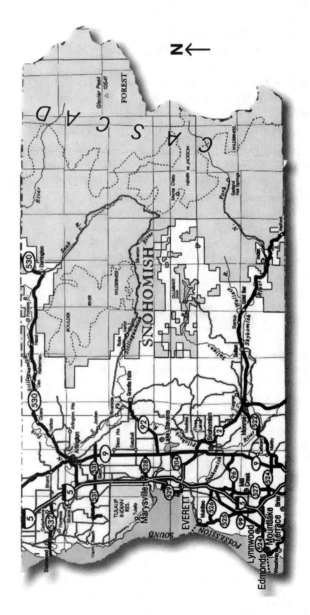

SNOHOMISH COUNTY

ARLINGTON

Stillaguamish Valley Pioneer Museum
Pioneer Park, 20722 67th Ave. NE, Arlington (360) 435-7289

Shingle manufacturing no longer ranks as the major manufacturing activity in this small western Washington community. But the city's ties to the lumber industry haven't been forgotten. On the grounds of this pioneer park is: a c.1900 log cabin, an 11-foot section of a 700-year-old fir tree, a 1923 assembly hall (Pioneer Hall) made from peeled split timbers, and a giant Western Red Cedar Stump. In the new museum building, artifacts, photos and pioneer memorabilia reflect the natural, cultural, social, political economic and industrial history of Arlington and the surrounding Stillaguamish Valley.

Stillaguamish Valley Pioneer Museum, Courtesy of Stillaguamish Valley Pioneer Museum

Pioneer Hall, Courtesy of Stillaquamish Pioneer

EDMONDS

Edmonds Museum
118 Fifth Ave. North, Edmonds (425) 774-0900

The forests of cedar that surrounded this area in the 1870s attracted young George Brackett, a timber cruiser and logger. He bought 147 acres, founded the town of Edmonds, built a sawmill and wharf, and developed the waterfront into a major shingle production industry. A working model of the type of shingle mill that once lined the waterfront is one of the permanent exhibits of the Edmonds Museum. Original artifacts from the turn-of-the-century city clerk's office, a reproduced 1894 Stevens Hotel bedroom, an extensive collection of nautical memorabilia, historical documents and photos fill the former Carnegie Library that now serves as Edmonds' and South Snohomish County's museum of history. The 1910 brick and stone building, which was once used as both a library and city hall, is listed on the National Register of Historic Places.

Edmonds Museum

Old School Bell displayed outside the Edmonds Museum

213

Visitor Information Center
120 Fifth Ave. North, Edmonds

Possibly the "newest" log cabin in the state was built in 1930 on the Hanley Estate using material from the Seaview area. It was occupied until the estate was sold for development in 1970. The cabin was donated to the city and relocated here in 1975 for America's Bicentennial celebration. Today it houses the Chamber of Commerce and Visitor's Bureau. The city has identified many local places of historical significance and lists them in a guide available at the Center. Other interesting places to see include: the wildlife refuge in downtown Edmonds with boardwalk and viewing area, the state's first salt water pier built solely as a public fishing pier, and the largest charter fleet on Puget Sound.

Edmonds Visitor Information Log Cabin

Bracket's Landing Park
At the foot of Main St., Edmonds

The site where George Bracket came ashore and founded the city of Edmonds is commemorated by this 27-acre waterfront park. His pioneer sawmill and wharf attracted other businesses to the area and the city was born. Bracket's original wharf is gone, replaced in 1988 by a jetty. His waterfront was replaced by an under-water park, the first of its kind on the West Coast. In 1971, the park was designated a marine sanctuary and Bracket's Landing site was added to the National Register of Historic Places.

Old Milltown
201 Fifth Ave. South, Edmonds (425) 778-4477

Allen Yost built the city's opera house, operated a stage line to Seattle and ran an early Ford automobile agency from this building in the early part of the twentieth century. In 1973 his building and some adjoining structures were converted into shops and restaurants. Throughout most of the interior, which was preserved during the renovation, are antiques and relics from the city's past. A covered boardwalk connects the buildings in this turn-of-the-century setting.

Allen Yost's former Ford Automobile Agency

Edmonds Congregational Church (Site)
American Legion, Frank Freese Post No. 66, 601 Dayton St., Edmonds

The first church to be built in Edmonds was constructed at this site in 1889, a year before the city was incorporated. In 1930 it was sold to the American Legion. Post members removed the steeple, dug a basement and moved the building 40-feet to its present site. A plaque commemorates the site of the city's first organized church.

215

EVERETT (EV-er-it)

Site of Vancouver's Landing
Grand Avenue Park, 1800 Grand Ave., Everett

Grand Avenue Park was designed as a place where visitors could view the "City of Smokestacks," but it is also one of several parks in the city where local historic events are commemorated. It was at a site below this bluff in 1792 that Captain George Vancouver landed and took possession of this area for Britain and his king, George the Third. A complete list of other parks in the Everett area, and the events they mark, can be obtained by calling the Parks and Recreation Department at (425) 259-0300

On Grand Avenue, between 8th and 24th Sts. are a number of grand homes built between 1890 and 1920. Among them is the 1910 Georgian Revival-style home built by investment banker William Butler at 1703 Grand where former U.S. Senator Henry M. Jackson lived. Also in the area at 2320 Rucker is the 1911 Colonial Revival-style home of the former governor of Washington, Roland Hartley, a National Registered Historic Landmark.

Totem Pole
44th St. and Rucker Ave., Everett

Chief William Shelton of the Tulalip Indian Reservation carved this 80-foot totem pole to honor the memory of the Salish Indian Chief, Patkanim. Chief Patkanim was one of four chiefs to sign the Mukilteo Treaty in 1855 which ceded to the United States the lands from Elliott Bay to the Canadian border. A relief bust of this great Indian Chief appears on the commemorative plaque at the base of this monument.

Historic Weyerhaeuser Office Building
Everett Area Chamber of Commerce, 1710 W. Marine View Dr., Everett
(425) 252-5181

In 1899 James J. Hill, of Great Northern Railroad fame, arranged for Frederick Weyerhaeuser to purchase 900,000 acres of Northern Pacific land at $6 an acre. Weyerhaeuser, in turn, constructed a mill on the Everett waterfront that grew to become the world's largest sawmill. At the time when this Tudor-style headquarters building was dedicated in 1923, Weyerhaeuser had two additional mills in operation in Everett and another under construction. Twice in its history the building has been "floated" by river. First in 1938 when it was barged from downtown Everett to the company's second mill site. And, it 1984 when it was moved to its present location. Today the first floor of this authentically restored building is home to the Everett Area Chamber of Commerce. Old photographs depicting commerce, waterfront activity and the lumber industry in early Everett can be seen throughout the building. The "Weyerhaeuser Room," the former office of W.H. Boner, contains historical exhibits.

Weyerhaeuser Building

Everett Public Market
2804 Grand Ave., Everett (425) 252-1089

Everett's 1900 Mayor, James E. Bell, operated this turn-of-the-century brick building as a stable for horse and buggy travelers and as a garage the emerging horseless-carriage trade. Horses were stabled in the basement and goods were brought to the top floor by the freight elevator that's still in use in this historic building. During World War II, Boeing used the building as an aircraft subassembly plant. Today, the restored building houses a number of antique dealers, specialty shops and restaurants in an early 1900s setting.

217

Rucker Hill Park
621 Laurel Dr., Everett

This park serves as a gateway to the city's historic residential district where many of the city's prominent pioneer families built stately mansions. Spectacular views of the Olympic and Cascade Mountains and Port Gardner Bay made this hillside the ideal Everett building location. The Rucker Hill district includes homes built on Laurel, Snohomish, Niles, Warren, Bell, Tulalip, 33rd and 34th Avenues, and is listed on the National Register of Historic Places.

Rucker Mansion
412 Laurel Dr., Everett

Arrival of the transcontinental railroad in Everett sparked the growth of this bayside community in the early 1900s. Bethel Rucker, and his business associate, William Swalwell, bought most of the land that is now Everett, and made their fortune in real estate. Rucker built this mansion in 1904 and sold-off parcels of the estate to other well-to-do families who built their homes in this scenic area. Rucker's Mansion is listed on the National Register of Historic Places.

Monte Cristo Hotel
Everett Center for the Arts at the Monte Cristo, 1507 Wall St., Everett
(425) 259-0380

On the day the 140-room Monte Cristo Hotel celebrated its grand opening in 1925 "The Everett Daily Herald" reported this hotel "means...community faith...community enterprise and community pride." For had it not been for the citizens of Everett, who purchased $120,000 in bonds for the hotel building fund, this hotel, the largest project of its kind undertaken in Everett, may never had been built. Conflict with fire codes closed the Monte Cristo 1973. In 1994, the completely restored six-story, Italian Renaissance-style building was reopened. The hotel's rooms were converted into 69 affordable living areas, but the historical integrity of the hotel's lobby and public areas was maintained. The grand lobby and mezzanine of this local and national historic site is a gallery of fine art featuring a permanent exhibit of blown glass from the Pilchuck Glass School.

Monte Cristo Hotel

A number of the Everett's historic buildings can be seen in the area around the Monte Cristo:

Everett Theatre, 2911 Colby Ave. (425) 258-6766 A completely renovated 1901 vaudeville theatre that once hosted such notable performers as Helen Hayes and George M. Cohan. This theatre is listed on the Washington Heritage Register.

Snohomish County Courthouse, Wetmore Ave. between Wall St. and Pacific Ave. When the city's 1897 Romanesque-style courthouse burned down in 1909, it was replaced by this red-tiled roof, white stucco Mission-style building. It's one of the few Spanish-style public buildings in the state. The courthouse is listed on the National Register of Historic Places.

Swalwell Building, 2901 Hewitt Ave. William Swalwell, one of the city's major pioneer investors erected this building in 1892 for the First National Bank. It remains today as one of the downtown area's best-preserved commercial buildings. Swalwell also constructed the adjoining commercial buildings, which are included on the National Register of Historic Places.

Boeing Commercial Airplane Company Assembly Plant
Paine Field on Hwy. 526, west of I-5 via exit 189, Everett

In 1916, on the shores of Lake Union in Seattle, William Boeing began what was to become the state's largest employer, the Boeing Commercial Airplane Company. During World War II, Boeing produced the famous B-17 and B-29 bombers. In 1958 Boeing introduced the 707, the first successful jet plane to enter commercial service. Today, visitors (12 and older) can take a 90-minute guided tour and see how prefabricated sections of Boeing's 747 and 767 jumbo jets come together in this sprawling assembly plant, the world's largest industrial plant (measured in cubic feet).

GRANITE FALLS

Granite Falls Historical Museum
Union and Wabash, Granite Falls (360) 691-7395

Lead and silver ore from Monte Cristo mines was shipped by rail through Granite Falls to the smelter at Everett. The town's growth never materialized from the nearby copper, silver and gold mines, but came instead from the region's other natural resource; its attraction as a recreation destination Relics preserved from the region's past are displayed in this museum of local history.

INDEX

Bush House
Index Ave. and Fifth St., Index

Copper, gold, silver and a number of other minerals mined from the surrounding hills brought a "boom" economy to the town of Index in the late 1890s. A number of businesses flourished, including the Bush House, a three-story inn built in 1898. The boom is long-over, but guests can still stay in one of the inn's ten rooms. The Bush House, the second-oldest building in Snohomish County, is listed on the Washington Heritage Register.

Red Men Hall
Index Ave. and Sixth St., Index

A lodge hall for the Improved Order of Red Man was erected here in 1903. The fraternity, founded in 1765, is one of the oldest fraternal orders in the United States. The 3-story hall, called the Red Man Wigwam, is still in use today for community and social events, and is listed on the National Register of Historic Places.

MARYSVILLE

Tulalip Indian Agency Office
3901 Mission Beach Rd., Tulalip Reservation, Marysville

With the signing of the Mukilteo Treaty in 1855, Tulalip Reservation was established for Indians of the Skykomish, Snohomish, Snoqualmie and Stillaguamish tribes. This Indian agency office was erected in 1912 and used by government agents until 1951. It's one of the last remaining agency buildings on the reservation and is listed on the National Register of Historic Places.

Chief William Shelton of the Tulalip Reservation carved an 80-foot totem pole commemorating Chief Patkanim, one of four chiefs who signed the Mukilteo Treaty that ceded to the United States all land between Elliot Bay and the Canadian border. The totem pole stands in Everett, and Chief Patkanim's gravesite can be visited at Mission Beach Cemetery on the reservation.

St. Anne's Roman Catholic Church
Mission Beach Rd., Tulalip Reservation, Marysville

Two years after this reservation was established, Father F.C. Chirouse founded a boarding school for the Indian children and built a mission church. His school

221

would be the first in the nation to be awarded a formal federal contract to provide boarding and education for Native American children. This Victorian Gothic-style church was erected in 1904 to replace Father Chirouse's original mission church after it was destroyed by fire. The old mission bell hangs in the belfry of St. Anne's, a National Historic Site.

Big Cedar Stump Historic Marker
Highway Rest Area, Exit 207 off I-5, North of Marysville

"This famous stump remains as evidence of the giant trees which once forested this area. Over 20 feet in diameter and 200 feet tall, the huge "Western Redcedar" is believed to have been more than 1000 years old. Discovered by early settlers of the area, the following is a resume of its recorded history.

1892 – The stump was killed by a fire which started in its hollow base.

1916 – After the top was removed, Paul Wangmo and Ole Rodway cut and chopped three spines from the core and cut archways through the stump.

1922 – After cutting the stump off at its base, Ole Reinseth and Slim Husby used horse teams to drag it north 150 yards where it was set on a concrete base.

1939 – The stump, by now cracked, was taken apart and pieced back together just north of Portage Creek, alongside the newly completed U.S. 99. On May 27, Crown Prince Olay and Princess Martha of Norway drove through the stump.

1971 – The stump's final move brought it here."

Indian Shaker Church
North Meridian Ave., Tulalip Reservation, Marysville

The Indian Shaker religion, a mix of Christian and Indian beliefs, (not affiliated with the Shakers sect based in Eastern and Midwestern states) was founded northeast of Olympia in 1882. The popularity of this new religion won wide acceptance among the Indian tribes and soon spread from reservation to reservation. In 1896, Johnny Steve and his wife brought the Indian Shaker religion to the Tulalip Reservation. This Indian Shaker Church, which is listed on the National Register of Historic Places, was erected by members of the congregation in 1924 and is one of the best preserved examples of the architectural style of this sect.

MUKILTEO (MUHK-il-TEE-oh)

Mukilteo Lighthouse
915 Second Ave., Mukilteo

Near the landing where ferry boats shuttle to and from Whidbey Island stands a 1906 Victorian-style lighthouse. The wood-frame station, with its original, French-made Fresnel lens and fog horn, is still operated and maintained by the U.S. Coast Guard. Visitors can tour this Nationally Registered Historic Site most weekends.

Mukilteo Lighthouse

Mukilteo Treaty Grounds
Point Elliott Peace Treaty Site, south of Mukilteo Lighthouse, 915 Second Ave.,
Mukilteo

A half-century before construction began on the Mukilteo lighthouse, leaders from
22 American Indian tribes met at this site with Washington territorial governor,
Isaac Stevens, to sign the Point Elliott Treaty of 1855. With the signing of that
agreement, Indians gave up rights to most of their lands between Seattle and the
Canadian border. The site of this important event in the state's history is listed on
the Washington Heritage Register.

Mukilteo Historical Museum
Rosehill Community Center, 304 Lincoln Ave., Mukilteo (425) 355-9656

After the Point Elliott Treaty was signed in 1855, Mukilteo quickly developed into
a major lumbering community. By the 1870s salmon was being packed here and
the first commercial cannery to operate on Puget Sound was opened. Ferry boats
soon plied the state's waterways transporting passengers and freight from city-to-city.
Old photographs that trace the maritime development of Puget Sound, marine
artifacts, and miniature models of Puget Sound ferry boats and terminals are displayed
in this museum of history.

Mukilteo Historical Museum

SNOHOMISH (snoh-HOH-mish)

Snohomish Historic District
Ave. "E", Fifth St., Union Ave., Northern Pacific Railroad and Snohomish River, Snohomish   Walking tour guide available from the Chamber of Commerce, 116 Ave. "B", Snohomish

When Congress elected to build a military road from Steilacoom to Fort Bellingham in 1853, five Steilacoom residents began acquiring land claims along Snohomish River by the proposed ferry crossing. One of those residents, E.C. Ferguson, built a pre-fabricated house in Steilacoom and moved the house, along with enough goods to stock a store, by sidewheel steamer to his homestead on the banks of the Snohomish River. When the military forts at Bellingham and Steilacoom were closed, the plan for a military road, and ferry crossing, were abandoned. However, a townsite was established in 1859 and served as the county seat for 35 years. Ferguson's pre-fab home and scores of other early homes and buildings have been preserved or restored in this historic district. A Snohomish Walking Tour Guide (available from chamber of commerce or Blackman Museum) identifies 75 places of historic interest in the city, from 1890s Victorian homes to turn-of-the-century businesses. Among the places listed are:

Snohomish Iron Works, 1910 - Oldest continuously operated business in the city.

Snohomish City Mall, 1927 - Former city hall.

1st Bank Antiques - First reinforced concrete structure in the county.

Eagles Hall, 1904 - Ballroom has floating dance floor; first of its kind built west of the Mississippi.

Snohomish Public Library, 1910 - Carnegie library with cross section of large fir tree (took 14 log trucks to bring the whole log to town).

City Hall, 1938 - Styled after Independence Hall in Philadelphia.

Country Manner, 1880 - One of last original false front buildings.

Snohomish Hardware, 1911 - Contains a water-powered elevator.

225

Linert Residence, 1908 - B&B listed on Washington Heritage Register.

Methodist Church, 1885 - 66-foot-high belfry contains county's first church bell.

Stevens House, 1887 - Built for John Stevens for whom Stevens Pass was named.

Vestal House, 1889 - Queen Anne home of first Washington State Senator.

Stevens House

Blackman House Museum
Snohomish Historical Society, 118 Ave. "B", Snohomish (360) 568-5235

Hyrcanus Blackman, a successful lumber mill operator and the town's first mayor, with his wife, Ella, built this Victorian home in 1878. Visitors to this authentically restored house museum are treated to an inside view of a well-preserved 1890s home. Many Blackman family artifacts and period furnishings are exhibited including: Mrs. Blackman's piano that was shipped around the *Horn*, their "everyday" china, original wall coverings and family photographs.

Tours of other Snohomish historic homes are offered through the Historical Society at various times of the year. Call the Society for specific information.

Blackman House Museum, Courtesy of Blackman House Museum

*Front Parlor, Blackman House Museum,
Courtesy of Blackman House Museum*

Pioneer Village Museum
118 Ave. "B" at 2nd and Pine (in the J.C. Penney Shopping Center behind Payless Drugs), Snohomish (360) 568-5235

Around the remains of the city's pioneer cemetery stand seven early Snohomish structures that have been relocated to this outdoor museum for preservation. The collection of restored buildings include: an 1875 log cabin, 1889 pioneer home, 1902 Victorian cottage, 1910 general store, blacksmith shop and weaver's shop.

227

STANWOOD

D.O. Pearson House & Museum
102nd Ave. N.W. and 271st St. N.W.,west side of Stanwood (360) 629-3352

Whidbey Island pioneer, D.O. Pearson, founded the first store in Stanwood in 1877, across the Stillaguamish River from the region's first trading post. Pearson became the town's first mayor and, in 1890, built this notable 3-story mansion. His home was noted for its unusual architectural distinctiveness, and considered one of the finest in the region. A museum addition was built behind the Pearson Mansion in 1991 to accommodate new exhibits, large artifacts and a library.

D. O. Pearson House and Museum

Whatcom County

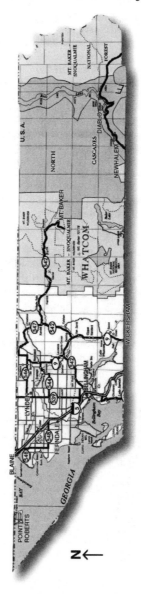

WHATCOM COUNTY

BELLINGHAM

Bellingham Bay Historical Marker
On the west side of I-5 east of Donovan St., in the south city limits of Bellingham

"In 1792 this sheltered harbor was discovered by the English explorer, Captain George Vancouver, and by him named in honor of an officer of His Majesty's Navy, Sir William Bellingham. Beyond the Bay in Puget Sound lie the 172 picturesque islands which compose the San Juan Archipelago, unrivaled for its scenic grandeur and natural beauty. The subject of territorial controversy in the boundary dispute of 1846, the San Juan Islands were awarded to the United States when Emperor William I of Germany, acting as international arbiter, located the present boundary."

Whatcom Museum of History and Art
121 Prospect St., Bellingham (360) 676-6981

In 1903 the four Bellingham Bay communities of Whatcom, New Whatcom, Fairhaven and Sehome merged to form the city of Bellingham. A year later this ornate Victorian brick building, erected as New Whatcom's City Hall in 1892, would serve the new city of Bellingham as its seat of government. Since 1941 the old City

Hall has been home to the Whatcom Museum. An extensive 12-year restoration project was completed in 1974 following a fire that nearly destroyed this historic landmark. Northwest Coast Indian artifacts, Victorian period rooms, and displays depicting the "boom and bust" history of the region and its early industries are among the museum's permanent exhibits.

Spinning Wheel exhibited inside Whatcom Museum of History and Art

General George E. Pickett Memorial Home
910 Bancroft St. between "E" and "F" Sts., Bellingham

Captain George Pickett was dispatched to Fort Bellingham in 1856 with a company of infantry to protect settlers from the Haida Indians. He built Fort Bellingham, the town's first bridge, and this wood-frame home for him and his Indian wife. In 1859, Pickett stood fast against the British who were claiming the San Juan Islands during the "Pig War" boundary dispute with the United States. But his nationwide fame came during the Civil War when, as a General in the Confederate Army, he led his well-known charge against the Union center at Cemetery Ridge during the 1863 Battle of Gettysburg. His home, one of the state's oldest landmarks, is listed on the National Register of Historic Places.

Pickett House

231

Fort Bellingham (Site)
1346 Marine Dr., Bellingham

U.S. Army presence in this region was established by Captain George Pickett and his men with construction of Fort Bellingham at this site in 1856. The Fort became the most prominent U.S. military location in the Puget Sound area. From this headquarters, Pickett directed the building of the first bridge across Whatcom Creek and construction of the road between the fort and the town of Whatcom. In 1860, after the "Pig War" boundary dispute, Fort Bellingham was abandoned. Nothing remains today of the fort or the massive blockhouses that once stood here.

Roeder Home
2600 Sunset Dr., Bellingham (360) 733-6897

The Roeder name is deeply engraved in the history of Whatcom County. Henry Roeder and his wife Elizabeth were the first white settlers in Whatcom County. Henry built the region's first sawmill at Whatcom Creek in 1852, and platted the town of Whatcom. His son, Victor, founded Bellingham National Bank and, in 1903, built this magnificent Craftsman-style house. Finely-crafted oak woodwork and hand-painted murals are among the features found in this well-preserved, turn-of-the-century home. The Victor Roeder home, which is listed on the National Register of Historic Places, was donated to the county in 1971 for use as a community cultural and social center. A guide to other early-1900s homes in the Bellingham area is available here.

Roeder Home

Eldridge Avenue Historic District
The area bounded by Eldridge Ave. and Washington St., between Vale and "F" Sts. Guide available from Bellingham Municipal Arts Commission or the Visitor Information Center, 904 Potter St., Bellingham (360) 671-3990

Several 1880-1910 Victorian homes that line the streets of this historic district remain as a reminder of the prosperity achieved by the city's pioneer families. The homes of two of the city's founders, Henry Roeder and Edward Eldridge, no longer remain, but others in this historic district have been preserved including: the James Bolster House, 2820 Eldridge, a Queen Anne-style building constructed of brick; and the George Bacon home, 2001 Eldridge, designed by George's cousin, Henry Bacon, architect of the Lincoln Memorial in our Nation's Capitol. The district also includes homes on the National Register of Historic places and turn-of-the-century designed Elizabeth Park, the oldest public park in Whatcom County.

Fairhaven Historic District
The area bounded by 10th and 13th Streets, Columbia and Larrabee Aves., Bellingham. Walking tour guide available at information gazebo at 12th and Harris Sts. or Old Fairhaven Association (360) 647-8661

In a period of just one year, from 1889 to 1890, 125 commercial buildings were erected in Fairhaven in anticipation of the city becoming the terminus of the

transcontinental railroad. When the Great Northern ended its line at Tacoma instead, dreams of Fairhaven becoming the "next Chicago" died and new construction ceased. Many turn-of-the-century red brick buildings remain in use today in this preserved historic district including: the Terminal Building, the oldest surviving commercial structure in Fairhaven. In 1895, Mark Twain lectured at the Lighthouse Theatre. During his visit, Twain stayed at the Fairhaven Hotel, which stood at 12th and Harris until it was destroyed by a fire in 1953. Many of the remaining historic buildings in this district are identified with brass plaques that tell a little of the building's history.

233

Roland G. Gramwell House
1001 16th St., Bellingham

The city's finest Victorian home was built by Roland Gramwell in 1890-92. Handsome returns from investments Gramwell made in Fairhaven are reflected in his elaborate mansion. When built, the exquisite three-story home featured the finest interior woodwork, stained-glass windows and the most modern electric and gas appliances available. Gramwell, one of the city's most influential men, entertained Mark Twain during his 1895 visit to Fairhaven.

James F. Wardner House
1103 15th St., Bellingham (360) 676-0974

Millionaire Jim Wardner invested some of his Idaho silver fortune in Fairhaven properties at the time when this city was expected to be the terminus for the transcontinental railroad. He built this elaborate 21-room mansion in 1890, but lived here only a year. Wardner sold all his Fairhaven properties shortly before the Crash of 1893. Today the well-preserved and maintained "Castle" is operated as a "bed and breakfast" replete with Victorian period antiques. "Wardner's Castle" is listed on the National Register of Historic Places.

Larrabee House
Lairmont Manor, 405 Fieldstone Rd., Bellingham

The Larrabees left their mark on the Pacific Northwest. Charles Larrabee, a successful businessman who made his fortune in banking, mining, railroads and real estate, donated the land for Fairhaven Park, which is located at the northern terminus of beautiful Chuckanut Drive. The Larrabees also donated nearly 1,900 acres at the southern end of Chuckanut Drive which would become Larrabee State Park, the first state park in Washington. Construction of the four-story Larrabee mansion was completed by Francis Larrabee in 1916, three years after Charles' death. The three structures that have been erected on this large estate are now used for multiple purposes and are administered by the Lairmont Manor Trusteeship. The primary family home is listed on the National Register of Historic Places.

Mt. Baker Theatre
106 N. Commercial, Bellingham (360) 734-6080

All the features remain that made this Moorish-Spanish-style theatre a source of city pride when built in the mid-1920s: an 80-foot interior dome, open-beamed lobby, chandeliers, and the original 215-pipe organ that once played for Vaudeville acts and silent movies. Live theatre and movies have been continuously presented since the 1,500-seat theatre opened. In 1978, this elaborately designed entertainment center was added to the National Register of Historic Places.

Leopold Hotel
1224 Cornwall, Bellingham

In the early 1900s this was one of the region's finest places to stay. Many distinguished visitors who came to the city were guests at this landmark hotel. Leopold Schmidt purchased the hotel in 1910, and expanded it in 1913. The original hotel, built as the Byron House in 1899, no longer stands, but its 1913 addition remains. Some of the hotel's early features can be found in the renovated addition, which is listed on the National Register of Historic Places.

Old Whatcom County Courthouse
1308 "E" St., Bellingham

The state's oldest brick building was constructed at this site in 1858 using bricks made in Philadelphia. It was originally designed as a bank to hold gold brought down from the Fraser River. In 1865, it was purchased by the county and converted into a courthouse and jail. A number of businesses and organizations have occupied the building since, but its part in the early history of the region earned it a listing on the National Register of Historic Places.

Western Washington Outdoor Sculpture Museum
Western Washington University, 516 High St., Bellingham (360) 676-3000

The first formal school in what is now Washington State was opened in Vancouver in 1832 for sons of the officers and employees of the Hudson's Bay Company. Twenty two years later, the first Territorial legislature mandated public education for children between the ages of 4 and 21. A year following Washington's admission as a State, the first state normal school opened in Cheney. A second normal school was opened in Ellensburg in 1891, and a third in Bellingham in 1899. Today they are known as Eastern, Central and Western Washington Universities. The original Romanesque-style school building, a National Historic Site lovingly referred to as "Old Main," now houses the administrative offices for this 189-acre campus. On the grounds are sixteen works of art by local and nationally-known sculptors. A guide to the location and description of each piece is available at the Visitors Center at the South College Drive entrance to the university.

Old Telegraph Road Historical Marker
North side of Guide-Meridian Rd., two blocks east of the Lynden exit off I-5

"Penetrating northward through this point, toward wilderness areas of British Columbia and Alaska, a telegraph line was partially built in 1865-67 to connect New York with London via a Bering Strait cable and a line across Russia. A single wire pole followed a fifty-foot clearing through heavy forests and across frozen Tundra. Western Union telegraph company dropped this project abruptly in 1867 when satisfactory trans-Atlantic cable service was established. Russian-American cooperation in building this line facilitated our purchase of Alaska in 1867."

BLAINE

International Peace Arch
Peace Arch State and Provincial Park, I-5 at the United States and Canadian border, Blaine

One of the oldest and best-known landmarks in the Pacific Northwest, the "International Peace Arch," marks more than just the site of the U.S. and Canadian border. It was erected to commemorate one hundred years of peace and friendship between the two countries. Sam Hill, who constructed the first paved road in the state, was the driving force behind this international project. In 1920-21 construction

236

crews from both countries used donated cement from Victoria and steel from New York to build the 67-foot high arch, the only one of its kind in the world. Resting within the arch on the American side is a piece of the Mayflower, the ship that brought the first Pilgrims to the New World in 1620. Within the arch on the Canadian side is a section of the Beaver, the first steam-powered vessel to navigate the Pacific Ocean. Two massive iron gates within the arch are permanently open. They are a symbol of the "firm and lasting peace" established between these two nations with the signing of the Treaty of Ghent on Christmas Eve, 1814. This monument proclaims that "the peace then established has never been broken."

International Peach Arch

Semiahmoo Park and Interpretive Center
9261 Semiahmoo Parkway, Blaine (360) 371-5513

Before the turn-of-the-century this was the site of the Alaska Packers Association's cannery, one of the largest salmon canneries in the west. Square-riggers would anchor here long enough to unload their cargo of Alaskan sockeye salmon, take on new provisions, and return north to the bountiful waters off British Columbia. The Raven-Salmon Woman Totem Pole and a few remaining restored buildings from the original cannery are part of this interpretive center. Exhibits focus on the Semiahmoo Indians, regional history, salmon fishing and the canning industry.

For more information, contact the **Blaine Visitor Information Center,** 215 Marine Dr., Blaine (360) 332-4544 or (800) 624-3555

DIABLO (dee-AHB-loh)

Diablo Dam Visitor Center
Hwy. 20, Diablo — Skagit Tours, 500 Newhalem St., Rockport (206) 233-2709

In 1917, construction began on the first of a series of three hydroelectric dams to be built along the upper Skagit River, south of Ross Lake, to provide electricity to Seattle and the Gorge, Diablo and Ross dams. During construction of Diablo and Ross dams, the nearby Incline Railway, that now whisks visitors 560-feet up the 68% gradient of Sourdough Mountain, shuttled men and material to the summit for the final leg to dam construction sites. A small museum features the history of Lucinda Davis and her three children who homesteaded an area near the dam site in 1898, built a waterwheel to generate electricity for their family farm, and operated a workingman's inn. Guided tours of the dam include an interesting video presentation on the history of the Skagit Project, a ride up the incline, a walk across Diablo Dam, and a close-up view of the beautiful emerald-green Diablo Lake.

FERNDALE

Pioneer Park
One mile west of I-5 via exit 262 to First Ave. Turn left to park entrance in Ferndale (360) 384-6461

The Pacific Northwest's largest collection of original cedar log cabins are preserved at this site along the Nooksack River. The Old Settlers Association 1920 building, which serves as the park headquarters, was the only cabin originally built at this site. The other structures were relocated here over a period of several decades to save them from destruction. Whatcom County's oldest church was built near Blaine in 1876 by Rev. W.M. Stewart. Rev. Stewart was a personal friend of President Lincoln and helped form the Republican Party after the Civil War. The church was relocated here in 1968. The Holeman cabin was built in 1890 on their homestead on the west side of the Nooksack River. It was relocated here in 1985 and furnished as a one-room schoolhouse typical of the period. Other cabins which range from the years 1873-95 feature antique printing equipment, general store memorabilia, old farm tools, nineteenth century bank relics, a veterans museum and postal artifacts.

Old Settlers Association Building at Entrance to Pioneer Park

1876 Log Church Building

Foster House

Pioneer Park

Pioneer Park

Hovander Homestead Park
5299 Neilsen Rd., Ferndale (360) 384-3444

Soon after Swedish immigrants, Hakan and Louisa bought this 60-acre farm along the banks of the Nooksack River in 1898, Hakan began designing the beautiful, two-story, Scandinavian-influenced cedar home that stands here today. The linseed oil finished woodwork, original flooring, cabinets, hardware and some of the family's original furniture were preserved and maintained by four generations of the family until ownership of this National Historic Site was transferred to the Whatcom County Park system in 1971. The Hovander's barn contains antique farm implements and is surrounded by flower and vegetable gardens and a fruit orchard. In addition to the history that has been preserved here, there are farm animals, hay fields, hiking trails, fishing facilities and activities for the entire family to enjoy.

Hovander Home

Tennant Lake Natural History Interpretive Center
5236 Neilsen Rd., Ferndale (360) 384-3444

Adjacent to the Hovander Homestead Park is the pioneer Neilsen homestead farm, where 200 acres of marshlands have been preserved as a wildlife habitat. The former three-story Neilsen home has been adapted as an interpretive center. A Fragrance Garden next to the Center has been specially designed for visually impaired guests. A half-mile nature trail with boardwalks and a bird-watching tower overlook the riverside marsh.

241

Anderson House Bed & Breakfast
2140 Main St., Ferndale

The former 1897 home of the city's first banker was restored as a bed & breakfast in 1986. Period furnishings accent this early Frank Lloyd Wright design American Foursquare home.

LYNDEN

Lynden Pioneer Museum
217 W. Front St., Lynden (360) 354-3675

Although the Dutch influence is prominent throughout the town of Lynden, the Dutch weren't the first to homestead here. It was Holden and Phoebe Judson from Ohio who crossed the plains, settled here and named the town. The history of this pioneer family, who began their westward journey in 1853, is exhibited here along with: an 1880s farmstead display, complete with relics from the period; the story of the Clamdiggers Association who first met in Judson's Hall in 1891; and the arrival of the Dutch who arrived here in the mid-1890s and made Whatcom County the state's largest milk producer.

This museum, one of the largest in the state, also features: Fred Polinder's Antique horse-drawn buggy collection; a large collection of well-preserved vintage automobiles; old John Deere tractors and other farm machinery from the Puget Sound Antique Tractor & Machinery Association; a replica of Lynden's 26 Main Street shops as they appeared in the 1920s and 30s; Northwest Indian artifacts; and military memorabilia from the Civil War to the Vietnam era.

Berthusen Park
8837 Berthusen Rd., Lynden (360) 354-2424

Clearing giant cedars from 100 acres of land was the mammoth task undertaken by Hans Berthusen when he homesteaded this property in 1883. He built his first home and barn from split cedars, raised crops of hay and grain, and ran a dairy. In 1901, Berthusen erected the county's largest barn; a structure that measured 128 feet by 188 feet and 50 feet high. When he died in 1944 the entire homestead was willed to the city as a memorial park. While Berthusen was alive, he maintained 20 acres of virgin cedar timber on his homestead as a "visible testimony to what the county was like when he first came here." His grove of trees are preserved as part of this city park along with his homestead barn which is listed on the Washington Heritage Register.

Dutch Mothers Restaurant
405 Front St., Lynden (360) 354-2174

The culture of the Dutch, who settled here in the mid-1890s and made this the largest Dutch settlement in the state, can be seen in the home and businesses that line the city's streets, and in the people who live in this well-kept community. "A Little Bit of Holland" fills this restaurants three main rooms: the Bloemen Kamer (flower room), Theologie Kamer (theology room), and the Borderij (farm room). Preserved in the interior of this 1909 building, which was first partitioned-off for two businesses, a drug store and ice cream parlor, is the original pressed metal ceiling, skylight and sections of fir flooring.

MOUNT BAKER

Mount Baker Historic Marker
Heather Meadow, between Maple Falls and Glacier on Hwy. 542 (Mount Baker Highway)

"The gleaming crest of Mount Baker, impressive northern buttress of the Cascade Range, rises skyward to the lofty elevation of 10,750 feet. Its Indian name 'Kulshan' means steep. Lieutenant Joseph Baker, Vancouver's valiant officer, sighted the snowy eminence from far out toward the sea on April 30, 1792 and the Captain of the expedition named it in his honor. Beyond Heather Meadow where stands this marker, looms Mount Shuksan, Mount Baker's sister peak, 9,038 feet in height, still retaining the Indian name which describes it ruggedness."

Mount Baker, the center of the Mount Baker-Snoqualmie National Forest, is the most visible landmark in Northwest Washington. Indians called Mount Baker the "Great White Watcher," for they could see its year-round, snow-capped peak from points as distant as Vancouver, British Columbia.

NEWHALEM (NOO-hay-luhm)

Skagit River Railway Engine No. 6
In the center of Newhalem

The first hydroelectric plant in the North Cascades was completed at Newhalem in 1921 to serve Seattle City Light employees who were building nearby Gorge Dam. In 1924, the year the Gorge Dam (a wooden structure) was completed, rail service between Rockwood and Newhalem was initiated. For thirty years, this Baldwin steam engine hauled carloads of equipment, supplies, Seattle Light employees and tourists between Rockport and Newhalem. It was retired after Hwy. 20 was completed between the two towns in 1953.

POINT ROBERTS

Point Roberts Boundary Historical Marker
Tyee Road at the U.S./Canadian Border, Point Roberts — To reach Point Roberts, cross the border at Blaine into Canada and follow the Canadian freeway to the Tsawwassen/Point Roberts exit. Continue south and back across the border.

"One mile west stands a granite obelisk, the first of a series of similar markers along the 49th parallel, defining the Canadian-American line from the Strait of Georgia to the summit of the Rocky Mountains. The official survey, begun at Point Roberts in 1857, was a joint venture by American and British boundary commissions. Completed in 1862, it carried out provisions of the Treaty of Washington (June 15, 1846), and virtually ended the old dispute between Great Britain and the United States over sovereignty in the Pacific Northwest."

Boundary Marker Number One
Monument Park, Marine Dr. and Roosevelt Rd. U.S./Canada border, Point Roberts

Archibald Campbell, U.S. Commissioner of the Northwest Boundary Survey, and his Canadian counterpart began marking the 49th parallel, the official border between the two nations, at this site in 1857. Several granite obelisks were erected along the border to commemorate the commission's survey, but this is the only one remaining today. When the Treaty of Washington established the 49th parallel as the international boundary, the five-square-mile community of Point Roberts, the most northwesterly part of the United States, was cut-off by land from the American mainland.

244

Boundary Marker Number One

Lighthouse Marine County Park
811 Marine Dr., Point Roberts (360) 945-4911

While this simple metal framework lighthouse lacks the grace and beauty of other lights found along the Pacific Coast, it does mark the most northwesterly point in the United States. The park surrounding the light includes a boardwalk, interpretive displays, and a 30-foot observation tower. The tower offers visitors a panoramic view of Georgia Strait where an occasional orca whale can be sighted.

WICKERSHAM - ACME

Lake Whatcom Railway
NP Rd., east off Hwy. 9, 11 miles north of Sedro Woolley, Wickersham
(360) 595-2218

The last steam engine to be operated in Seattle, Northern Pacific's 1907 switch engine number 1070, has been semi-retired to Wickersham where it pulls vintage excursion cars over a former Northern Pacific branch line. Two plush 1913 day coaches, a business car with rear observation platform, wooden caboose and other rolling stock can be seen at the depot. The train, which operates on a limited Summer schedule, travels through scenic back-country near the foothills of Mt. Baker.

1907 Northern Pacific Switch Engine, Courtesy of Lake Whatcom Railway

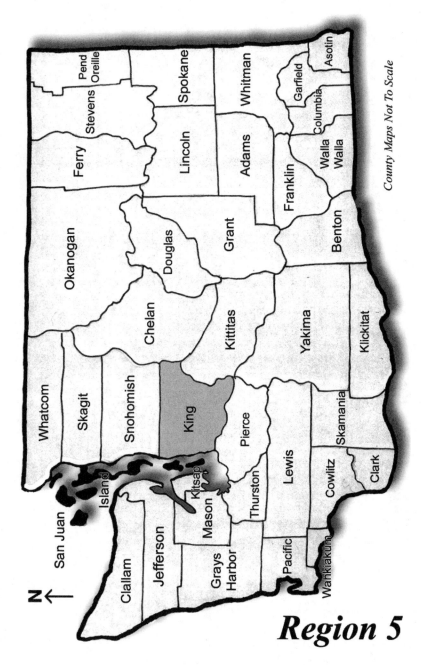

County Maps Not To Scale

Region 5

King County

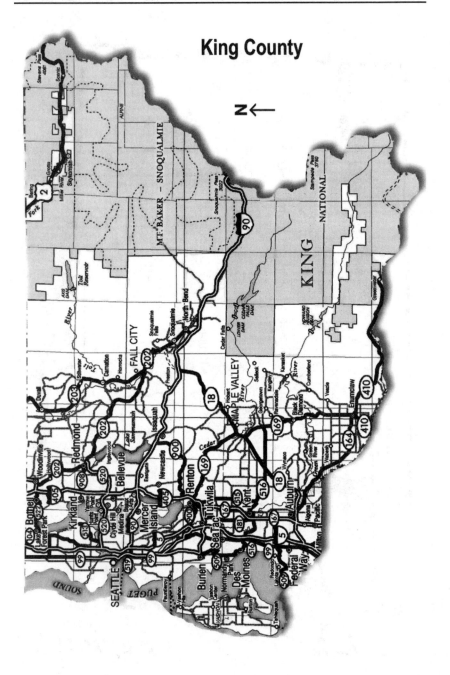

REGION 5

KING COUNTY

AUBURN (AW-burn)

White River Valley Historical Museum
918 "H" St. SE, Auburn (253) 939-2783

The valley's vast prairie land and dense forests attracted pioneers who settled the White River area in the mid-1850s. But, life in the valley wasn't as tranquil as the setting would suggest. Many feared the local Indians. The events that justified that fear, and the history of the White River Valley communities of Kent, Auburn, Algona and Pacific are chronicled in this museum's collections. Pioneer relics, Indian artifacts, photographs, and old newspapers are exhibited with a primary emphasis on the valley's agricultural heritage.

Aaron Neely Mansion
12303 Auburn-Black Diamond Rd., Auburn (253) 833-9404

Aaron Neely was a seven-year-old when he crossed the plains from Tennessee in the 1850s with his parents and settled in the Kent area. In 1876, he acquired a 120-acre land claim just west of Auburn. As the years passed he acquired more land and became one of the valley's leading fruit growers. Neely built this large, two-story Queen Anne-style Victorian home from lumber cut and milled on his property and lived here until 1900. His home, which is listed on the National Register of Historic Places, has been restored by the Neely Mansion Association and is open for tours by special appointment.

Pioneer Memorial
Lt. Slaughter Memorial
30th St. NE and Auburn Way N., Auburn

News quickly spread through the Puget Sound area in the fall of 1855 telling the tale of settlers and soldiers that were killed by Indians in the White River Valley. For nearly a year, western Washington was at war. The two monuments that were erected near the site of these tragedies were later relocated to this small city park. One honors the memory of the eight pioneers who were killed. The second is dedicated to Lieutenant William A. Slaughter and Corporals Barry and Clarendon, who lost their lives while pursuing the attackers. An additional distinction was paid Lt. Slaughter when the residents named the present city of Auburn "Slaughter" in his honor.

BELLEVUE

The Rosalie Whyel Museum of Doll Art
1116 108th Ave. NE, Bellevue (425) 455-1116

More than a thousand of the world's most exquisite, museum-quality dolls, from the mid-nineteenth century to the present are exhibited in this internationally recognized museum. The 13,000 square-foot museum building was designed with a Victorian-style architectural theme, replete with an English garden. It's a perfect setting for the treasures displayed in its galleries. Teddy bears, miniatures and other childhood memorabilia are also featured. Other exhibits focus on the history of doll making as well as the artistry of the dolls themselves.

Rosalie Whyel Museum of Doll Art, Courtesy of Rosalie Whyel Museum of Art

Bellevue Art Museum
301 Bellevue Square, Bellevue (425) 454-3322

First-time visitors looking for this museum will be pleasantly surprised to find that, instead of being located in a typical "museum-style" building, it's on the top floor of the city's downtown mall. And it's a fitting location for a city that's grown from a forested wilderness to metropolis. Although the museum's collections focus primarily on the arts, exhibits regularly include historic themes that relate to the region or state as a whole.

BLACK DIAMOND

Black Diamond Historical Museum
32627 Railroad Ave., Black Diamond (360) 886-1168 or (360) 886-2142

Victor Tull, an employee of the Black Diamond Mining Company of Nortonville, California, discovered rich veins of coal in the Black Diamond locality in 1882. A tent city was established to house the company's miners while houses and a narrow-gauge railroad were being constructed. By 1885, commercial-quality coal was beginning to be shipped by rail to Seattle ports. Within 10 years, Black Diamond was the county's largest coal producer. The restored 1883 Columbia & Puget Sound Railroad Depot now houses the town's historical museum. Original artifacts from the community, mining tools, and replicas of a western jail, country's doctor's office and mine entrance are among the museum's featured exhibits. The depot is listed on the State Register of Historic Places.

1883 Columbia & Puget Sound Railroad Depot, Black Diamond Historical Museum, Courtesy of Black Diamond Historical Museum

Black Diamond Bakery
Railroad Ave., Black Diamond

The original bakery, although expanded, continues to prepare quality bread and pastries using the building's original wood-fired brick ovens. It's the state's oldest operating bakery.

Union Stump
Roberts and Morgan Rds., Black Diamond

In 1907, when a miners union was being proposed, employees were told they couldn't meet on Company property. They chose to hold their meetings around an old tree stump located west of town. The original stump has been encased in cement and preserved as a state historic site. The United Mine Workers of America membership certificate, issued in 1907 when the miners joined Local 2257, is displayed at the Black Diamond Museum.

BOTHELL (BAH-thuhl)

Bothell Landing Park
18120 NE Bothell Way, Bothell (425) 486-1889

In the city park that was once the town's steamship landing, memories from the town's past are safeguarded in three pioneer structures:

The restored 1893 home of the city's former postmaster and mayor, William Hannan, contains turn-of-the-century furnishings and is operated as a historical museum by the Bothell Historical Society.

An 1885 hand-hewn log cabin, constructed by Swedish immigrants Andrew and Augusta Beckstrom, was the birthplace of the first child born in Bothell. The small 190- square-foot cabin, which housed the ten members of the Beckstrom family, is listed on the Washington Heritage Register.

The 1890s Lytle House was the home of Bothell's first physician.

Hannan Home, 1890 School Bell and Beckstrom Log Cabin

CARNATION

Carnation Research Farm
Nestle Training Center, Carnation Farms Rd., Carnation (425) 788-1511

Hop farming and logging in this region gave way to dairies in 1910 when Elbridge Stuart, owner of the Carnation Milk Company in Kent, established a 350-acre research dairy farm at this site. Stuart's objective was to breed high-producing cows; a goal he achieved in ten years. To mark the accomplishment, a statue was erected to "Possum Sweetheart," who set a world production record of 37,381 pounds of milk in 1920. Her record was eclipsed in 1936 when "Ormsby Butter King" produced 38,606 pounds. A self-guided tour of the farm, milking parlor, maternity and calf barn is offered.

ENUMCLAW (EE-nuhm-klaw)

Naches Trail

Federation Forest State Park, 49201 Enumclaw-Chinook Pass Rd., 17 miles east of Enumclaw on Hwy. 410

Through the wilderness that was once Washington, Native Americans and emigrants blazed trails connecting the eastern part of the state with Puget Sound. A section of one of those early trails, the Naches Trail, which linked Fort Walla Walla and

Fort Steilacoom, has been identified and maintained at this state park. The Catherine Montgomery Interpretive Center contains exhibits that describe the wide contrasts in the state's plant life and its seven climatic zones.

FALL CITY

Fall City Hop Shed
King County Community Park, Fall City (425) 392-1979 or (425) 222-7484

The first white men to settle in this area were Washington Territorial Volunteers who came here in 1856 to prevent native warriors from crossing Snoqualmie Pass. As the years passed, and peace was achieved, lumbering and hop farming became prominent occupations in the Snoqualmie Valley. George Rutherford constructed one of the region's pioneer hop curing sheds at a steamboat landing on the Snoqualmie River in 1888. It was relocated to this county park for restoration and preservation.

FEDERAL WAY

Enchanted Village
36201 Enchanted Parkway South, Federal Way (253) 661-8001

Although Enchanted Village's 1906 carousel was built in Abilene, Kansas, most of its operating years has been in the Pacific Northwest. In 1921, Weston Betts purchased the 50-foot portable carousel for his Amusedrome at Redondo. After a 30-year run, Betts took his 36-horse carousel on tour, stopping at a number of sites including Woodland Park Zoo, Point Defiance Park and the Seattle World's Fair. In 1977, Weston Beets II opened Enchanted Village with the carousel as the amusement park's centerpiece. Of the three carousels of this type built by Colonel C.W. Parker at the turn-of-the-century, this is the only one remaining.

The Mystery Cabin
At the entrance to Hylebos Wetlands State Park, Fourth Ave. South and South 348 St., Federal Way

Neither vintage photographs city records nor newspaper reports have been able to authenticate the exact history of this old log cabin. Some reports credit Chief

Seattle with building it in the 1860s near the city that now bears his name. Other reports indicate that it was the Mercer family home from 1850 to 1855. What is known is that Seattle pioneer, David Denny remodeled it in 1889 for use as a real estate office. In subsequent years, the building was used as a church, school and tavern. Today, it's being preserved as the oldest existing log house to survive Seattle's great fire of 1889.

*Mystery Cabin, photographed before it was relocated to
Hylebos Wetlands State Park*

ISSAQUAH (IS-uh-kwah)

**Gilman Town Hall Museum
Issaquah Historical Society Museum**
165 SE Andrews St., Issaquah (425) 392-3500

Before dairy farms, a chocolate factory and street festival, Issaquah was a coal-mining community. The growth of the city, from the first discovery of coal in 1859 and the arrival of the railroad, to the present day is displayed in this historical museum. Old photographs, railroad tools, artifacts, a pioneer kitchen and an early grocery store gives visitors a glimpse of the town's past. Among the long-standing buildings preserved by the museum are the 1889 town hall,1889 train depot and 1902 town jail. The Darigold Plant, salmon hatchery and Issaquah Trail Center are other interesting sites located in the nearby historic downtown district.

1889 Gilman Town Hall

1889 Issaquah Train Depot

Gilman Village,
300 block of NW Gilman Blvd., Issaquah

A collection of renovated vintage homes and buildings from the city's early days have been brought together in a pioneer village setting replete with a wooden boardwalk. These old-time buildings now house a number of specialty shops and restaurants.

256

KIRKLAND

Peter Kirk Building
620 Market St., Kirkland

English immigrant, Peter Kirk, planned to make this a major West Coast steel-producing region. Construction of a large steel mill, with four blast furnaces, began in 1891. That same year, this building was erected to house some of the mill's offices. No steel was ever produced as the Panic of 1893 brought an end to Kirk's plans before the mill was finished. The Peter Kirk Building is now an arts center. One block away, two 1890s commercial buildings have also been preserved. All three are listed on the National Register of Historic Places.

Peter Kirk Building

MAPLE VALLEY

Maple Valley Historical Museum
23015 SE 216th Way, Maple Valley (425) 433-3470

Household items from the early 20s; a 1926 fire engine — the city's first; school pictures that span the period from 1930 to 1964; and memorabilia from the city's past are exhibited in this c.1920 school building.

NORTH BEND

Snoqualmie Valley Historical Museum
320 North Bend Blvd. South, North Bend (425) 888-3200

Jeremiah Borst converted Fort Alden's blockhouse, abandoned at the conclusion of the Indian war of 1856-57, into a barn when he homesteaded here in the late 1850s. Borst was the valley's pioneer hop farmer. Within a decade after selling his 1,000-acre ranch, an aphid infestation ended hop growing in the state. Artifacts from the hop-growing era, pioneer possessions, early carpentry and logging tools, Native American baskets and relics, historic photos, and a 1910 kitchen and 1912 parlor are exhibited.

Snoqualmie Valley Historical Museum

REDMOND

Marymoor Museum
Marymoor Park, 6046 W. Lake Sammamish Pkwy. NE, Redmond (425) 885-3684

The sprawling, 28-room country home of former Seattle banker, James Clise, now houses a collection of historical artifacts that relate to the Seattle region known as "Eastside." Clise originally planned the home to be a 5-room hunting lodge on an 80-acre parcel that included a waterfowl preserve. He expanded not only the Tudor-style home, but his acreage as well. Clise moved here with his family in 1907 to raise prize-winning Ayshire cattle and Morgan horses. Today, the Marymoor Museum occupies part of the mansion and features an extensive collection of historical photographs that document the life style and development of the Eastside communities of Bellevue, Kirkland and Redmond.

James Clise County Home, Marymoor Museum

Also on the grounds of Marymoor Park is the Dutch windmill Clise constructed following a visit to the Netherlands, and a prehistoric Indian site located on the

banks of the Sammamish River. Artifacts uncovered in archaeology digs at the site are exhibited at the museum. Both the Indian site and Clise's mansion are listed on the National Register of Historic Places.

The Yellowstone Road
196th St. between Fall City Hwy. and 80th NE, Redmond

Before the invention of the automobile, our nation's roadways were little more than Indian trails and wagon roads. At the turn-of-the-century, construction of four transcontinental highways began. This 1.3-mile length of roadway was laid in 1901 as part of Washington State's segment of the national highway system and is listed on the National Register of Historic Places.

RENTON

Renton Historical Society Museum
235 Mill Ave. South, opposite Renton City Hall, Renton (425) 255-2330

It would be twenty years after coal was first discovered here before Renton would become a major coal mining town. Although coal was plentiful, economical transportation didn't exist until the railroad arrived in 1877. The history of this important industrial center, from a coal mining company town to Boeing airplane manufacturer, unfolds in the displays in this museum of local history. Included are: coal mining artifacts, turn-of-the-century coal car and logging equipment, a 1927 Cooper fire engine (the city's first), pioneer clothing and furnishings, and an extensive photographic collection.

Renton Historical Society Museum   *1927 Howard Cooper Fire Engine*

Bust of Chief Seattle

SNOQUALMIE (snoh-KWAHL-mee)

Pacific Northwest Railway Museum
38625 King St., Snoqualmie (425) 746-4025 or (425) 888-0373

One of the most magnificent railroad depots in the state sits in the heart of Snoqualmie's historic district. The 1889 Victorian-style Snoqualmie Depot, built by the Seattle, Lake Shore and Eastern Railroad Company, is listed on the National Register of Historic Places. It has been completely restored by the Puget Sound Railway Historical Association which operates the depot's museum, bookstore and interpretive railway. Their collection of Northwest railway equipment is one of the largest in the country, numbering nearly 100 pieces of rolling stock. A steam-powered rotary snowplow, wreck crane, an Army hospital kitchen car, a 45-ton diesel locomotive, interurban and streetcars are among the interesting pieces that line the track. Railroad artifacts displayed inside the depot museum include: dining car china, old menus, lanterns, signs and memorabilia. Volunteers operate vintage equipment on a regular schedule between Snoqualmie and North Bend. In addition, they conduct training programs for people interested in becoming volunteer brakemen, conductors, firemen and engineers.

1889 Snoqualmie Depot, Pacific Northwest Railway Museum

Rolling Stock exhibited at the Snoqualmie Depot,
Pacific Northwest Railway Museum

Snoqualmie Pass Wagon Road
Near the Denny Creek Campground, Snoqualmie National Forest, 17 miles southeast of North Bend

Still visible at this site is a 1.5-mile section of the first wagon road to cross the Cascade Mountains between Walla Walla and Seattle. The road was charted by Lt. Abiel Tinkham in 1854, and completed in 1868. Early settlers and freight wagons used this section of the road to get across Snoqualmie Pass.

Snoqualmie Falls Generating Station
Snoqualmie Falls, Hwy. 202, one mile northwest of Snoqualmie

The first major hydroelectric project in the state was constructed in 1898, 250 feet below the surface of the Snoqualmie River in a cavity hollowed out of solid rock. Since 1899, its original generating equipment has provided power for the street railway systems in Seattle and Tacoma. The generating station is listed on the National Register of Historic Places and has been designated a Civil Engineering Landmark by the American Society of Civil Engineers.

One of the major scenic attractions in the state is the 268-foot **Snoqualmie Falls** that thunder past this generating station. An observation deck, built 300 feet above the Snoqualmie River affords visitors a panoramic view of the falls, generating station and Salish Lodge (a 1988 remake of the original 1916 roadside inn). A one-mile trail can be hiked to the base of the falls.

Snoqualmie Falls, Generating Station and Salish Lodge

WOODINVILLE

Hollywood Farm
Chateau Ste. Michelle
14111 NE 145th St., southeast of Woodinville (425) 488-1133

Seattle lumberman Frederick Stimson constructed Manor House, an eight-bedroom, Craftsman-style home, in 1912 as the centerpiece of his 125-acre Hollywood Farm. Stimson's farm was an agricultural masterpiece. He raised a preferred stock of Holstein dairy cattle that produced record-breaking quantities of cream and butter. His swine commanded top dollar. And he raised thousands of chickens under tightly regimented conditions. His home and carriage house are preserved on 87 acres of his original estate, which is now home to the award-winning Chateau Ste. Michelle winery. The Olmstead family, the world-famous landscape architects, designed landscaping for the Stimsons. Visitors to the winery are welcome to tour the grounds. Stimson's home and gardens are listed on the National Register of Historic Places.

Hollywood Schoolhouse
14810 NE 145th St, Woodinville (425) 481-7925

When Hollywood School was built in 1912 to replace a smaller wood building that had burned, no one realized that, within 10 years, the school would close for lack of students. In subsequent years the school building served as a community meeting hall, grange, a Japanese language school, and for a number of commercial and retail businesses. In 1975, Hollywood School was added to the Washington Heritage Register. Today, the restored building is furnished with antiques and is used as an event facility.

Woodinville Elementary School
Woodinville City Hall, 13209 NE 175th St., Woodinville (425) 489-2700

After the all-wood school building burned in 1912 it was replaced by a brick structure similar to the Hollywood Schoolhouse. The building was remodeled by the Works Progress Administration in 1935 and today serves at the city hall. The Woodinville Historical Society exhibits some of their collection of local artifacts and historic photographs in the main entry hall.

Woodinville Memorial Park
Corner of NE 175 St. and 132nd Ave. NE, downtown Woodinville

Ira and Susan Woodin, who settled here in 1871 and established the town, deeded an acre of land for use as a community cemetery. One corner of this pioneer cemetery, known as Potter's field, is where paupers and unknown persons were buried. Johann Kock, the town blacksmith, has the most recognized burial plot in the cemetery. His anvil was used as his headstone.

SEATTLE

Alki Homestead (site)
2717 61st Ave. S.W., Seattle (206) 935-5678

Twenty-four pioneers from Illinois landed at Alki Point in the Fall of 1851, with dreams of establishing a major city in the three-year-old Oregon Territory. Two members of the party, David Denny and John Low, had scouted this area some two months earlier and selected this point for their settlement. The settlers called it "New York,Alki." (Alki meant By-and-By in the Chinook language.) The region's plentiful timber, and a San Francisco "Gold Rush" market hungry for lumber, provided a strong economic base for the new community. When they found that the waters of nearby Elliott Bay offered a deeper port, they moved their families to what is now Pioneer Square and renamed their village "Seattle" to honor the great Suquamish Indian Chief, Sealth, who befriended them during their first winter. A monument commemorating the founding of Seattle at this site was erected at Alki Ave. and 63rd Ave. S.W.

Alki Point Light Station
3201 Alki Ave., Seattle (206) 932-5800

Years before an "Official" light was installed here, Hans Hanson, out of concern for his fellow man, established the point's first beacon: an oil lantern mounted on a 10-foot pole. Hanson, his brother-in-law Knud Olson, and their families took turns trimming the lamp until the U.S. Lighthouse District established a light station in 1887. The present Coast Guard light station, a picturesque white masonry building with a 37-foot octagonal tower, was built in 1918.

Fort Lawton
West Point Lighthouse
Daybreak Star Indian Cultural Center
Discovery Park, W. Government Way and 36th Ave. Lighthouse (206) 282-9130
Visitor Center (206) 625-4636 — Daybreak Center (206) 285-4425

Only a few buildings remain today from the 640-acre U.S. Army post that was established at this site in 1897. For its first five years, Fort Lawton served as one of the state's coast artillery posts. In the years that followed, the fort was used by the infantry, engineers and transportation corps. It played a major role as an embarkation and debarkation center during World War II and as a support center for Puget Sound Air Defense activities. Discovery Park now covers most of what used to be Fort Lawton.

A road to the beach below old Fort Lawton takes visitors to the old West Point Lighthouse. At first the 1881 station was a simple wooden structure illuminated by lamps that burned fish and whale oil. It was upgraded in 1901 and, in 1985, became one of the last lighthouses to become fully automated. The register that, for 104 years, recorded the names of guests from around the world who visited this station, was officially retired in 1985 when the light was automated.

The works of contemporary Native American artists are displayed at the park's Daybreak Star Indian Cultural Center.

Northwest Seaport Maritime Heritage Center
1002 Valley St., Seattle (206) 447-9800

Four historic vessels that once plied the waters of the Pacific Northwest are anchored just minutes from downtown Seattle at this Maritime Heritage Center on Lake Union's southern shore. All four are listed on the National Register of Historic Places. They have been completely restored and are open to the public for tours.

S.S. San Mateo - This steel-hulled ferry was constructed in 1922 and, for the next 47 years, she transported cars and passengers across Puget Sound. At the time of her retirement in 1969, the *San Mateo* was the last operating steam-powered auto ferry in the nation.

Wawona - The largest schooner built in North America was launched at Fairhaven, Calif., in 1897. Initially her cargo hold was filled with lumber from the Pacific Northwest for destinations as far south as California. In 1914, the *Wawona* sailed to the Bering Sea where her cargo changed to Alaskan cod. During the World War II years, this beautiful sailing ship was pressed into service to her country as a military barge. The restored, three-masted, 165-foot schooner is the last surviving commercial sailing ship in the Pacific Northwest and the first ship honored with a listing on the National Register of Historic Places.

Relief - In 1904, this 129-foot lightship began a tour of duty that would span 56 uninterrupted years of service along the Pacific Coast. For most of those years, she sailed from station-to-station where she would serve as a floating lighthouse; her oil lamps and 1000-pound bell signaling warnings to mariners. During World War II, the *Relief's* role changed when the Navy installed guns on her decks and she began patrolling marine traffic in harbor areas. The *Relief* is one of the oldest lightships in the country, and the only one equipped with her original steam engine. In addition to her 1975 listing on the National Register of Historic Places, the *Relief* was declared a National Landmark in 1989.

Arthur Foss - When this steam-powered tugboat was put into service in 1889, she steamed to the mouth of the Columbia River and began a history-filled career that would gain her recognition as a National Historical Landmark. In her 80 years at sea, this mighty tug would pull ships across the infamous Columbia River bar; tow barges between Seattle and Skagway, Alaska during Alaska Gold Rush; become *Narcissus* in MGM's 1933 movie, *Tugboat Annie*; and escape capture in the South Pacific during World War II. The *Arthur Foss* came out of retirement in 1984 and sailed to Alaska to represent Washington State's Governor at Alaska's 25th anniversary of statehood. She was designated Washington State's Centennial Flagship in 1986 and represented the state at EXPO '86 in Vancouver, B.C.

Center for Wooden Boats
1010 Valley St., Seattle (206) 382-2628

Wooden shipbuilding skills of the past haven't been lost in today's modern world, at least not here at the Center for Wooden Boats. Inside this replica of a Victorian-era boat building shop, shipwrights build classic small craft (up to 30 feet in length) that visitors can rent for an outing on Lake Union. Small craft models, photographs, and videos show the history of these boats and the expertise it took to build them. Talented staff members conduct workshops on the fine art of steam-bending a boat's rib, casting an oarlock and other skills needed to recreate these authentic replica craft.

Ye Olde Curiosity Shop and Museum
Pier 54 on the Seattle Waterfront, 1001 Alaskan Way, Seattle (206) 682-5844

Curios and oddities from all parts of the world fill the store and museum established by Joe Standley in 1899. His friendship with Alaskan explorers, sea captains, prospectors and Indians, enabled him to acquire a fine collection of Northwest and Alaskan relics that he showcased in his museum which he originally named, "Standley's Free Museum." In 1900, Standley changed the name to "Ye Olde Curiosity Shop." Today, the family-owned business is said to house the world's largest collection of curios.

Museum of Flight
9494 E. Marginal Way South, Seattle (206) 764-5720

William Boeing's "Red Barn," where the Boeing Aircraft Company was founded in 1916, is now part of the largest air museum on the West Coast. The restored building, where Boeing manufactured Band W and Navy training planes during World War I, contains a number of interesting exhibits and priceless photographs from the dawn of aviation. The "Red Barn," which is listed on the National Register of Historic Places, together with the 11-story, steel and glass Great Gallery, displays an impressive assemblage of vintage and modern, civilian and military aircraft. The history of aviation is traced through exhibits of more than fifty aircraft from a replica of an early Wright Brothers glider, to the first Air Force F-5 supersonic fighter, to an Apollo spacecraft. The first United Airlines mail plane; a 1929 18-passenger tri-motor; a Douglas DC-3; a World War II-era B-47 bomber; and a Navy Blue Angels jet are among the other aircraft displayed here.

Birthplace of the Boeing Airplane Co.

The Underground Tour
Doc Maynard's Public House, Pioneer Square, 610 First Ave, Seattle
Information (206) 682-1511 Reservations (206) 682-4646

On June 6, 1889, the wooden-frame buildings that comprised the 25-block downtown Seattle area burned to the ground in an all-consuming conflagration. As the city was being rebuilt with brick and stone, city fathers decided to raise the downtown streets one story higher and solve the old problem of street flooding and backed-up sewers caused by the incoming tide. The plan worked. The streets no longer flooded, but all the new ground floor storefronts, laundries, and movie theatres now faced underground sidewalks and eventually had to be abandoned. When the city later sealed off the subterranean area, "Underground Seattle" was created. Today, visitors can take a humorous, 90-minute historical tour of the underground city that originates in Pioneer Square at Doc Maynard's Public House, a restored 1890-era saloon. (Reservations recommended. Dress for the weather. Wear comfortable shoes. And you may want to bring a flashlight.)

Pioneer Square Historic District
Roughly bounded by the waterfront, King, 4th and Cherry Sts., Seattle
Guide available from the Visitor Center at 117 S. Main St.

This is where it all happened; where the city's pioneers put down their roots in 1852 and started building the "Queen City of the Pacific Northwest." Seattlites have long cared for their birthplace. They constructed 50 new Romanesque Revival-style buildings when this entire district was destroyed by fire in 1889. And saved them from demolition in the 1960s, by undertaking a major restoration and rehabilitation project. What stands here today in this 25-block historic district are vivid reminders of the city's pioneer, Victorian, turn-of-the-century and early twentieth century periods.

Pioneer Place Park
Yesler and 1st Sts., Seattle

The site of Seattle's first permanent settlement is memorialized in this city park that includes: a 50-foot Alaskan Indian red cedar totem pole carved in 1939 to replace the 140-year-old pole that was destroyed by fire; a turn-of-the-century drinking fountain for men, women, horses and dogs topped with a bust of Chief Seattle; a replica of a gas street light that illuminated this area during the Gold Rush days; and the elaborate glass and cast-iron pergola erected in 1909 at what was then the city's transportation hub.

Klondike Gold Rush National Historic Park
117 S. Main, Seattle (206) 442-7220

On July 17, 1897, the coastal steamer *Portland* arrived in Seattle with sixty-eight wealthy prospectors and two tons of gold from the Klondike gold fields of Alaska. The Klondike Gold Rush was on! And Seattle became a major outfitter to the thousands of prospectors who stopped here to buy their required year's supply of food, clothing and tools before heading north. Historic photographs, tools and gold mining artifacts depicting the city's role as the West Coast's primary Yukon staging area are displayed in the Klondike Museum.

Smith Tower
506 2nd Ave., Seattle (206) 682-9393 (Smith Tower Museum (206) 324-1125)

When this 42-story building was constructed in 1914 for typewriter magnate, Lyman Smith, it was one of the tallest structures in the world. Only New York City's skyscrapers were taller. It remained Seattle's grandest structure until 1962 when the Space Needle was erected for the Seattle World's Fair. An observation deck and reproduction of a Chinese Temple on the building's 35th floor are generally open to the public.

U.S. Coast Guard Museum
Pier 36, 1519 Alaskan Way South, Seattle (206) 442-5019

Rare and unusual maritime artifacts and thousands of historic photographs dating to the early 1800s are exhibited at this museum of Coast Guard history. Lighthouse and buoy lenses, models of Coast Guard cutters, old and new uniforms, relics from captured German submarines and ships, and pieces of wood from two famous vessels: the USS *Constitution* (Old Ironsides); and the HMS *Bounty*, are included in this museum's collection. Four Coast Guard ships: two, 400-foot icebreakers and two, high-endurance cutters are homeported at this pier and are usually open to visitors on weekends.

Museum of History and Industry
McCurdy Park, 2700 24th Ave. "E" (206) 324-1126

One of this museum's featured exhibits makes it possible for guests to travel back in time, walk a downtown street of 1880s Seattle, look into 3/4-scale storefronts, and see what part of the city was like before the Great Seattle Fire of 1889 destroyed more than 60 blocks of the city's commercial district. Another gallery features maritime artifacts of the Pacific Northwest, ships models and figureheads. Displays of nineteenth and twentieth century costumes are shown in the fashion gallery. Many relics and priceless memorabilia from the city and county's early years are exhibited including an old mail plane from the Boeing Aircraft Company.

Pike Place Public Market Historic District
1431 1st Ave., Seattle (206) 682-7453

Farmers have brought their produce to sell direct to the public at this open market since 1907, making this the oldest continuously operating farmers market in the United States. In the early years, everything was sold off the back of trucks. Now, permanent buildings and stalls cover this seven-acre national historic site where fishermen, butchers, antique dealers, restaurateurs, florists, and merchants share space with the families of truck farmers who started it all.

Hiram M. Chittenden Locks
Ballard Locks, 3015 N.W. 54th, Seattle (206) 783-7001

More than 100,000 marine vessels use these locks annually to pass between the salt water of Puget Sound and the inland fresh waters of Lake Union and Lake Washington. Hiram Chittenden, a major in the U.S. Corps of Engineers, supervised the design and construction of the locks between 1911 and 1916; during the time the Panama Canal was being completed. The only locks on this continent that exceed the capacity of these locks are in the Panama Canal. A small museum at the Visitor Center tells the history of this project and illustrates how commercial ships and pleasure boats are raised and lowered as they pass through the canal between the two bodies of water. An underground viewing room at the Center shows salmon and trout fighting their way up a 21-level fish ladder to get to fresh water to spawn. Nearby is the 7-acre Carl English Ornamental Gardens.

Seattle Waterfront Historical Photography Exhibit
Ivar's Acres of Clams, Pier 54, Seattle (206) 624-6852

This famous Seattle eatery boasts a collection of more than 500 historic photographs, maps and mementos that document the ships, events and people that comprise this city's past. An artist's drawing of 1889 Seattle, from its busy waterfront to the commercial district and Cascade foothills, is one of the interesting pieces on display. It shows the buildings in the 66-block area that were completely destroyed by fire shortly after the artist completed this work.

Other points of interest can be found along the city's waterfront. The **Coleman Dock**, at Pier 52, was once home port to Puget Sound's **Mosquito Fleet**. One of the last surviving vessels from the Mosquito Fleet, the *Virginia V*, is anchored at Pier 55. A marker at Pier 58 commemorates the arrival of the *Portland* on July 17, 1897, with a "ton of gold" from the Klondike, the event that began the Alaska Gold Rush.

Nordic Heritage Museum
3014 N.W. 67th St., Seattle (206) 789-5708

"The Dream of America" exhibit in this unique museum portrays the quest for a better life and the promise of a new land, a vision shared by the thousands of

Scandinavian immigrants who journeyed to this country between 1840 and 1920. The hardships they endured, the traditions they brought with them, and their contribution to the communities where they lived are vividly displayed with life-size exhibits in the museum's galleries. The former 1907 red brick schoolhouse, where children from the Nordic nations of Denmark, Finland, Iceland, Norway and Sweden were educated, is now the largest ethnic museum in the Pacific Northwest.

"Waiting to Leave for America" exhibit at the Nordic Heritage Museum,
Courtesy of Nordic Heritage Museum

272

Lake View Cemetery
North end of Volunteer Park, 1400 E. Prospect St., Seattle

After the city's first park and cemetery, Denny Park, was regraded in 1928, the remains of settlers interned in the pioneer cemetery were re-buried here. Among the early graves are some of the city's first residents: The Denny family, the city's first settlers; David "Doc" Maynard, a city founder and its first physician; Henry Yesler, whose sawmill was the city's first major commercial enterprise; and the Indian princess, Angeline, daughter of Chief Seattle. Lake View is also the final resting place for martial arts film star, Bruce Lee, who died mysteriously in 1973, and his son Brandon, who was killed on a movie set in 1993.

Pacific Science Center
200 Second Ave. North   (206) 443-2001

One day after the 1962 World's Fair closed in Seattle, the Pacific Science Center opened in the five buildings that were originally constructed as the Fair's U.S. Science Pavilion. It was the first museum in the nation founded as a science and

technology center and today features more than two hundred interactive science exhibits where visitors of all ages can experience hands-on adventures in science. The Center, which stands in the shadow of the Space Needle, also includes an IMAX Theater, laser light show and planetarium.

Pacific Science Center's High Rail Bike,Photo by Dick Milligan, The Olympian

273

Seattle Children's Museum
Seattle Center House, 305 Harrison St., Seattle (206) 441-1768

Hands-on experiences designed for youngsters from preschool through sixth grade are packed into this fun-packed children's museum. A child-sized town, with bank, grocery store, fast food restaurant, doctor's office and bank is one of the museum's most popular attractions. Others include Mountain Forest, Cog City, Global Village and Discovery Bay. Workshops and other creative activities spark the imagination of the museum's young visitors.

Seattle Aquarium
Pier 59, 1483 Alaskan Way, Seattle (206) 386-4300

A glass-enclosed underwater dome, with a 360-degree view of nearly four hundred species of Puget Sound's marine life, is one of the major attractions of this award-winning aquarium. A tropical Pacific coral exhibit, tidepool, outdoor tanks and freshwater pond add to the aquarium's variety of aquatic displays. Of special interest is the fully-operational salmon hatchery and working fish ladder.

Nippon Kan Theater
622 S. Washington, Seattle (206) 624-8800

Since 1909, all the sights, sounds and traditions of the Japanese culture have been relived through performances on the stage of this community theater. Through the music, dance, drama and ethnic events presented here, the rich heritage of the Japanese who live here has been preserved and fortified. The theater was designated a National Historic Site in May, 1978.

Wing Luke Asian Museum
407 Seventh Ave. "S"., Seattle (206) 623-5124

Seattle's Asian community was established just up the hill from Pioneer Square in 1860, within a decade of the city's founding. Today it's known as the Chinatown International District and is comprised of citizens and immigrants of Chinese, Japanese, Filipino, Southeast Asian, Korean and Pacific Islander descent. This museum, which was named in honor of Wing Luke, a Chinese Seattle councilman who died in an airplane crash, chronicles this community's history from the 1860s to the present. Asian folk art, a 50-foot dragon boat, photographs and documents pertaining to Pacific Northwest Asian-Americans, Yao Taoist ritual scrolls, Chinese court robes, and calligraphy are among the featured exhibits.

Seattle Goodwill's Memory Lane Museum
1400 S. Lane St., Seattle (206) 329-1000

Realistic depictions of Seattle life styles between 1860 and 1960 can be seen in collections of this local history museum. Miss Bardahl, the renowned world champion hydroplane that won three gold cups before she was retired in 1965, is one of the major exhibits. An old time garage and gas station, household items including Fiesta dinnerware, china and glassware, and an extensive collection of vintage clothing are also featured. Goodwill's traveling vintage fashion shows are presented to community groups and encompass periods from the turn-of-the-century to the 1950s.

Space Needle
Seattle Center (206) 443-2100 or (206) 443-2111

It was the tallest building west of the Mississippi when it was built for the Seattle World's Fair in 1962. Since then, the Space Needle has been eclipsed in height, but not in distinction. It has become the symbol of the City of Seattle and is one of America's most recognized landmarks. In addition to being the tallest building, the Space Needle also set other records during its construction. It took 467 cement trucks an entire day to fill the foundation hole; the largest continuous concrete pour ever attempted in the West. And the motor for the revolving restaurant has the

highest gear ratio in the world: 360,000 to 1. An interpretive "Compass Northwest" display on the observation deck describes places of interest in and around the Emerald City that can be seen from this vantage point. Celebrities who have visited the Space Needle include George Burns, Carol Channing, Michael Douglas, President Richard Nixon, Elvis Presley and John Wayne.

Camp Fire Boys and Girls Museum
8511 15th NE, Seattle (206) 461-8550

Two rooms at the Camp Fire Boys and Girls Administration Building have been set aside as a museum and archives to showcase the Camp Fire's 85-year history as a youth organization in the Central Puget Sound area. Uniforms, awards, photographs, scrapbooks, local crafts, and memorabilia that exemplifies their motto, "The First Fire We Light is the Fire Within," are exhibited. All items in the collection were donated by Camp Fire Alumni and their families. The museum is open normal business hours by appointment.

Tillicum Village
Blake Island Marine State Park, tour departs from Pier 56, Seattle (206) 329-5700 or (206) 443-1244

A cruise to this recreated Indian village on Blake Island affords travelers the chance to experience some of the culture of ancient Indians who lived on this island for centuries before the arrival of white explorers. Tillicum Village, built in 1962 near the site of the ancestral fishing camp of the Suquamish Indians, features a large cedar longhouse where guests are treated to a traditional salmon bake. As dinner from the alderwood fires is served, several Northwest Coast Indian dances are presented by costumed performers.

The Burke Museum
University of Washington, Visitor Information Center, 4014 University Way NE, Seattle (206) 543-5590 or (206) 616-2036

In 1861, ten years after Seattle's first settlers landed at Alki Point, a Territorial University was dedicated. The university started in a single white building that stood on a ten-acre plot (site is marked at Seneca Street between 4th and 5th Avenues). It moved to its new campus in 1895 and now consists of 128 buildings on nearly seven hundred acres. The Burke Memorial Washington State Museum is the oldest university museum in the West and houses one of the finest collections of anthropology, geology and zoology in the United States. Northwest Coast Indian art and artifacts, cultures of Pacific Rim countries, gems, minerals, and a permanent display of Northwest dinosaurs are featured exhibits.

The Vintage Telephone Equipment Museum
U.S. West Building, 7000 E. Marginal Way South, Seattle   (206) 767-3012 or (206) 789-4761

On May 8, 1923, telephone "dial" service was made available to Seattle residents for the first time. One of the three Panel Central Offices that made that historic event possible has been completely restored and is a featured exhibit in this 11,000-square-foot telephone museum. Other operational telecommunications equipment on display include: telegraph (key and sounder/morse code), teletype, toll transmission, central office switching, switchboards, and magneto (crank) telephones. Telephone memorabilia and a number of historic photographs are also displayed. The museum, which occupies two floors of this building, is open on a limited schedule, but may also be toured by appointment.

Northwest Puppet Center
9123 15th Ave. N.E., Seattle   (206) 523-2579

Who could imagine that, behind the doors of this restored, one-time church, in this quiet residential neighborhood, lurk dragons, and knights, lions and princesses, and a bevy of folk tale characters from around the world.   They're all here, sharing space in this unique setting, awaiting their turn on stage at the Pacific Northwest's only permanent puppet theater and museum of international puppet exhibits.

Professional puppeteers also produce regularly scheduled shows where antique and contemporary rod and hand puppets from around the world, and hand-carved, 3-foot-tall marionettes entertain audiences of all ages.

Stephen and Chris Carter Performing Carter Family Marionettes, Photo by Mark Aalfs, Nothwest Puppet Center

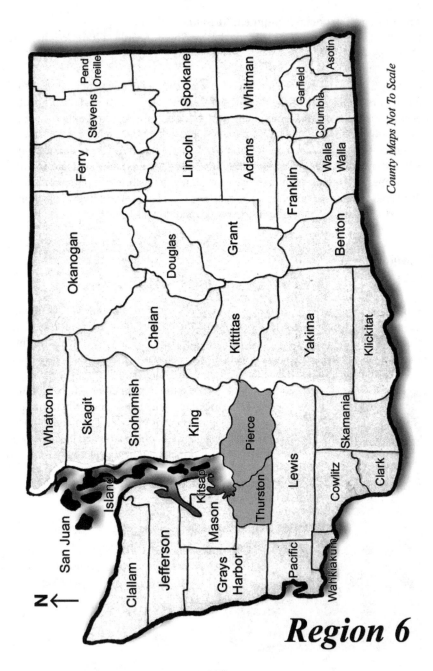

County Maps Not To Scale

N ←

Region 6

Pierce County

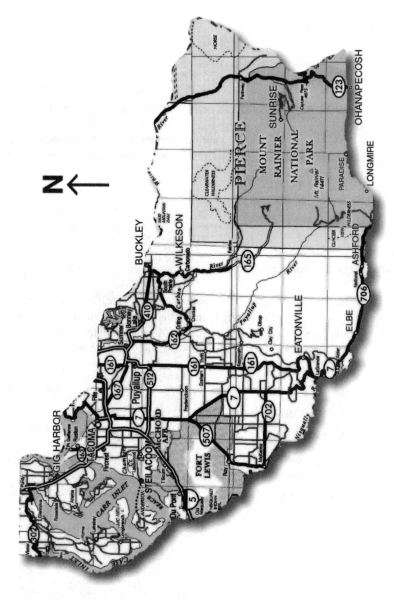

REGION 6

PIERCE COUNTY

ANDERSON ISLAND

Anderson Island Historical Society Museum
9306 Otso Point Rd., Anderson Island (253) 884-2135

Access to the 1912 Johnson Farm, the home of the Anderson Island Historical Society Museum, requires a short ferry ride across Puget Sound from the port at Steilacoom. The Johnson's home and a number of outbuildings house educational exhibits, antique farm machinery, early twentieth century household furnishings and a collection of children's toys and dolls.

ASHFORD

Ashford Mansion Bed & Breakfast
Mt. Tahoma Canyon Rd., Ashford

British immigrant, Walter Ashford and his American-born wife, Cora, homesteaded in the Nisqually Valley in 1888. They founded the town of Ashford in 1891 and established a store, post office and dance hall. In 1903 they built the home that now serves as a bed and breakfast inn. Ashford's mansion is listed on the National Register of Historic Places.

Alexander's Country Inn
37515 Hwy. 706E, Ashford (253) 569-2300 or (800) 654-7615

Tiffany lamps, handmade quilts, stained glass windows, and old family photographs add to the atmosphere of this 1912, Victorian-style country inn. The completely restored inn is operated today as a bed and breakfast. Its first-floor restaurant is open to the general public.

BUCKLEY

Foothills Historical Society Museum
River St., 1/2-block north of Main, Buckley (360) 829-1533

Development of the community's economic base, from early timber related industries to premiere fruit orchards, is represented in the collections of the city's historical society's museum. A comprehensive assemblage of relics from the community's past is displayed.

DUPONT

DuPont Historical Museum and Cultural Center
207 Barksdale Ave., DuPont   For information call City Hall at (253) 964-8121

DuPont has two distinctively separate historical periods: the Fort Nisqually age, and the era of the DuPont Power Works.

The Hudson's Bay Company established Fort Nisqually as a trading post at two sites in the present city of DuPont. The first fort was built in 1833. It was moved one-half mile from its original location in 1843. Fort Nisqually was the setting for a number of "firsts" in Washington's Puget Sound history: It was the first white settlement; the first white couple were married and first white child was born here; first commercial enterprise; and the first cattle, sheep and chickens were raised here. The first American home built north of the Columbia River was also erected here. Two surviving buildings from the original fort: the factor's house and a log granary, the oldest buildings on Puget Sound, were relocated to Tacoma's Point Defiance Park in 1934.

Old Fort Nisqually Marker

An important exhibit of this museum features the *Beaver*, the ship that worked Puget Sound from Fort Nisqually. It was the first steam-powered vessel to navigate the Pacific and the first on Puget Sound. A section of the *Beaver* was placed inside the Canadian side of the International Peace Arch when the Arch was constructed at Blaine in 1921-22. The opposite arch, on the American side, contains a section of the *Mayflower*, the ship that brought pilgrims to the New World in 1620.

In 1906, E.I. duPont de Nemours Company purchased the present city of DuPont, along with adjacent land, and began construction of an explosives plant. During the next 70 years, millions of pounds of black powder and nitroglycerine were manufactured here. Most of the homes that line DuPont's streets today were built in 1909 as housing for the plant's employees and their families. To make the "village" complete, a church, schools, stores and shops were erected. The entire city of DuPont is listed on the National Register of Historic Places.

The town's former butcher shop and city hall building is now home to the historical museum and cultural center. Among the museum's interesting exhibits is a collection of DuPont Company artifacts including wooden sparkproof shovels and a machine that packed powder into dynamite sticks.

DuPont's Former Butcher Shop and City Hall

EATONVILLE

Eatonville Historic Walking Tour
Visitor Information Center, 220 Center St. East, Eatonville (360) 832-4000

Just off the highway to Mt. Rainier lies the town of Eatonville, founded by T.C. Van Eaton in 1889. Van Eaton established the region's first trading post along an ancient Indian trail and conducted most of his business with local Indians. In 1904 when the railroad laid tracks to the town, commercial lumber business began. A guide to historic places in this once-rich timber region is available from the Visitor Information Center.

Pioneer Farm Museum and Ohop Indian Village
7716 Ohop Valley Rd., Eatonville (360) 832-6300

Two original pioneer log cabins are the hub of this 1880s farm museum. The hand-hewn cedar cabin that now serves as the museum office, tour center and gift shop, was originally built in 1887 by Robert Sampson McCimans. The second log cabin was erected by Orsamus Stubbs in 1888 for his wife, Mary and their three children. The Sidham family of five moved into the cabin after the Stubbs left. Photographs of the Stubbs and Sidham families, original family antiques, furnishings, housewares and memorabilia are exhibited in the restored Stubbs-Sidham cabin. Other buildings house antique implements and machinery that's still used by visitors to this hands-on museum to churn butter, card wool, grind grain and perform other daily farm chores. A variety of pioneer farm tours are offered, including overnight stays. A Native American "seasons tour" and Indian heritage tour provide a hands-on

opportunity to experience what life was like for Native Americans who lived in this region in the 1800s. Original and replica Indian artifacts are exhibited in the Ohop Indian Village.

Four miles north, at **Northwest Trek**, visitors can take a one-hour, five-mile guided tram tour through a 600-acre wildlife preserve where caribou, elk, moose and other native Northwest animals can be observed in a natural setting. An interpretive center is also on the grounds. Call (360) 832-6116 for schedule and fees.

ELBE (EL-bee)

Mt. Rainier Scenic Railroad
Hwy. 7, Elbe (253) 569-2588, or (888) STEAM II

A breath-taking view awaits guests who travel on this scenic railroad to the foothills of Mt. Rainier. Powered by a vintage steam locomotive, the fully-restored, 1920s passenger train with tourist and open cars makes an hour-and-a-half excursion from Elbe to Mineral Lake on the mountain's south slope. A short stop at the lake gives visitors time to view the antique logging equipment that's displayed there. A number of old locomotives are on exhibit at the Elbe station where an old mail car serves as train station and ticket office.

FORT LEWIS

Fort Lewis Military Museum
Building Number 4320, Fort Lewis (253) 967-7206

Nearly 200 years of U.S. Army history in the Pacific Northwest is preserved and exhibited in this imposing museum building. Three main galleries focus on distinctive historical periods: Soldiers of the Northwest Gallery, 1804-1917; America's Corps Gallery, 1918 to present; and The Fort Lewis Galley, 1917 to present. Uniforms, weapons, equipment and a collection of Fort Lewis memorabilia is displayed inside the 10,000 square-foot museum. A large outdoor display includes: tanks, armored cars, missiles and other large pieces of military equipment.

The museum building was constructed in 1918 by the Salvation Army to provide services to soldiers at Fort Lewis and accommodations for their wives, mothers, relatives and friends who were visiting. At that time, the 150-room building was known at the Red Shield Inn. Ownership of the building was transferred to the U.S. Army in 1921 and it remained in service as an inn until 1972. The old inn is listed on the National Register of Historic Places.

Fort Lewis was established through the generosity of the citizens of Tacoma and Pierce County. They passed a bond issue that was used to purchase the land, which they, in turn, donated to the Federal Government for the building of Camp Lewis. It was the first military installation in the nation's history to be established on land donated by private citizens.

Fort Lewis Military Museum, Courtesy of Fort Lewis Museum

Fourth of July Celebration Site
Near Sequalitchew Lake, North Fort Lewis

In 1841, the first public observance of the July Fourth holiday held west of the Mississippi took place at this site. Lt. Commander Charles Wilkes, who was surveying and charting the lower Puget Sound, used this occasion to let the British at Fort Nisqually feel the presence of American forces in the region. As part of their daylong celebration, two brass howitzers were brought on shore and fired to signal a 26-gun salute; one round for each state then in the Union. A monument was erected at this site in 1906 to commemorate the 65th anniversary of this historic event.

FOX ISLAND

Fox Island Historical Museum
1017 Ninth Ave., Fox Island (253) 549-2239

The story of Fox Island's inhabitants, from the Indians who were forced to live here on a temporary reservation in the mid-1850s, to the settlers who developed maritime and agriculture opportunities, is preserved in this museum of local history. From a small collection of family artifacts, photographs and letters, the museum has grown to be one of the finest in the region. An early 1900s kitchen, Victorian parlor and children's bedroom, a farm shop, an early post office and a rare collection of farm machinery are among the featured exhibits. Military equipment from the Civil War to World War II, heirloom collections and mementos from the state's first female Governor, Dixy Lee Ray can also be seen.

On the grounds of the museum is the 1908 **Acheson Family cabin**. It was the summer home of Rev. Acheson, a Presbyterian minister. His daughter Lisa, who also used the cabin, married DeWitt Wallace and together they created and published the world-famous Reader's Digest Magazine.

Acheson Family Cabin on the Grounds of Fox Valley Historical Museum

Fox Island School
Nichols Community Center, 690 9th Ave., Fox Island (253) 549-2434

Fox Island School, the fourth school in the history of the island was constructed as a WPA project in 1934 on the condition that it would always be available for community use. In 1960, when the district began bussing students to Gig Harbor, the school building was converted into a community center. It was later renamed in honor of Col. Frederic H. Nichols, founder of the Fox Island Water Company, Editor of the island's weekly newspaper, the *Grapevine*, and an activist in the Grange and all other community organizations. The building is listed on the National Register of Historic Places.

Fox Island Church
United Church of Christ, 400 6th Ave., Sylvan (Fox Island) (253) 549-2420

A. J. Miller, the first settler in the Fox Island community of Sylvan, began teaching Bible classes in 1889. A year later, construction of the island's first church was completed. Although its had different names, from the First Congregational Church of Sylvan to the present United Church of Christ, its offered continuous services since it doors first opened.

Fox Island Church

Fox Island Ferry Dock
Fox Dr. and 9th Ave., Fox Island

Construction of the Fox Island Bridge in 1954 connected Fox Island to the peninsula and ended the ferry service that began in 1914. Remains of the old ferry landing can still be seen at this intersection.

GIG HARBOR

Old St. Nicholas Church
Peninsula Historical Society Museum
3510 Rosedale St., Gig Harbor (253) 858-6722

St. Nicholas Church

One of the oldest active fishing fleets on Puget Sound can be found at Gig Harbor, the sheltered bay discovered by the 1841 Wilkes Expedition. The fleet's roots can be traced to Samuel Jerisich, a Yugoslavian fisherman who settled here in 1867. Exhibits that focus on the history of the local fishing and logging industry can be seen at the historical society museum located in the lower level of the Old St. Nicholas Church. Among the other items of interest in the museum's collection are antique musical instruments and building tools. Old photographs and slides preserve a broad visual history of the community.

St. Nicholas Church was constructed in 1913, with the first Mass offered on Easter Sunday, 1914. The sanctuary of the restored church is used today for various community events and historical society activities.

The Parsonage
4107 Burnham Dr., Gig Harbor (253) 851-8654

Volunteers built this house in 1892 to provide a home for the Parson of the First Methodist Episcopal Church. The church, which was originally located about 50 feet from the parsonage, was relocated to its present site on Harborview Drive in the early 1900s. In 1985, with a minimum of remodeling, the present owners converted the Parsonage into a bed & breakfast. It was the first bed & breakfast located within the city limits of Gig Harbor, but no longer takes guests.

First Methodist Episcopal Church
9324 N. Harborview Dr., Gig Harbor

William Peacock, who settled here with his wife and children in 1890, built the original one-room church building at a site near the Parsonage on Burnham Drive. Before that first church was built, the congregation attended services on board a steamer anchored in the bay. In 1916, the church was dismantled and moved board-by-board to its present location. Today, the building, which has been extensively remodeled and expanded, is used as an assisted living facility.

William Peacock Home
Peacock Hill Restaurant, 9916 Peacock Hill Ave. NW, Gig Harbor (253) 851-3134

Antiques are featured throughout the former home of William Peacock, one of Gig Harbor's early settlers. Peacock and his wife Anna arrived here from Maine with their children in 1890. They began construction of this three-story home in 1898 and lived here until 1929. From that time to the present, Peacock's one-time home has been primarily used as a restaurant.

Gig Harbor Peninsula Historic Homes

A number of turn-of-the-century homes and businesses can be seen in the Gig Harbor vicinity:

Arletta School, 36th St. and Ray Nash Dr., Arletta. The first school district on the Peninsula was established in Arletta in 1886. This building, the third schoolhouse erected in the district, was built as a WPA project in 1938 using local granite and timber. Today, its used as a community building.

Artondale features two historic sites: the **Wollochet-Point Fosdick School**, which is listed on the National Register of Historic Places and the **Wollochet Bay Store**. The school building has been converted into a private residence, 1804 34th Ave. NW. The original store building, one of the first on the Peninsula, was located near the site of the bay's former steamer stop. At the site today is a building erected after the original store burned in the 1970s.

Scott House, North Harborview Dr. & Peacock Hill, Gig Harbor. Western America-style 1895 frame home with original leaded windows. Scott operated a livery service and was one of the first in Gig Harbor to own an automobile.

The Harbor Heights community boasts several historic spots. **Jerisich Park**, named for the first family to settle in Gig Harbor, features a monument commemorating the gig that sailed into Gig Harbor from the Wilkes' expedition in 1841. Next to the park, on Harborview Drive, is the **Skansie Home**, constructed in 1908 using 16,000 bricks. Remains of the **Skansie Shipbuilding Company** can be seen on the property next to their home. The 1908 **Hunt Mansion** at the foot of Soundview Dr., now houses the **American Gallery of Quilt and Textile Art**. Reed Hunt, who grew-up in this mansion, was the former chief executive of Crown Zellerbach.

Skansie Home

Glen Cove Hotel, 9418 Glencove Rd., Key Center. The original home was built in 1897 on 32 acres for H. Nicholas and Anges Paterson who operated it as a pioneer inn; providing home-cooked meals and accommodations for their guests. Many of the exquisite features of the home have been preserved and can be seen in the present-day hotel. Glen Cove Hotel is listed on the National Register of Historic Places.

The Midway School, at 38th St. NW and Murphy Dr., opened in 1893 as a one-room schoolhouse. In 1915, the former Madrona Grange Hall was moved to the school site for use as a recreational hall and for after-school programs. The school, which closed in 1941, is listed on the National Register of Historic Places.

LAKEWOOD CENTER

Fort Steilacoom Museum
Western State Hospital, 9601 Steilacoom Blvd. SW, Lakewood Center
(253) 756-3928

The killing of an American pioneer in 1849 brought the U.S. Army to this region of Puget Sound to protect the growing number of Americans who were settling here. A number of log buildings were the first to be constructed, but traditional fort walls and gates were never built at the site. In 1857, new buildings were erected including the four constructed along officers' row that remain today. When the post was vacated in 1868, the property was deeded to the Washington Territory government for use as the Western State Hospital for the Insane.

The four restored 1857 officers' quarters on the hospital grounds have been preserved and are open for tours with a docent. One is furnished as a married officer's quarters; another is a bachelor officer's quarters; one is an interpretive center; and the other is used for community meetings and events. The site of Fort Steilacoom and remaining buildings are listed on the National Register of Historic Places.

LONGMIRE (See Mt. Rainier National Park)

MCCHORD AIR FORCE BASE

McChord Air Museum
100 Main St., McChord Air Force Base (253) 984-2485 Visitors need to show drivers license, proof of insurance, current registration or rental car agreement at the visitors center to enter the base.

The story of McChord AFB, from its construction in 1938 to the present is told in exhibits within the museum building and vintage aircraft in outdoor displays. Among the aircraft exhibited is the B-23 *Dragon*, one of 9 remaining from the 38 originally built; Fairchild C-82A *Packet*; Douglas (T)C-47D; NorthAmerican F-86D *Sabre* (Sabre Dog) that served with the Yugoslavian Air Force; Lockheed T-33A *Shooting Star*, the last T-33 built for the U.S. Air Force; and the last flying C-124C *Globemaster II*. A B-18 *Bolo*, the first type of aircraft assigned to McChord, is presently being restored.

Displays inside the museum include old uniforms, unit exhibits, armaments, photos, aircraft models and an F-106 flight simulator available for visitor's use.

Many events contributed to the history of McChord AFB since it was established in 1938: British aircrews were trained here in 1941; the first operational deployment of B-25 bombers was from McChord; and Colonel Doolittle trained members from McChord to fly in his famous raid on Tokyo during World War II. Squadrons from McChord participated in military action from Korea to Desert Storm as well as peacetime relief efforts, both foreign and domestic.

MT. RAINIER NATIONAL PARK

Before the first white man set eyes on it, Nisqually Indians called the mountain Tahoma, their meaning for "white mountain." When Captain Vancouver discovered it in 1792, he named it Regnier, for British Admiral, Peter Regnier. Today, Washingtonians, and visitors who travel here from around the world, call it Mt. Rainier. At 14,410 feet, Mt. Rainier is the state's highest peak, has more glaciers than any other mountain in the contiguous United States, and is the state's best-known National Park. Four park visitor information centers recount the history of Mr. Rainier through exhibits, history walks and preservation of some of the park's early buildings.

LONGMIRE

Longmire cabin. The last remaining pioneer settlement cabin in the park was erected by the Longmire family in 1888 as a meat house for the hotel they were building. It was later used as part of the Longmire's medical spa.

Longmire Museum (253) 569-2211. Was built in 1916 as Mt. Rainier's first park headquarters. Today, its one of the oldest museums in the National park service. It contains a fine collection of Indian baskets from the Klickitat, Skokomish and Thompson River tribes and historic photographs from the 1930s. Outside the museum is a section from a 670-year-old Douglas fir tree.

National Park Inn (253) 569-2411. This rustic wooden building was constructed in 1917-18 as an annex to the first National Park Inn. In 1926, the first hotel's main building burned to the ground. After the fire, the annex was relocated across the street and became the new National Park Inn. Today, the completely renovated 25-room hotel is the last of Longmire's three original hotels still in operation. Next to the inn is a 1911 structure, built from Douglas fir logs. It was restored in 1980 and is used today as a hikers center.

The Longmire area of Mount Rainier National Park has been designated a National Historic District. The former Administration building, community building and service station are registered as National Historic Landmarks.

PARADISE

Paradise Inn (253) 569-2413, was built in 1917-18 as a 33-room hotel. It is one of the largest hotels in the world to be constructed entirely from Alaskan cedar logs from a single forest. The hotel's two-story lobby has original hand-hewn woodwork, two large stone fireplaces, parquet wood floors and handcrafted Indian rugs. Its been expanded to 126 rooms and is a designated National Historic Landmark.

Henry M. Jackson Memorial Visitors Center. Exhibits tell the history of the park. The center's observation deck provides a breath-taking view, but the best sights can only be seen by hiking one of the parks many trails. Some are as short as a mile. Others, such as the 90-mile Wonderland Trail, take more than a week to cover. The nearby Paradise Glacier Trail, a six-mile trek, leads to the large ice-shrouded Paradise Ice Cave, one of the most beautiful sights in the park.

OHANAPECOSH (oh-HAN-up-pee-kahsh)

Ohanapecosh Visitor Information Center houses exhibits on the history of the park's forestlands. Rangers lead history walks to Hot Springs from the Center.

SUNRISE

Sunrise Visitors Center is located at the 6,400-foot level, the highest point in the park where automobile traffic is permitted. Historic buildings constructed between 1913-1943 include the Yakima Park Stockade Group, a National Historic Landmark. Exhibits at the Center feature the geology of the park. Trails from Sunrise lead to spectacular glaciers, including Emmons Glacier, one of the largest in the United States.

PUYALLUP (pyoo-AL-uhp)

Ezra Meeker Mansion, 312 Spring St., Puyallup (253) 848-1770

Marking and preserving the Oregon Trail was a quest Ezra Meeker pursued for nearly a quarter of a century at an age when most people are retired. Meeker first crossed the plains by covered wagon from Indiana in 1852, platted Puyallup, was elected the town's first mayor and earned the title "Hop King of the World" for being the most successful hop farmer in the state. In 1906, at the age of 76, Meeker, in an ox-drawn wagon, once again set out on the Oregon Trail. This time his goal was to retrace and mark the trail from Washington State to Nebraska in order to draw attention to the need to preserve this important pioneer road. Meeker made three more trips along the trail including one by car, and the last, at age 93, in an open cockpit airplane. Three years after his death at the age of 98, the Oregon Trail was designated a National Historic Highway.

The 17-room home that Meeker built in 1890 is one of the finest early-Victorian mansions in the state. It features rich woodwork, carved cherry wood staircases, stained-glass windows, hand-stenciled ceilings, and ornate fireplaces with imported mantelpieces. The home, which is listed on the National Register of Historic Places, contains original furnishings, period antiques and Meeker family memorabilia.

Pioneer Park, S. Meridian St. and Elm Pl., Puyallup

A life-size statue of Ezra Meeker stands in the center of this community park to honor the memory of this man from Puyallup who spent 23 years promoting preservation of the Oregon Trail.

Japanese-American Assembly Center, Puyallup Fair Grounds, Puyallup

After Japan declared war on the United States in December, 1941, all Japanese and Japanese-Americans on the West Coast were ordered to report to temporary detention camps for eventual relocation to permanent camps across the United States. They would be held in these camps until the end of World War II. A marker at the front gate to the fairgrounds memorializes those who were interned here.

Western Frontier Museum
Trails End Ranch, 2301 23rd Ave. SE, Puyallup (253) 845-4402

One of the Nation's largest collections of Western memorabilia is displayed in this museum of history. Pioneer relics, Indian artifacts, and logging equipment exhibits are showcased in an Old West setting.

Paul H. Karshner Memorial Museum
309 Fourth St. NE, Puyallup (253) 841-8748

Hands-on exhibits especially designed for young children are maintained by the Puyallup School District in this c.1920 school building. Elementary-aged students can use Indian tools and pioneer utensils, sit inside a Native American wigwam, or discover how early settlers traded with their Indian neighbors. Other fields of science are also represented in this children's museum of science and history.

Mount Rainier Historic Marker
5 miles south of Puyallup on the east side of Hwy. 162

"This monarch of the Cascade Range has been called the Great Pyramid of the United States. No other mountain on the continent exceeds Rainier in bulk of rock masses, number of glaciers (26 active) and extent of base. Nearly all of Mr. Rainier National Park's 337 square miles belong to the mighty mountain. Geologists believe the original peak lost 2,000 feet in a volcanic blast creating a crater three miles square. Three cinder cones grew together surrounding the crater rim: Columbia Crest, the central snowy dome, Point Success to the south and Liberty Cap to the north. The British explorer, Captain George Vancouver, discovered the mountain in 1792 and named it for a fellow naval officer, Peter Regnier, now spelled Rainier."

STEILACOOM (STIL-uh-kuhm)

Steilacoom Historic District
Between Nisqually St. and Puget Sound, Steilacoom

One of the oldest American settlements in the state was established here with the building of Fort Steilacoom in 1849. During the next decade, the community of Steilacoom grew to become the busiest port on Puget Sound, the seat of Pierce

County and a candidate for territorial capital. It was the first city incorporated in Washington Territory (1854), and the site of the first territorial courthouse, jail and library. The first American ship built in the region was constructed here as well as the first Catholic and Protestant churches north of the Columbia River. A guide to the old Victorian homes and commercial buildings preserved in this National Historic District is available from the Steilacoom Historical Museum and the Bair Drug and Hardware Store.

Steilacoom Historical Museum
112 Main St.(lower level of Town Hall), Steilacoom (253) 584-4133

Memorabilia from the first wagon train to cross the Naches Pass Trail in 1853, original volumes from the first territorial library, documents from the Indian Wars of 1855-56, relics and photographs from the first territorial jail, and an exceptional assemblage of Native American and Pioneer artifacts are included in the collections of this museum of local history. An excellent guide to thirty-four local historic buildings and monuments is available from museum staff.

The restored town hall building houses a permanent exhibit of enlarged photographs of early Steilacoom and a prized "Bicentennial Quilt." Community members made the quilt, which depicts local history, in 1976 for our Nation's Bicentennial.

Steilacoom Historical Museum

Bair Drug and Hardware Store
1617 Lafayette St., Steilacoom (253) 588-9668

The restored, 1895 Bair Store has been Steilacoom's gathering place for more than a century and continues to serve the community as both a museum and restaurant. Early pharmaceuticals, antique hardware merchandise, a replica of an early-day post office and an original 1906 soda fountain are housed in this historic structure. Breakfast, lunch and a Friday night dinner is served from the soda fountain which also dispenses olde-time sarsaparilla and phosphates.

Bair Drug and Hardware Store

Washington State Historical Road No. 1 Historic Marker
Byrds Mill Rd. and Union Ave., Steilacoom

"Byrds Mill Road. Established by Thurston County Oregon County Territory Legislature in 1852, and re-established by Washington State Legislature in 1941. This military road afforded the only route of escape from the Puyallup Valley to

Fort Steilacoom during the Indian War of 1855, and to the pioneers was a highway of great importance. Along this route in 1864 there was built the Russian-American telegraph line which was proposed to extend to Europe by way of Bering Strait and Asia."

First Protestant Church in Western Washington Monument,
Behind the Bair Drug and Hardware store, on Wilkes between Lafayette and Commercial Sts., Steilacoom

A large stone monument commemorating the first Protestant Church built north of the Columbia was dedicated at this site in 1908. The original bell from the 1853 Methodist Church's belfry is encased in the monument.

Immaculate Conception Catholic Mission
1810 Nisqually St., Steilacoom (253) 584-4133 (Steilacoom Museum)

The first Catholic Church built north of the Columbia River was erected in 1857 on the grounds of Fort Steilacoom. When the fort closed in 1864, after the outbreak of the Civil War, the church was moved about a mile southeast to its present location. The restored church, which has been in continuous use throughout its existence, is listed on the National Register of Historic Places.

Steilacoom Tribal Cultural Center
1515 Lafayette St., Steilacoom

History of the Steilacoom Indian Tribe, from its first contact with Europeans in 1792 to the present, is exhibited in this former church building. The Center operates one of the few tribally-run museums in Washington State. Permanent displays depict the tribe's life styles and the pre-history of the Tacoma Basin.

Steilacoom Tribal Cultural Center

Nathaniel Orr Home and Pioneer Orchard
1811 Rainier, Steilacoom (253) 584-4133 (Steilacoom Museum)

Nathaniel Orr built one of the town's best-known and most-frequented historic homes in 1857. Originally, the upper floor was used as living quarters and the first floor was Orr's wagon shop. In 1868, after his marriage, Orr remodeled the building and moved the wagon shop into a separate building. Orr's home, wagon shop and the pioneer orchard he planted is listed on the National Register of Historic Places. Preserved within the home are original furnishings brought from Victoria by Mrs. Orr in 1868 and pieces handcrafted by Nathaniel Orr. Unfortunately, the home was extensively damaged while undergoing restoration and is not presently open to the public.

SUMNER

Ryan House Museum
1228 Main St., Sumner (253) 863-8936 or (253)863-6155

George Ryan, while not the founder of Sumner, played a major role in the development of the town. Ryan emigrated to the West from Wisconsin in 1873. He used money he earned as a bookkeeper to buy 40 acres in Sumner from the town's first schoolteacher. Ryan farmed his land, owned a sawmill, was the town's first mayor, built a large section of the business district, and was instrumental in bringing the Northern Pacific Railroad to Sumner. He built this modest, three-room frame farmhouse in 1875 using locally milled cedar. In 1926 the Ryan family donated the house to the city for use a local library. When a new library was constructed in 1979, the house was restored to its 1890s style replete with period furnishings and opened as a house museum. Historical documents, photographs and artifacts are preserved by the Sumner Historical Society at this pioneer home. Ryan House is listed on the National Register of Historic Places.

TACOMA (tuh-KOH-muh)

Washington State History Museum
1911 Pacific Ave., Tacoma (888) 238-4373

Next door to the renovated Union Station is the Washington State History Museum. But, unlike its neighbor, the museum is a new, 106,000 square-foot, state-of-the-art facility utilizing multimedia technology that brings the state's history to life. Visitors can interact with historical figures or see what life was like in a Japanese internment camp, a Southern Coast Salish plank house, or in a Hooverville shack. For the action-minded there's a video ride down the Columbia, the experience of a cave-in

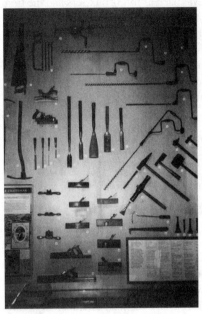

at a Roslyn coal mine, or the thrill as a full-size B-17 soars overheard. Through computer animation guests can watch the birth of the region's great mountain ranges or see the floods that once cascaded down the face of present-day Dry Falls. "Encyclopedia Washingtonia" and "Electronic Journals" lets visitors explore and collect information about the state's history either geographically or by topic. An enormous "tree of wood products" display on the museum's first floor links everyday wood products to the state's timber industry.

Antique Tool Collection from the Washington State History Museum

Union Station
1713 Pacific Ave., Tacoma

The coming of the railroad meant prosperity for every town fortunate enough to be chosen as a stop along the mainline. The ultimate reward, one that many cities sought, was selection as the terminus of the transcontinental line. When Tacoma beat-out Seattle, Mukilteo, Steilacoom, and Olympia, and was named the western terminus of the Northern Pacific Railway, city fathers wanted to build a station equal to the honor. They contracted with the firm of Reed and Stem, the architects of New York City's Grand Central Station, to design the beautiful, copper-domed station that stands here today. In 1986, the 1911 station was restored and transformed into a federal courthouse. The rotunda of this Nationally Registered Historic Site is open to the public and features a magnificent exhibit of fine glass sculptures.

Union Station

Karpeles Manuscript Library Museum
407 S. "G" St., Tacoma (253) 383-2575

In the era before e-mail, word processing and typewriters, most communication was in the form of handwritten letters and documents. Preserved within this museum are original drafts, letters and documents handwritten by some of the great men and women who changed and shaped the history of our nation. The seven Karpeles museums located across the United States contain original works that are studied by scholars or just simply admired by visitors. Although you won't find the Declaration of Independence in the museum's collection, you will see the cover letter John Hancock wrote. They also have Wagner's draft of the "Bridal Chorus;" the proposal draft of the Bill of Rights; and the Declaration of Allegiance of all Indian tribes to the United States, the final peace treaty signed by 968 Indian Chiefs representing all of the Nation's 189 Indian tribes.

Fort Nisqually Historic Site
Point Defiance Regional Park, N. 54th and Pearl Sts., Tacoma (253) 591-5339

In 1933, one hundred years after Fort Nisqually was constructed by the Hudson's Bay Company near present-day DuPont, the fort's two remaining buildings were relocated here and restored as a WPA project. The 1845 square-log granary, the state's oldest existing building, and the 1854 factor's house are the original buildings among the ten structures in this reconstructed, full-scale fort. Other buildings, while not originally built within the fort, are representative of the construction methods utilized during the period. Some of the structures were built using hammered scrap iron door hinges and latches salvaged from the fort's original buildings. Both the Granary and factor's house are listed on the National Register of Historic Places. Hudson's Bay Company trade goods and artifacts, agricultural implements, blueprints, maps, charts and photographs are exhibited in the fort's museum. A self-guiding brochure, available from the museum, illustrates the early exploration and fur trade eras of Washington state history when the Hudson's Bay Company dominated the region.

Fort Nisqually Historic Site

Camp Six Logging Museum
Western Forest Industries Museum
Point Defiance Regional Park, 5400 N. Pearl St., Tacoma (253) 752-0047

Replicated within the nation's only old growth forest located in a city park is an authentic logging camp typical of those found in the state during the period from 1880 to 1940. Original Kapowson bunkhouses; Quinalt camp cars; a 110-foot rigged Spar tree; the last remaining 300-ton Lidgerwood Skidder; and other movable, steam-powered logging equipment are among the interesting sites in this 20-acre recreated camp. A Shay steam locomotive operates on a mile and a half track around the site and offers weekend train rides in season. Exhibits in the camp's museum contain logging related artifacts and historic photographs. Camp Six is listed on the National Register of Historic Places.

Camp Six Logging Museum

Job Carr Log Cabin
Point Defiance Regional Park, 5-mile Dr., Tacoma

Along the five-mile drive that winds through the park's 500 acres of natural forest is a 1918 replica of the first house built by a white man in Tacoma. Job Carr arrived in Tacoma in 1864 and built his cabin at the foot of McCarver Street. He became the city's first postmaster and its mayor. In 1868 he sold most of his land to the Northern Pacific Railroad which selected Tacoma as its Western terminus. Carr's cabin is listed on the State Heritage Register.

Pantages Theater
9th and Commerce, Tacoma (253) 591-5890

In the heart of the Broadway Theater District is the former Vaudeville theater built by Alexander Pantages in 1918. W. C. Fields, Mae West, Charlie Chaplin and the Marx Brothers were some of the entertainers who performed on the stage of this lavish theater. "The Pan," as it was affectionately called, became a movie house in 1926 and remained a movie theater for the next 50 years. Today, the restored, 1186-seat Greco Roman-style theater is home to the Tacoma Symphony and is listed on the National Register of Historic Places.

Pantages Theater

Rialto Theater
In the Broadway Plaza at 310 South 9th St., Tacoma (253) 591-5890

Two theater buildings have stood at this site. The Olympus opened in 1892 and was twice remodeled and renamed before it burned to the ground in a 1909 fire. It reopened as the Rialto in 1918. The Broadway Theater District undertook refurbishing the 742-seat Beaux Arts-style theater in 1991. Many of the original features of this popular attraction were restored or were replicated during restoration. A year after the Rialto reopened, the theater was placed on the National Register of Historic Places.

Rialto Theater

Shanaman Sports Museum of Tacoma
Tacoma Dome, 2727 E. "D" St., Tacoma

One of the city's best-known and most recognized landmarks is the 15-story Tacoma Dome. This arena, the world's largest wood-domed structure, is home to the Shanaman Sports Museum of Tacoma. Exhibits depict the evolution of sports in Tacoma and Pierce County through written and visual displays. The museum is open before and after all sports events held at the Tacoma Dome.

St. Peter's Episcopal Church
2910 Starr St., Tacoma

In the city's Old Town Historic District stands the town's first church. The small board-and-batten, Gothic Revival-style church was erected in 1873 and served as a center for citizens of all faiths religious, social and community activities. The church's organ and bell were shipped round the Horn shortly after the church was erected. Sunday School children in Philadelphia raised money for the 965-pound bell, which sits atop an ivy-covered, 40-foot-tall cedar trunk next to the church. St. Peter's is listed on the National Register of Historic Places.

Slavonian Hall
2306 N. 30th St., Tacoma

Among the turn-of-the-century buildings preserved in this historic district is Slavonian Hall. It was built in 1902 as a community center for the many European immigrants who settled here. A history of the community is displayed within the building, a Nationally Registered Historic Place. Other early buildings in this district now house shops and restaurants.

Stadium High School and Bowl
111 North "E" St., Tacoma

Constructed as a luxury hotel in 1891 for the Northern Pacific Railroad, the Tacoma Land Company Hotel never opened as planned. The Depression that gripped the Nation in 1893 halted construction and a fire gutted the half-completed building the same year. In 1906, the Chateauesque-style hotel was converted into a high school; the most grandiose high school on the West Coast. Its copper-tipped towers, multiple turrets and early French Renaissance architecture has earned it the nickname "The Castle." Adjoining the school, which is still used as a high school, is Stadium Bowl, an amphitheater that was the first of its type on the Pacific Coast. Three former Presidents spoke here as well as sports giants Babe Ruth and Jack Dempsey.

Within the Stadium Historic District adjacent to Stadium High School are more than 100 Victorian houses. Among them are stately mansions once owned by Tacoma's wealthy railroad, timber and shipping families. Many are open during the city's annual "Grand Homes of Tacoma" tour. This historic district is listed on the State Heritage Register.

Commencement Bay Maritime Center
705 Dock St., Tacoma (206) 272-2750

Tacoma's maritime heritage is graphically displayed in this center's exhibits. Another reminder of the city's connection with the sea is a 1929 Fireboat, one of the oldest on the West Coast, that's displayed in a small park on Ruston Way, the scenic drive that parallels Commencement Bay from Tacoma's Old Town District to Port Defiance.

1929 Fireboat

W.W. Seymour Botanical Conservatory
Wright Park, 6th Ave. and "I" St., Tacoma

The centerpiece of Wright Park is a graceful, twelve-sided, glass-domed conservatory. Built in 1908, it's one of three late Victorian era conservatories remaining on the West Coast. W.W. Seymour, a former mayor of Tacoma, for whom the building is named, donated the conservatory to the city. Hundreds of orchids and other exotic plants are grown here. The surrounding arboretum, one of the oldest in the country, contains more than 100 varieties of native and foreign trees. Both the park and conservatory are listed on the National Register of Historic Places.

Temple Theater
47 St. Helen's Ave., Tacoma (253) 272-2042

The state's largest ballroom and one of the largest stages on the West Coast are two prominent features of this restored 1926 Art Deco-style theater. Its the city's largest performing arts theater and can accommodate more than 1600 patrons.

Old City Hall
Seventh Ave. between Commerce and Pacific Aves., Tacoma

From 1893 until 1959 this Italian Renaissance-style building was the seat of Tacoma's city government. The landmark clock tower, with its 2-ton clockworks, remained intact when renovation of the Old City Hall began in 1972. Today, professional offices fill the historic building. The Old City Hall building and surrounding historic district is listed on the National Register of Historic Places.

The Old City Hall Historic District, roughly bounded by St. Helens Court, Seventh and Ninth Avenues, was the city's first formal commercial district. The 1916 Elks building, 1889 University Hilton Club and 1888 Northern Pacific Headquarters are three of the city's better-known landmarks found in this district.

Tacoma Public Library
1102 Tacoma Ave. South, Tacoma (253) 591-5688

More than half a million volumes on Northwest history are housed in this 1903 Carnegie library building. A fine collection of World War I posters is also preserved here.

Tacoma Totem Pole
Fireman's Park, 9th and "A" Sts., Tacoma

Alaskan Indian sculptors from the Eagle Tribe were brought to Tacoma in 1903 to carve the totem pole that stands today in this park. The restored pole was carved from a single cedar tree and is one of the tallest in the nation. Figures depict the tribe's order of succession.

Tacoma Totem Pole

Tacoma Art Museum
12th St. and Pacific Ave., Tacoma (253) 272-4258

In addition to its fine collection of art works by American and internationally known artists, the museum also features eighteenth century furniture and period artifacts displayed in a typical living room setting. American glass and ceramics are also part of the museum's permanent exhibits.

Nihon Go Gakko
Japanese Language School, University of Washington Tacoma Campus, 1715 S. Tacoma Ave., Tacoma

Most visitors to this newest campus of the University of Washington are unaware of the significance of this vacant building. It's appropriate that it shares common ground with an institute for learning; for it was here that hundreds of "nisei," (American-born, second generation Japanese) received formal education in Japanese language, cultural traditions, and supplementary English classes. When the first Tacoma school was established in 1911, it was one of an estimated sixty that would

309

be constructed along the West Coast during the first two decades of the twentieth century. This building was erected in 1922 by "Issei," the first-generation Japanese immigrants, with funds raised within the Japanese community. A major addition was made to the building in 1926 to accommodate the school's growing student body. In 1942, the school closed as the city's Japanese-Americans were forced to evacuate to internment camps. Although occupied for brief periods, the building has virtually been vacant since the end of World War II.

The Tacoma Narrows Historic Marker
Hwy. 16 at the northwest end of the Tacoma Narrows Bridge, Tacoma

"The first white explorers of these waters made camp ashore on the night of May 20, 1792 near this site. The campers were from the British expedition under Captain George Vancouver. Lieutenant Peter Puget was in charge of this part. His mission was to chart the sea in the forest to its southern limits. Vancouver named the maze of waterways "Puget Sound," a name given later to the entire inland sea. Beyond the mile-long suspension bridge can be seen Tacoma and Mount Rainier."

The first suspension bridge constructed at this site now lies at the bottom of the Narrows. Nicknamed "Galloping Gertie," the original bridge would catch the wind like a sail, causing the road surface to roll and undulate. Four months after the bridge opened in 1940, a 42-mile-per-hour windstorm pulled the bridge apart. The

replacement bridge that spans the Narrows today was completed in 1950. At 5,979 feet, it's one of the longest suspension bridges in the world. The sunken remains of "Galloping Gertie" were listed on the National Register of Historic Places in 1992 to protect the ruins from salvagers.

The New Tacoma Narrows Bridge

310

Browns Point Lighthouse and Keeper's Cottage
201 Tulalip NE, Tacoma

Since 1887 a light at this site has warned sailors of the perils of steaming through these waters. Many changes were made to the light in the ensuing years including the addition of a fog signal. Even with the light and horn, several ships were lost in the waters off this point before the present lighthouse was erected in 1933. Browns Point Light is listed on the National Register of Historic Places.

WAUNA (WAW-nuh)

Wauna Store/Post Office
Across the bridge from Purdy, on the water's edge of Hwy. 302 at Goodrich Dr. NW, Wauna

For more than 80 years the Wauna store served the community as both store and post office. In 1982, the store closed and the building was used exclusively as a post office. The building, erected by the White family in 1899, is being preserved as a local historical landmark. Any repairs to the building must match the original construction material and style.

WILKESON

Coke Ovens
Off Hwy. 165 past the school and behind the railroad tracks, southeast of Wilkeson

Coal was discovered in this region as early as 1862, but it would be another eleven years before commercial mining began. In 1885 the first of 160, 12-foot high brick ovens were built to turn coal into coke. For the next 50 years Wilkeson was the sole producer of coke in the Northwest. Wilkeson's coal reserves are vast. It's estimated that more than 220 million tons of coal remain underground in the immediate vicinity of Wilkeson. Forty of the original ovens remain and are listed on the National Register of Historic Places.

Wilkeson School
Wilkeson Elementary School, Hwy. 165, Wilkeson

Sandstone from the town's quarries was used in the construction of the capitol dome and other structures on the Capitol Campus in Olympia as well as for this impressive local school building. Erected in 1912-13 by Dolph Jones, this school is still in use today and is listed on the National Register of Historic Places.

Holy Trinity Orthodox Church
433 Long St., Wilkeson

Slavic coal miners and their families raised money and donated labor to erect this wood frame church in 1895-98. Throughout the years the original church building, which was founded in 1895 by the Russian Orthodox Mission to America, has remained unaltered and in its original state. Only periodic maintenance has been required. The chapel retains its original Russian Orthodox Mission set of brass candlesticks, processional cross and main icons, which were supplied to the church by the Patriarchate of Moscow under the patronage of the Tsar. Holy Trinity is listed on the National Register of Historic Places and has an active congregation.

Wilkeson Town Hall
Wilkeson Library, 540 Church St., Wilkeson   Town Hall (360) 829-0790
Library (360) 829-0513

This Wilkeson sandstone building was constructed in 1923 as a community center and Episcopal Church. Today, it houses the town's library, police station, city clerk's office and city council chambers. Of particular interest is the fence that surrounds the building. It's made of the saw blades that were once used to cut sandstone for many of the state's better-known buildings.

Thurston County

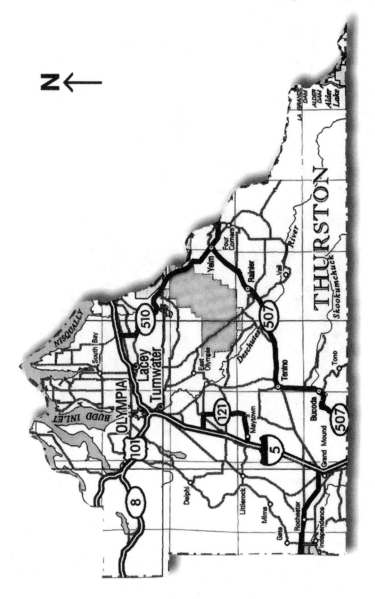

THURSTON COUNTY

BUCODA (byoo-KOH-duh)

Seatco Prison (site)
Parking area at 12th and Factory Sts. overlooks the site that was east of Bucoda near the Skookumchuck River

Washington's first territorial prison was erected at this site in 1878. Up to 93 prisoners were incarcerated within its massive wooden walls until construction of a permanent penitentiary was completed at Walla Walla in 1887. Inmates were often shackled and forced into hard labor in the prison's shops or in the neighboring coal mines and logging camps. The prison site is listed on the National Register of Historic Places. A plaque at this site honors the workers who were employed by the **Mutual Lumber Company** that once stood here.

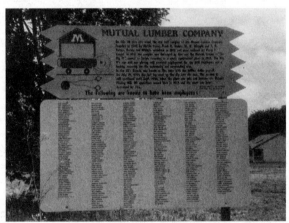

Mutual Lumber Company Plaque

Oliver Shead House (site)
206 N. Main St., Bucoda

Pioneer businessman and investor, Oliver Shead, built the home that once stood here and another for his sister (210 N. Main St.) in the mid 1880s. Shead provided land and building materials for construction of the Seatco Prison and, in return, received a share of the profits from inmate labor. Only the home of his sister remains today. Her home is listed on the State Heritage Register.

LACEY

Lacey Museum
827 1/2 Lacey St., Lacey (360) 438-0209

In 1881, when the city was called Woodland, one of the best sulky horse racing tracks in the west was opened here. Lake resorts, dance halls, and campgrounds followed, making Lacey a major recreation destination. During the same era, Lacey became home to St. Martin's College, founded by Benedictine monks in 1895. A member of the college faculty pioneered radio broadcasting in the Pacific Northwest. And, in 1922, station KGY was licensed as the first radio station in the state. The 1928 Russell farmhouse, that once housed Lacey's city hall and fire department when it was located on Pacific Ave., is now home to the city's museum of history where an old time radio exhibit, relics and old photographs from the community's past are preserved.

Lacey Museum

LITTLEROCK

Mima (my-muh) Mounds Natural Area Preserve
Waddell Creek Rd. north of 128th Ave. SW, one-mile west of Littlerock
(360) 748-2383

Before this area was developed, hundreds of thousands of regularly spaced symmetrical earth mounds covered the open prairie. Many theories have been made over the years to explain the existence of these mysterious earth mounds, but no agreement has been reached among those who have examined these strange phenomena. In the 1970s, 445 acres of open prairie containing these mounds were purchased by the Nature Conservancy and given to the state for preservation. A self-guided interpretive trail, nature trail and hiking trails weave through the preserve. The mounds are a registered National Natural Landmark.

Mima Mounds Interpretive Kiosk

NISQUALLY (nis-KWAL-ee)

Nisqually Historic Marker
On I-5, 1/2-mile west of the Nisqually River Bridge, Nisqually

"Here, in the Nisqually Valley, on the bank of McAllister Creek, also known as Medicine Creek and by the Indians called She-Nah-Nam, is the memorable spot where Isaac I. Stevens, first territorial governor of Washington, sat in counsel with the chieftains of the lower Puget Sound Indian tribes, principally the Nisquallys, Puyallups and Squaxons, December 24 to 26, 1854. The resulting Medicine Creek Treaty purchased land for white settlers, awarded reservations to the Indians, and concluded the first in a series of important Northwest Indian treaties."

OLYMPIA

Old Capitol Building
600 S. Washington St., Olympia (360) 753-6725

Washington state purchased the 1892 Thurston County Courthouse in 1901, added a wing for legislative chambers and, for the next 23 years, used the building as the state's capitol and seat of government. The renovated, copper-domed building, which is listed on the National Register of Historic Places, now houses the offices of the superintendent of public instruction.

Preserved near the Old Capitol Building, in Sylvester Park (Legion and Capitol Way), is **Olympia's original 1850s town square.** Presidents Theodore Roosevelt, William Taft and Franklin Roosevelt, and other famous visitors to the town addressed Olympia's citizens from this town square. A statue of former Governor John Rogers, who spearheaded the conversion of the Thurston County Courthouse into the capitol's legislative building (Old Capitol Building), stands in the center of the park. Governor Rogers was elected in 1896. He died shortly after his re-election in 1900.

Old Capitol Building

Washington State Capitol Campus
Capitol Way, Olympia (360) 586-3460 (Visitor Center) or (360) 586-8687 (Tour information)

Although construction of the present capitol began in 1893, it would take nearly 50 years to finish all the buildings that now comprise the Washington State Capitol Campus. A national depression, attempts to move the capitol, and a lack of funding caused the original plans to be reconsidered. What evolved was a main legislative building (the domed building at the center of the Campus) and several surrounding buildings that were erected over the years as needed.

Washington State Capitol Building

Legislative Building - The first foundation for this building was laid in 1893 at the site of the original 1855 wooden territorial capitol building. But construction stopped the next year when funds dried-up in the wake of a national depression. It would be 25 years before construction resumed. The 22-story Legislative Building, the fifth highest all-masonry building in the world, was completed in 1928 using locally quarried sandstone from Wilkeson, granite from Index and Alaskan Tokeen marble. The 42 steps leading to the second floor entrance symbolize Washington's admission to the Union as the 42nd state.

A guide that describes the many noteworthy features of the capitol is available from the first floor Visitor Center. Of particular interest are: the scenes depicted on the six solid bronze entry doors; replicas of the statues of Mother Joseph and Marcus Whitman that were sent to Statuary Hall in our Nation's Capitol; the five-ton chandelier suspended from the dome; Tiffany light fixtures, the last large commission created by Louis Comfert Tiffany; the state seal reproduced on railing and doorknobs throughout the building; and the "Documents of Liberty" display in the Secretary of State's office that includes the original state constitution, a letter handwritten by George Washington, and the telegram declaring Washington a state.

A time capsule was imbedded in the center of the floor at the main entrance in 1976, to commemorate our country's bicentennial. Among the items placed in the capsule, which will be opened in the year 2076, are: student essays forecasting what life will be like in Washington when the capsule is opened, seed samples from the state's trees, Indian artifacts, water and air samples, photographs, a can of salmon, and a can of Olympia Beer.

Temple of Justice Building, the first Campus building to be completed, has been home to the State Supreme Court and the State Law Library since the building was first occupied in 1920. The State Library was originally housed in the building's basement.

The 1908, Georgian Revival-style **Governor's Mansion**, while not designed as part of the original Campus, sits on a knoll in the shadow of the Legislative Building. The chief executive's 17-room home was remodeled in 1974 and is furnished in antiques donated by citizens of the state.

Other Campus buildings include the 1921 **Insurance Building**, 1934 **Institutions Building,** 1937 **Public Lands Building**, 1940 **House Office Building** and the 1959 **State Library**, where a fine sculpture collection, a free-standing mosaic wall, murals and other works of art by Northwest artists is exhibited.

Four memorials have been erected on the 55-acre Campus to honor the brave men and women from Washington State who gave their lives for their Country. The War Memorial Fountain and Monument, north of the Insurance Building, was dedicated

in 1938. Nestled in the hillside east of the Insurance Building is the 1987 Vietnam Veterans Memorial. The latest monuments are: the 1993 Korean War Veterans Memorial, located on the East Campus across the footbridge from the State Capitol Visitor Center; and the Medal of Honor marker.

Medal of Honor Memorial

319

Washington State Capitol Museum
Delbert McBride Ethnobotanical Garden
211 West 21st Ave., Olympia (360) 753-2580

Clarence J. Lord, a prominent banker and former mayor of Olympia, built this 32-room, Italian Renaissance Revival-style mansion as his family home in 1923. After his death in 1937, Elizabeth Lord deeded the house to the state for use as museum. The elegance of this former estate is quite evident, from the formal gardens to the variety of fine interior woodwork selected by the architect, Joseph Wohleb. Today, the house is an official repository for territorial and state government manuscripts and the collections of the Washington State Historical Society. Permanent exhibits present the political history of the capitol and the culture of the state's early pioneers and Native Americans. Lord's mansion is listed on the National Register of Historic Places.

The ethnobotanical garden on the mansion grounds was created to "provide an understanding of the food, medicine and tool uses of plants by American Indians in Western Washington." Thirty-four varieties have been planted and identified. A guide, available at the museum, explains how these plants and trees were used to make Indian baskets, dyes and other everyday essentials ranging from tonic tea and hand cleaner to insect repellant.

Clarence J. Lord Mansion, Washington State Capitol Museum

Henry McCleary House
111 West 21st Ave, Olympia

Next door to the Clarence Lord Mansion is the Jacobean-Renaissance Revival-style home Henry McCleary erected in 1923. McCleary, a mill operator who was once allegedly refused a loan by Lord's bank, contracted with Lord's architect, Joseph Wohleb, to build him an even more luxurious home. McCleary's Mansion, which is listed on the National Register of Historic Places, has been converted into a number of offices.

Henry McCleary Mansion

Women's Club of Olympia
1002 Washington SE, Olympia (360) 753-9921, (360) 491-7713 or (360) 943-1099

The oldest women's club on the West Coast has its headquarters in this 1907 Four Square-style building. The club was organized in March, 1883, and first met in the pioneer home of Edmund Sylvester. Members were active in women's suffrage and other state and national concerns. The building is listed on the National Register of Historic Places.

321

Olympic Collegiate Institute
Central School
South Adams and Union, Olympia

This Greek Revival-style building was built in 1858 to house the Puget Sound
Wesleyan Institute. After the school closed in 1861, the building was used for
almost ten years as the Thurston County Courthouse. It then served as the Union
Academy, Olympia Collegiate Institute 1862-71, and the old Central School, the
first district school house. In the late 1940s, after the building had been converted
into residences, this book's author, Jan Roberts (Janice Hall), lived here with her
family. The building was added to State Heritage Register in 1985.

Formerly housed the Puget Sound Wesleyan Institute,
County Courthouse, and three Schools

Historic Downtown Olympia
Bounded by Water and Franklin, State and 7th — Guide available from the City of
Olympia Heritage Commission, in the City Hall at 900 Plum St., Olympia

Renovation of turn-of-the-century buildings and identification of historic sites in
downtown Olympia has preserved the area's early history for future generations to
enjoy. Among the two dozen places catalogued by the Commission are thirteen
that are listed on the National or State Register of Historic Places.

322

Old Daily Olympian Building
Capitol and State Sts., Olympia

Joseph Wohleb, the well-known architect who moved here from California in 1911, designed this 1930 stucco building using Spanish detailing that was typical of early California architectural schemes. The "Olympian," the first Washington Territory newspaper was published here.

The Spar
114 E. 4th Ave., Olympia

This 1935, Joseph Wohleb-designed building was built as a downtown restaurant and meeting place. Many of the building's original interior features can be seen in this Olympia Heritage Site along with old photos and period memorabilia.

Talcott
420 Capitol Way, Olympia (360) 357-9339

The fourth brick building erected in Olympia after the 1882 fire was constructed for the Talcott's as a variety store. In 1889, Talcott, the state's oldest jeweler, designed and manufactured the Washington State Seal. Inside today's store is a display of rare documents and photography entitled "Olympia's First Century."

Percival Landing
Water St. between Thurston and 4th Aves., Olympia

Samuel Percival came to Olympia in 1853 from Massachusetts. He ran a store, built a sawmill and constructed the first dock on Puget Sound. A boardwalk and observation tower marks the site of this important city landmark.

TENINO (ti-NEYE-noh)

Tenino's Historic Sandstone Buildings and Sites
Sussex St. between Hodgden and Ritter and 300 block of Park St., Tenino
(360) 264-5075

Sandstone from the old Tenino Stone Company quarry was used to construct a number of prominent buildings throughout the West during the period between 1888 and the 1930s. Although the sandstone buildings erected along the section of

Pacific Highway (old Hwy. 99) that runs through this part of the city are no match for the courthouses, city halls, churches, libraries and other grand structures carved from Tenino sandstone, they serve as a lasting monument to the labor of the craftsmen who once worked the quarry and helped build the town. The site of the old quarry became a living war memorial following World War II and is now a 95-foot deep municipal swimming pool. A guide to the city's historic sandstone buildings and sites is available from the chamber of commerce and museum.

Tenino Depot Museum
399 W. Park St., Tenino (360) 264-4321

Before sandstone was discovered at Tenino, the railroad was here. The first depot, erected in 1872, was little more than a stop on the line where passengers could connect to a narrow-gauge line to Olympia. With the discovery of high-grade sandstone and access to rail transportation, the city grew. The third station was constructed of sandstone in 1914 and served the community until the 1960s. Today, the depot, which is listed on the National Register of Historic Places, houses the collections of the South Thurston County Historical Society.

Tenino Depot Museum, Courtesy of the Tenino Depot Museum

During the Great Depression, when Tenino residents' savings were frozen in the Citizens Bank, the chamber of commerce promoted a script made of wood that could be used to buy goods and services in the community. All the local merchants and businesses accepted the wooden script, the only Depression-era script to receive approval of the U.S. Comptroller. The expression, "Don't take any wooden nickels," wouldn't be heeded today, for that old wooden script is valuable. The machine used to make the rare wooden script is exhibited here along with other permanent exhibits that include: logging, quarry and railroading tools; a c.1927 kitchen and millinery shop.

1930 Doctors Office exhibit inside the Tenino Depot Museum,
Courtesy of the Tenino Depot Museum

Oregon Trail Marker
Northwest corner of Sussex and Sheridan Sts., Tenino

Ezra Meeker came West from Indiana across the Oregon Trail by ox team in 1852, pioneered hop growing in Puyallup, was Washington Territory's first bee-keeper and became one of the state's most prosperous men. He wrote books on pioneer life and spent the last 23 years of his life promoting preservation of the Oregon Trail. In 1906, at the age of 76, Meeker once again traveled by an ox-drawn wagon. But, this time it was to retrace and mark the Oregon Trail from Washington to Nebraska. He repeated the trip again in 1910, traveled over the Trail by automobile in 1924, and flew 1,300 miles along the Trail in an open-cockpit plane in 1924 at the age of 93. In 1931, three years after Meeker's death, the Oregon Trail was designated a National Historical Highway. The simple stone pillar at this site was the first maker placed by Meeker to commemorate this important pioneer trail.

Oregon Trail Marker, Courtesy of Tenino Depot Museum

Colvin House
16828 Old Hwy. 99, Tenino (360) 264-2132

Four generations of the Colvin family have lived here since the 2200-acre ranch was first settled in 1849 by Ignasius and Emma Colvin. Their pioneer home became a stage stop and layover point for travelers on the old road between Cowlitz and Tumwater. Some of the ground-floor bedrooms featured outside doors that guests could use to leave early without waking others. The restored Colvin home is listed on the National Register of Historic Places.

Colvin House, Courtesy of the Tenino Depot Museum

TUMWATER

Tumwater Historic Marker
Capitol Blvd. at the south end of the Deschutes River Bridge, Tumwater

"Here the Deschutes River cataracts into Budd Inlet, the most southerly point of Puget Sound, where ends the old Oregon Trail, arduous route of hardy pioneers of the west. With determined disregard for British opposition to their settlement north of the Columbia River, a small band of pioneers founded here in 1846 the town of New Market, first American community established on Puget Sound. The Indian name for the cataract was Spa-Kwatl but in Chinook jargon it was Tumwater, meaning throbbing water, which name New Market later adopted."

A monument to the 32 founders who came here in 1845 and established the first non-Indian settlement north of the Columbia River stands on the west bank of the Deschutes River near the west end of the Deschutes River Bridge.

Henderson House Museum
Pictorial Museum
602 Deschutes Way SW, Tumwater (360) 754-4163 (recorded message)

An outstanding collection of century-old photographs depicting the commercial and residential development of this Deschutes River community, period clothing, pioneer tools, and artifacts are featured in this restored 1905 Carpenter Gothic-style house. The museum's library includes a c.1895 Encyclopedia Britannica.

Henderson House Museum

327

Crosby House
509 Deschutes Way SW, Tumwater (360) 754-4160 (city of Tumwater)

The oldest house in Tumwater was built in 1858-60 by Captain Nathaniel Crosby III, grandfather of the late entertainer Bing (Harry) Crosby. Bing Crosby, who was born in Tacoma, supported a local fund drive in the 1940s to save the old house. Today, the restored, two-story, wood frame cottage-style house contains original Crosby family and period furnishings and is maintained as a city museum.

Crosby House

Tumwater Historical Park
Off Deschutes Pkwy. at the foot of Grant St., on the east side of I-5, Tumwater (360) 754-4160 (city of Tumwater)

The old Olympia brew house, a six-story, brick Italianate-style building and the 1905 Colonial Revival-style home of Olympia Brewery's founder, Leopold Schmidt's, were purchased by the Olympia Brewing Company and are preserved as part of this historical park.

Olympia Brewing Company
100 Custer Way, Olympia (360) 754-5177

Leopold Schmidt, a master brewer from Germany, constructed Tumwater's first brewery in 1896 after tasting the city's artesian well water. In additional to daily tours of the brewery, which is now owned by the Pabst Brewing Company, visitors can view the famous Pabst Stein collection that's on display at the visitor center.

Pabst Stein Collection, Olympia Brewing Company

Tumwater Falls Park and Interpretive Center
On the banks of the Deschutes River across from the Olympia Brewery, Tumwater
(360) 943-2550

The Michael Simmons party of 32 pioneers arrived here in 1845, established the
first American settlement north of the Columbia River, and founded the first industry
in the region. They built a water-powered gristmill at the base of the falls in 1846,
followed a year later by a sawmill. By the 1870s, a number of small factories and
mills were operating. Stone foundations from the 1883 electrical power plant, the
region's first, can be seen in the middle falls area. This park is included in the
Tumwater Historic District, a Nationally Registered Historic Site.

Bush Prairie
U.S. 99, 5 miles south of Tumwater

One of the members of the Simmons Party that settled Tumwater in 1845 was George Washington Bush, a freed slave from Clay County, Missouri. Bush initially planned to settle in Oregon Territory, which prohibited slavery. Their laws, however, also restricted blacks to a maximum two-year residency. Simmons and Bush continued north into territory that was under control of the British where no slavery laws existed. Bush was a highly respected man. He loaned provisions from his own stores to families who ran short during the long overland journey. He financed construction of Simmons sawmill, helped others with gifts of seed and food during hard times, and provided lodging for travelers between the Columbia River and Puget Sound.

When Washington Territory was established in 1853, many of Oregon's property laws were adopted by the new territory. Once again, Bush was not permitted to own the 640 acres of land he had settled. His many friends petitioned the Territorial Legislature and the U.S. Congress. Congress responded by passing special laws permitting him to keep his property. After Bush's death in 1863, his sons (their sixth son was the first non-Indian child born north of the Columbia River), and their children continued to farm the land for more than 100 years.

The Bush Prairie region was named to memorialize George Bush, an outstanding Washington pioneer.

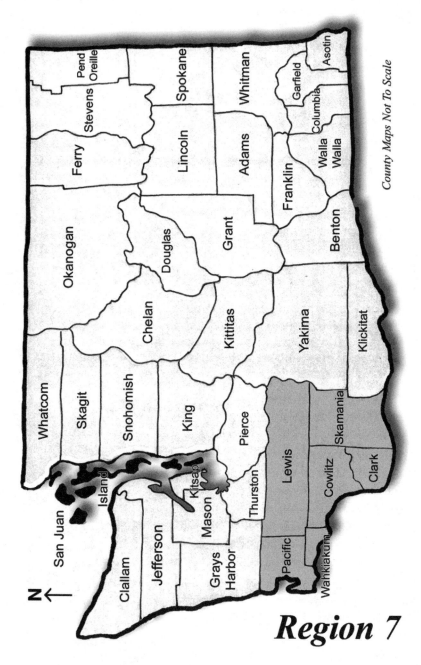

County Maps Not To Scale

Region 7

Clark County

REGION 7

CLARK COUNTY

AMBOY (AM-boy)

North Clark Historical Museum
Hwy. 503 and Munch Rd., Amboy (360) 686-3841

Restoration of Amboy's 1913 Community Church Building has been underway for several years. When completed, the old church building will serve the community as a museum of local logging history.

North Clark Historical Museum

Mount Saint Helens National Volcanic Monument Visitors Center is also located in Amboy. For a recorded message call (360) 247-3900. Refer to the Mount St. Helens listings in Cowlitz County for more information about the Monument.

Cedar Creek Gristmill

9 miles east of Woodland, northwest of Amboy — From Woodland cross the bridge over the Lewis River and turn left on N.E. Hayes Rd. Continue east as road becomes N.E. Cedar Creek Rd (County Road 16). Turn left on Grist Mill Rd. down a tree-lined gravel road across a covered bridge to the mill. (360) 225-9552

On the banks of Cedar Creek is a completely restored, waterwheel-powered grist mill built by George Woodham in 1876. A wooden flume extends 650 feet up the creek to catch water that powers the mill's grindstones and turns grain into flour. Over the years the mill had several owners, each adding to, or modifying the mill's interior to fit their needs: a shingle mill and blacksmith shop was added, the first floor converted into a machine shop, and the upper floor became an apartment. The "Friends of the Cedar Creek Grist Mill" began restoration of the mill in 1980, and returned it to its original function in time to grind wheat in celebration of the state's centennial in 1989. The mill, which is listed on the National Register of Historic Places, is located in one of the most picturesque spots in the state.

Cedar Creek Gristmill

BATTLE GROUND

Lewisville (Site)
Lewisville Park, 26411 NE Lewisville Hwy., Battle Ground

This 158-acre regional park on the banks of the East Fork of the Lewis River is the county's oldest park. It was built by the WPA in 1936-40 on what was once the site of the town of Lewisville. The only structure remaining from the town is the Green home and barn, located about one-half mile from the park on the opposite side of the river. The site of this former pioneer town is listed on the National Register of Historic places.

Albert and Letha Green House and Barn
25716 NE Lewisville Hwy., Battle Ground

The only remaining structure from the town of Lewisville is the former home of Albert and Letha Green. The Greens built their home in 1884, four years before the city of Battle Ground was founded. Albert Green was a traveling music teacher. Their son, Vernon, was an internationally-known cartoonist who created "Bringing Up Father." The house, which isn't open to the public, is listed on the National Register of Historic Places and can be seen from the highway bridge that crosses the Lewis River.

Lewis & Clark Railway Co.
215 S. Grace St., Battle Ground (360) 687-2626

A 21-mile rail excursion from Battle Ground along the Lewis River takes guests to Moulton Falls, the site of ancient Native American meeting grounds. Along the way, travelers cross a historic wood trestle and pass through a 340-foot tunnel that was blasted out of Yacolt Mountain in 1902. Guests can also take a longer, 38-mile trip to Chelatchie through the historic logging town of Yacolt, book rides on afternoon and evening dinner trains or take special holiday trips. The railway operates classic cars pulled by diesel-powered engines.

RIDGEFIELD

Arndt Prune Dryer
2109 NW 219th St. (follow Pioneer Rd. to South 9th), Ridgefield

At the turn-of-the-century, prune production was this community's prominent agricultural activity. Drying sheds, such as this, were used throughout the valley to turn acres of harvested plums into dried prunes. This 1898 prune dryer, the last operating dryer in Ridgefield, is listed on the National Register of Historic Places but not accessible to the public.

Lancaster House
End of Lancaster Rd.(follow West Main to 61st which becomes Lancaster), north of Ridgefield

Judge Columbia Lancaster was an important political figure during the time that Washington was emerging as a State. He arrived in the Pacific Northwest in 1847, served as Chief Justice of the Provisional Supreme Court of Oregon, Joint Councilman to the Territorial Legislature, and the first delegate to Congress from the newly-formed Washington Territory. Lancaster's well-preserved 1850 mansion is now a private residence. The home is an excellent example of Greek Revival-style architecture and is listed on the National Register of Historic Places.

A number of historic buildings in Ridgefield and vicinity have been preserved and listed on the National Register of Historic Places. The **William Henry Shobert**

home, built in 1905 (621 Shobert Ln.), the old **Lambert School** (21814 NW 11th), and the **Sara Store** (17903 NW 41st Ave.) which was added to the register in 1995.

Lancaster House

Basalt Cobblestone Quarries District
Ridgefield National Wildlife Refuge, Carty Unit, NW Main and NW 291st Sts., Ridgefield (360) 887-4106

Portland's streets were paved with cobblestone quarried from here in the 1880s and 1890s. Today, the abandoned quarry is part of the 3,000-acre wildlife refuge where thousands of birds and waterfowl spend their winter months. The quarry district was added to the National Register of Historic Places in 1981.

VANCOUVER (van-KOO-ver)

Fort Vancouver Historic Marker
At the former tourist information center turnout on northbound I-5, 1/2-mile north of the Interstate Bridge, Vancouver (not presently accessible by motor vehicle)

"Hudson's Bay Company established Fort Vancouver in 1824 within the area of present-day Vancouver, 83 nautical miles from the Pacific Ocean. Forty wooden buildings were enclosed within a 20-foot log palisade. Until the treaty of 1846 set the international boundary at the 49th parallel, this fort supplied Hudson's Bay Company posts west of the Rocky Mountains. The fort became part of the U.S. military system in 1848 as Columbia Barracks, later changed to Vancouver Barracks. Vancouver is recognized as the oldest settlement in the state."

Fort Vancouver National Historic Site
Visitor Center, 1501 E. Evergreen Blvd., Vancouver (360) 696-7655

From 1824 to 1848, Fort Vancouver was the Hudson's Bay Company headquarters and main post for its vast Pacific Northwest fur-trading empire. Fur brigades, 50 to 200 strong were dispatched from here with supplies for their year-long beaver trapping expeditions. Fort Vancouver was run by Chief Factor John McLoughlin, who made it the region's most important social, cultural and political center. Although the British wanted McLoughlin to keep the Americans from settling in the territory, he befriended them. Then, in 1846 when the U.S. and Canadian boundary was established north of here, McLoughlin retired, moved to Oregon City, Oregon and became an American Citizen.

Hudson's Bay Company moved out in 1860 and by 1866 fires had destroyed all the original buildings. Excavation of the site produced more than a million artifacts which aided researchers and historians when they began reconstructing the fort in 1966. The stockade walls, bastion, chief factor's residence, blacksmith shop, bakery and other buildings within the partially reconstructed fort have been authentically rebuilt at their original locations. Docents in period costume demonstrate pioneer crafts in the bakery and blacksmith shop. Outside the fort's main gate is an interpretive garden with examples of the types of seasonings and foods grown here by early settlers.

Fort Vancouver

Officers' Row Historic District
Between Fort Vancouver Way and East Reserve, Vancouver (360) 693-3103

Across from the Vancouver Barracks parade grounds are 21 homes of former post officers; the nation's largest assemblage of restored officers quarters on a single row. The houses, which are listed on the National Register of Historic Places, were constructed between 1849 and 1907 and reflect several architectural styles that were popular during that period. A Walking Tour of Officers' Row (guide available at the Grant or Marshall House) describes the special features or treatments to look for when viewing these homes.

Grant House
Grant House Folk Art Center & Cafe, 1101 Officers' Row, Vancouver
(360) 694-5252, Cafe (360) 699-1213

The first house erected on Officers' Row was built in 1849-50 for the post commander, Colonel Hathaway. A few years later, the two-story log building was covered with a clapboard siding and a double wrap-around veranda was added. Its original log walls can be seen on the north side of the building. Today, the home is called Grant House, in honor of President Ulysses S. Grant's visit here in 1879. Grant served as the post's quartermaster in 1852-53 while a Captain in the U.S. Army, but never lived in the house that now bears his name. Original and period furnishings and antiques fill the home.

Headquartered here is the **Grant House Folk Art Center** which celebrates the creative heritage of the region's early settlers and the officers and their families who lived on Officers' Row.

Grant House

Marshall House
1301 Officers' Row, Vancouver (360) 693-3103

General George C. Marshall lived in this grand 8,000-square-foot, 1886 Queen Anne Victorian-style home in 1936-37 when he served as Commander of the Department of the Columbia. Marshall was promoted to Army Chief of Staff in 1939 and then General of the Army (a five-star general) during World War II. After the war he was appointed special ambassador to China and served on the President's cabinet as Secretary of State and Secretary of Defense. In 1953, he earned the Nobel Peace Prize for fostering the European Recovery Program (best-known as the Marshall Plan) that promoted postwar economic recovery. The Marshall Home has been restored to its 1880s appearance and is open to the public.

Other homes on Officers' Row are privately owned and not open to the public but are identified by interpretive plaques.

Marshall House

Vancouver Barracks
Fort Vancouver Way, south of Evergreen Blvd., Vancouver

Camp Vancouver was established by the U.S. Army in 1848-49 on part of the grounds formally owned by the Hudson's Bay Company. Over the years it was renamed Columbia Barracks, Fort Vancouver and, in 1885, Vancouver Barracks. Initally, the presence of U.S. Army troops was needed to protect American interests and preserve the peace. As the population of the Northwest grew, so did the importance of this post. It became the regional command of the Army's Department of the Columbia; an area that consisted of Oregon, Washington, Alaska and most of

Idaho. Ulysses Grant, Phillip Sheridan, George Marshall and Omar Bradley are some of the better-known Army officers who served at this post.

Vancouver Barracks

Cannon Replica Project
Vancouver Barracks, Fort Vancouver Way, south of Evergreen Blvd., Vancouver

On a small plot of land, overlooking the parade ground, barracks and officers' row, is a monument to four soldiers buried in **Vancouver Barracks Cemetery**, the oldest active Army cemetery in the Pacific Northwest. All four men were awarded our Nation's highest military honor, the Congressional Medal of Honor, for their uncommon valor. The two cannon that flank the memorial are exact, non-firing, replicas of Napoleon light field cannon. They were constructed in 1990-92 as a Mountain View High School metalworking and woodworking class project and

placed here by Troop 328 Eagle Scouts. The cannon were dedicated to the memory of Medal of Honor winners: William McCammon, Civil War; James Hill and Moses Williams, Indian Campaigns; and Herman Pfisterer, Spanish-American War.

341

Medal of Honor Memorial

John Murdock Aviation Center (formerly the Pearson Air Museum)
1105 E. 5th St., Vancouver (360) 694-7026

Vintage operating aircraft and aviation artifacts are on display at this air museum which is located on Pearson Airpark, the oldest operating airfield in the United States. History of the airfield that witnessed its first dirigible landing in 1905 and first airplane flight six years later, is commemorated in this museum's exhibits.

Next to the Center is a monument to the three Russian aviators who made the first nonstop flight across the North Pole from Moscow, Russia to this field in 1937. To acknowledge their successful 63-hour flight, the pilot and crew of the Chkalov

Transpolar Flight were honored guests of General George Marshall at his home on Officers' Row. Dedicated in 1975, the **Soviet Trans-polar Memorial** is the first commemoration of Soviet achievement in the United States.

342

Jack Murdock Aviation Center

Clark County Historical Museum
1511 Main St., Vancouver (360) 695-4681

Within the walls of the city's 1909 red brick Carnegie Library building is the history of Clark County; a great place to start your exploration of the state's oldest non-Indian settlement. Relics, photographs, dioramas and documents exhibited here tell the story of Lewis' and Clark's exploration (Clark County was named for Captain William Clark); the highly-successful Fort Vancouver, built by the British in 1824-25; the history of the U.S. Army's Vancouver Barracks, a major influence in this area after the 1846 Treaty brought present-day Washington into the Oregon Territory; and the contribution pioneers made in the development of this region. Other featured exhibits include antique dolls, railroad memorabilia, and an 1890 country store and

doctor's office. Centuries before Lewis and Clark camped along the banks of the Columbia, Native Americans lived on this land. Their history is also recorded here in the artifacts housed in this museum of history.

Vancouver U.S.A. Heritage

Tours
Vancouver/Clark County Visitors and Convention Bureau, 404 E. 15th St.,
Suite 11, Vancouver (360) 693-1313

A guide to 36 places of historic interest in Vancouver and Clark County published
by the bureau highlights the region's most significant landmarks. Driving tours of
Vancouver's central park and historic downtown district, and outlying towns in
east and north Clark County are easy to follow, illustrated and descriptive.

House of Providence
Providence Academy, 400 E. Evergreen Blvd., Vancouver

The largest brick building erected north of San Francisco wasn't designed by a pre-
eminent architectural firm. It was Mother Joseph, a Catholic nun of the Sisters of

Charity of Providence, who
was responsible for the design
and construction of Providence
Academy for Young Ladies in
1873. This was the first
permanent Catholic school in
the Northwest and the first
hospital, orphanage and
convent in Clark County. More
than 300,000 bricks from the
city's Hidden brick factory
were used in its construction.
In 1969, Robert Hidden,
grandson of Lowell Hidden
who built the brick factory in
1871, purchased the Academy
to save it from destruction and
converted it into retail shops
and a restaurant. The Academy
is listed on the National
Register of Historic Places.

The Hidden House
100-110 W. 13th St., (360) 693-1417 or (360) 696-2847

Was it bricks from Lowell Hidden's factory that turned Mother Joseph's dream of building Providence Academy into reality, or was it her dream that encouraged Hidden to build the factory? The answer can be found inside Lowell Hidden's 1885 home, which is now open to the public and serves as a gift shop, tea room and restaurant.

Mother Joseph Statue
In the courtyard of Vancouver's City Hall, 210 E. 13th St., Vancouver
(360) 696-8121

Fr. Blanchet called Mother Joseph, a French-Canadian nun, and four other sisters of her order to Fort Vancouver in 1856. In the ensuing years Mother Joseph's work impacted a vast area of the Pacific Northwest. In 1873, using the skills she learned from her father, Mother Joseph designed and built Providence Academy, at that time the largest structure north of San Francisco. Then, Mother Joseph traveled throughout the Northwest on horseback visiting remote mining and logging camps to raise funds to build other charitable institutions. She's credited with the construction of eleven hospitals, seven academies, five schools, and two orphanages. In addition, Mother Joseph helped build Vancouver's St. James Catholic Church, the oldest Roman Catholic congregation in the state. For her architectural accomplishments, she was designated First Architect in the Pacific Northwest by

the American Institute of Architects.

A century ago, every state in the Union was invited to send a statue of their two most inspirational people to the U.S. Capitol for display in Statuary Hall. The State of Washington selected Marcus Whitman and Mother Joseph.

Old Apple Tree,
Marine Park, Columbia Way, east of I-5, Vancouver (360) 696-8173

Dr. John McLoughlin, chief factor at Fort Vancouver, planted appleseeds he received from London in 1826. One of the seedlings he nurtured still bears fruit and is considered the oldest living thing planted by man west of the Rocky Mountains.

Kaiser Shipyard Memorial
Marine Park, Columbia Way, east of I-5, Vancouver (360) 696-8173

During World War II, thousands of men and women worked in Vancouver's shipyards. This memorial, viewing tower and intrepretive center was built to honor them, and industrialist Henry J. Kaiser, for the contribution they made to bring an end to the war that ravaged Europe and the Pacific for five years.

Slocum House
Esther Short Park
605 Esther St., Columbia and W. 8th Sts., Vancouver

The Joint Ownership Treaty of 1846 led to many disputed land claims between American and British settlers, the Hudson's Bay Company and St. James Mission. Amos and Esther Short, the first Americans to file a land claim in the area were burned-out three times and driven from the state. The Shorts returned and fought for their legal claim. In 1857, Mrs. Short donated five acres of their land claim to be used as a community park and public square. That park, named in honor of Esther Short remains the oldest city park west of the Mississippi. The original disputed land claim was awarded to the Short's ten children several years after their parent's death.

One of the city's first mansions, the 1867 Slocum House, was relocated here in 1966 from the residential section of Old Vancouver. Charles Slocum, a leading Vancouver merchant, built this Italianate villa to resemble their family home in Rhode Island. The home, which is listed on the National Register of Historic Places, is the last house remaining from that mid-1800s neighborhood. The home is now used as a community theatre.

Slocum House, Esther Short Park

Saint James Catholic Church
218 W. 12th St., Vancouver (360) 693-3052

With help from Mother Joseph, St. James Roman Catholic Church, the first Victorian Gothic Revival-style church in Washington Territory, was constructed at this site in 1885. A 150-foot bell tower with twin 80-foot towers on each side are two features that make this majestic structure one of the city's finest. Locally-fired brick from the Hidden brick factory was used in the construction of this masonry cathedral; the same brick used by Mother Joseph to build Providence Academy 12 years earlier. St. James is listed on the National Register of Historic Places and its Roman Catholic congregation is the oldest in the state.

347

Covington House
Leverich Park, 4201 Main St., Vancouver   (360) 695-6750 or (360) 695-4875

Richard and Anne Covington emigrated from London in 1846 to teach children of the Hudson's Bay Company employees at Fort Vancouver. In 1848 they built this hand-hewn log cabin at a site near Orchard (about five miles northeast of here). In the early 1850s the Covingtons operated a boarding school from their home; making it the oldest school building in Clark County. Young officers from Vancouver Barracks were often entertained by the Covingtons who had the region's only piano. (Their piano is exhibited at the Clark County Historical Museum.) The cabin, which is listed on the National Register of Historic Places, was moved here in 1931.

Vancouver Fire Department Museum
900 W. Evergreen Blvd., Vancouver (360) 696-8166

Vintage photographs and a restored Seagrave fire engine are featured in this fire-fighting museum.

WASHOUGAL (WAW-shoo-guhl)

Two Rivers Heritage Museum
One 16th St., Washougal (360) 835-8742

Nearly 3,000 years of Native American history has been uncovered by archaeological digs in this region. The museum, which is operated by the Camas-Washougal Historical Society, displays some of those findings. Stone tools, nearly six dozen Chinook Indian baskets, a pioneer exhibit, doll collection, glassware and farm tools

are featured. Information about the **Parkersville site** (Port of Camas/Washougal at the end of SE 9th), one of the oldest American settlements in the state, can be obtained from museum staff.

Washougal Woolen Mill
Pendleton Woolen Mills, 2 — 17th St., Washougal (360) 835-1118

Washougal Woolen Mill became a member of the Pendleton family of mills shortly after it opened in 1912. Since that time, virgin wool has been processed and woven into some of the world's finest fabric at this mill. Visitors to the mill can tour the facility, see the original mill buildings and powerhouse, and observe how wool is processed from dying to spinning and weaving to the final product.

Original Pendleton Woolen Mills Building

Mount Pleasant Grange Hall
Marble Road, just off Hwy. 14 at milepost 23, 6 miles east of Washougal

Agriculture gained prominence in Washington after the freezing winter of 1866-67, when thousands of cattle perished for lack of food. Hundreds of farmers moved to the state tripling the number of farms by 1870 (primarily in Eastern Washington). In 1873, the state's first Grange was organized. The Grange, for the most part, was a social and educational organization, but was politically active in the late 1870s. The Mt. Pleasant Grange is the oldest continuous operating Grange Hall in the state. A photographic history of this Grange's events and past officers is exhibited.

Mount Pleasant Grange Hall

YACOLT (YA-kawlt)

Pomeroy Living History Farm
20902 N.E. Lucia Falls Rd., Yacolt (360) 686-3537

Life on a farm in the 1920s, before rural electrification, is demonstrated for visitors to this, the Northwest's first living history farm. On open weekends (call for schedule) guests can be active participants; performing chores that were common activities on a typical farm. The 6-bedroom log house that E.C. Pomeroy and his son, Thomas, built in 1920 has been preserved. Their carriage house, pole shed, barn, granary, and a fully-equipped blacksmith shop are among the remaining out-buildings that can be toured. Horse-drawn farm implements and a large collection of farming and

logging tools is also displayed.

Sixty acres of the Pomeroy's 677-acre farm has been set aside as a living museum to preserve the past for the present to see. To further insure its preservation, the five generation Pomeroy farm has been placed on the National Register of Historic Places.

Cowlitz County

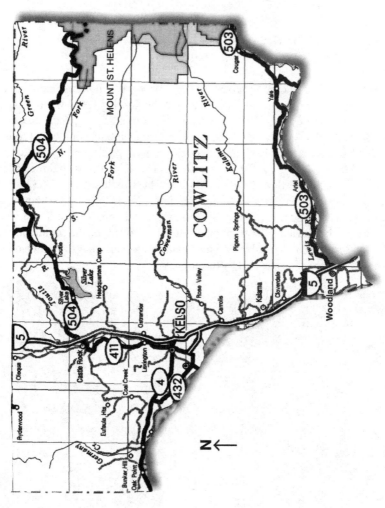

COWLITZ COUNTY

CASTLE ROCK

Castle Rock Exhibit Hall
147 Front Ave., NW, Castle Rock (360) 274-6603

The system of dikes built to protect the town from river floods couldn't stop the flow of mud and debris from cascading into the Cowlitz River when Mount St. Helens erupted in May, 1980. The river turned as thick as pancake batter. It overflowed its banks, covered the fairgrounds, local high school football and track fields, damaged or destroyed more than 200 homes, took out bridges and forever changed the city's history. This Exhibit Hall opened in 1990 with three galleries. The River Gallery is devoted to the history of the Cowlitz River. The Mountain Gallery tells the importance of Mount St. Helens to the local timber industry and features historic logging techniques, equipment and photos. Our Town Gallery dramatizes the impact of the eruption of Mount St. Helens on the community. One display (once taken on tour by the Smithsonian Museum) shows a portion of a tree that was sheared and shattered by the eruption.

Tree Sheared by Mount St. Helens Eruption, Castle Rock Exhibit Hall

Laughlin Round Barn
Cowlitz Round Barn
9240 Barnes Drive, Castle Rock   For information contact the Cowlitz Round Barn
Preservation Association, 405 Allen Street, Kelso

A "round" barn. It's a sight that's attracted visitors and tourists for years, for there's not many of them left in the United States. But, when Samuel Laughlin built his uniquely-designed barn in the late 1800s, it wasn't for the purpose of drawing crowds. The round design of the barn served a purpose. Its ground floor horse and cow stalls face inward for easier feeding. It also featured a system of horse-powered pulleys that were used to hoist hay to the loft for storage. The well-constructed barn has withstood the ravages of time and Mother Nature and has been recognized with a listing on the National Register of Historic Places.

COUGAR

Southern Gateway to Mt. Saint Helens
Hwy. 503, eastbound from I-5 at Woodland through Cougar to Mt. Saint Helens

Travelers can follow two state highways for a close-up view of Mt. Saint Helens: Hwy. 504 to the north, with its multi-million dollar visitor centers and Hwy. 503, the southern approach through the historic Lewis River Valley. Those who take Hwy. 503 may want to make a stop in Ariel, the town made famous by D.B. Cooper, or at Jack's Wildwood Inn and Ale House in Cougar for a view of logging antiques from the valley's early days. This southern road also leads to Ape Caves, the Trail of Two Forests and Lava Canyon. Adventurers who plan to scale the mountain can register and get a climbing permit at Jack's County Store in Ariel.

KALAMA (kuh-LAM-uh)

Totem Pole
Port of Kalama Marine Park, Exit 30 off I-5 to Geranium, Kalama

The world's tallest single-tree totem pole soars 140 feet from its base here in Marine Park. It was carved by Chief Laluska in memory of Janet Wineberg and dedicated in 1974. Native Indian legends and myths are portrayed in the symbols carved into this tree and replicate two totem poles that are displayed at the Royal Ontario Museum in Canada.

Base of World's Tallest Single-tree Totem Pole

Ezra Meeker's First Home Site
Oregon Trail Marker
Main St., Kalama

Ezra Meeker's passion for preservation of the Oregon Trail was unmatched by any other individual or organization of his time. In 1906, at the age of 76, Meeker set out on the Oregon Trail to retrace and mark the historic route between Washington and Nebraska. He made the trip in an ox-drawn wagon to draw attention to the

need to preserve this important pioneer trail. During the next 17 years he made three more trips including one by car and one in an open cockpit airplane. Eight years after he made his last trip, the Oregon Trail was designated a National Historic Highway. Meeker's first home site is located a short distance from this marker.

Saint Joseph's Church
Elm and Fourth Sts., Kalama   Chamber of Commerce (360) 673-6299

Northern Pacific Railway chose the city of Kalama as a terminus for its northern line in 1871. That decision brought a new importance to the city and helped spark

its growth. Today, Kalama is one of the largest dry-bulk tonnage ports on the West Coast. Many of the town's fine old homes and buildings are nestled in the hillside overlooking the Columbia River. Among them is the historic 1909 wood-frame Saint Joseph's Catholic Church, which is listed on the State Heritage Register. It replaced the church that was originally erected on this site in 1876.

Kalama boasts one of the largest selection of antique shops in the state. Numerous antique dealers can be found in the business district along the city's First Street and some of its adjacent streets.

KELSO

Cowlitz County Historical Museum
405 Allen St., Kelso (360) 577-3119

The city of Kelso owes much of its success to forward-thinking Peter Crawford, an emigrant from Scotland, who settled here in 1847 and platted the town around the Cowlitz River. Water transportation to inland ports and access to the Pacific Ocean via the Columbia River benefited the town's early growth. The story of how the settlement grew to become the county seat is told in the museum's exhibits. Cowlitz and Chinook Indian artifacts, the log cabin Ben Beighle built in the Toutle River Valley in 1884, remnants of the Oregon Trail, pioneer logging tools, and a replica steamboat dock and railroad depot are some of the museum's permanent exhibits. A 1916 Oregon Trail marker originally placed on Pacific Avenue near the Cowlitz River is displayed in the museum's parking lot.

Antique Truck Exhibit, Cowlitz County Historical Museum

Monticello Convention Site
Center of the Cowlitz River, Kelso

Members of the Monticello Convention met here in 1852 to petition Congress to establish Washington Territory from that portion of the Oregon Territory north of the Columbia River. Through the efforts of this Convention, and the Cowlitz Conventions that also petitioned Congress in 1851 and 1852, Washington Territory was created. The actual location of Monticello was virtually washed away during the floods of 1866-67. The site of this historic meeting is commemorated by the State and listed on the State Heritage Register.

Nat Smith House
110 W. Grant St., Kelso

Former steamboat captain and sawmill owner, Nat Smith, built this Victorian-style home around 1885 on part of the Seth Catlin land claim. In later years Smith's home was owned by Tom Fisk, an attorney who acquired purchase options on behalf of R.A. Long for all the land that is now the city of Longview. The Smith home is listed on the National Register of Historic Places.

Catlin Cemetery
Columbia Heights Rd. and Fishers Ln, Kelso

This hillside cemetery is the final resting place for many Kelso pioneers. Among those interned here are some of the early settlers who were members of the 1852 Monticello Convention. A guide to the headstones is available from the Cowlitz County Historical Museum.

First Methodist Church
Kelso United Methodist Church
206 Cowlitz Way, Kelso (360) 423-7480

Kelso's first church was built at this site in 1888-89 as the First Methodist Church. A brick building replaced the original structure in 1929 and was rebuilt again after a fire in 1938.

LONGVIEW

Longview Historic Walking Tour of the Civic Center Historic District
Bounded by Maple, 16th Hemlock and 18th, guide available from the Longview Chamber of Commerce, 1563 Olympia Way (360) 423-8400 and the City Planning & Building Department, 1525 Broadway, Longview (360) 577-3330

The Long-Bell Lumber Company came to this region from Kansas City, MO in the early part of the twentieth century in search of Douglas Fir to replace its depleted supply of Texas and Louisiana Southern Pine. Initially, 70,000 acres of timber tracts and 3,400 acres of the valley floor were purchased. Eventually, 14,000 acres, nearly the entire valley floor, was acquired and diked to prevent flooding. In the early 1920s the city of Longview was founded as one of the first planned cities in the West. R.A. Long Park, at the heart of the Civic Center, was the focal point of the new city. Surrounding the park is: the 1926 library, a personal gift from Robert Long, Chairman of the Long-Bell Lumber Company; the 1923 Georgian Revival-style Monticello Hotel; and the post office, built as a WPA project during the Great Depression. The park, hotel, post office and library are listed on the National Register of Historic Places. Several early downtown buildings that are also listed on the Longview and National Register of Historic Places are included in the walking tour guide.

In the lobby of the Monticello Hotel are original John Knowles Oil Paintings depicting Northwest settlement scenes. A Long-Bell, **1924 Shay Locomotive**, typical of the type used in logging the hills and back country of the Pacific Northwest, is exhibited on the west lawn of the library. An interpretive exhibit, surrounding the Long-Bell Steam Whistle in front of the 1300 block of Commerce, tells about the history of Longview. Although not historic, the "Nutty Narrows Squirrel Bridge" that spans Olympia Way near the northwest corner of the Civic Center, has become a popular local attraction since its appearance on "Ripley's Believe It or Not."

The Columbia River Mercantile (The Merk)
Commerce and Broadway, Longview (360) 636-0993

The former 1923 Long-Bell Lumber Company Store and office building has been completely restored and now houses retail stores and offices. Located in the historic downtown district, the Merk features a reading room where historic Long-Bell documents and photos of the world's largest lumber mill are displayed. A guide for touring the Merk is provided.

"The Merk," Courtesy of the City of Longview,
Planning and Building Department

Columbia Theater
Columbia Theater for the Performing Arts, 1231 Vandercook Way, Longview
(360) 423-1011

Restoration has returned this famous city landmark to its original splendor replete
with chandeliers and intricate ornamentation and grillwork. Appearing on stage
during the early days of this 1,000-seat theater were such well-known entertainers
as: John Philip Sousa and his band, Edgar Bergen and Charlie McCarthy, and
Ginger Rogers. The former 1925 Italian Renaissance-style vaudeville and movie
theater now features plays, concerts and community events. Its upstairs apartments
have also been remodeled and are now home to senior citizens.

MOUNT ST. HELENS MONUMENT

Mount St. Helens Visitor Center at Silver Lake
Spirit Lake Memorial Hwy. (Hwy. 504), 5 miles east of Castle Rock on the shores
of Silver Lake

The events that led to the May, 1980 eruption of Mount St. Helens is presented in
this National Forest Service Visitor Center. The Center was built above the Toutle
River Valley, one of the areas most affected by the explosion and the mud flows that
followed. Theater presentations and interpretive exhibits prepare visitors for their
visit to the Monument. Visitors can walk down inside a scale model of the Mount
St. Helens and experience, through special effects, what it would be like to be
inside an active volcano. The Center's nature trail offers an interesting side-trip to
the Silver Lake wetlands where waterfowl and wildlife can be seen in their natural
habitat.

Sediment Retention Structure
Sediment Dam Rd., exit at mile post 21 off Hwy. 504 (Spirit Lake Memorial Hwy.)
at the North Fork of the Toutle River about half-way between Castle Rock and the
Coldwater Ridge Visitor Center

Six years after the eruption of Mount St. Helens, the U.S. Army Corps of Engineers
began building a Sediment Retention Structure (SRS) to stop sediment from moving
downstream and causing navigation problems. SRS contains outlets that permit
water and fish to pass, but traps the sediment. It's estimated that by the year 2035,
258 million cubic yards of sand, gravel and sediment will be collected behind the
184-foot embankment. To get a sense of the tranquil valley that existed before the

eruption, follow the one mile, tree-lined trail that leads from the observation station to the embankment where sediment and debris collect. For many visitors, they'll long-remember that peaceful hike among the Douglas fir and alder trees.

Sediment Retention Structure

Hoffstadt Bluffs Visitor Center
Hwy. 504 at milepost 27

Panoramic views of the Toutle River Valley and Mount St. Helens are enjoyed by tourists who stop at this rest area and visitors center. The Center doesn't feature many exhibits, but offers the only full-service restaurant in the area. Opened 15 years after the eruption of Mount St. Helens, the Center overlooks what is considered the blast zone. As nature heals itself, the valley floor once again attracts herds of Roosevelt Elk and other wildlife that can be seen from the Center's wrap-around viewing deck. Helicopter rides and horse-drawn wagon tours of the adjacent elk refuge begin at the Center.

Mount St. Helens Forest Learning Center
Hwy. 504 at milepost 33, about halfway between the Sediment Retention Structure and the Coldwater Ridge Visitor Center

The history of Mount St. Helens before, during and following the May, 1980 eruption is presented in graphic detail that flirts with reality. Once inside the Center, visitors find themselves in an old-growth forest, surrounded by the sights and sounds of forest dwellers; from squirrels to a full-size elk. An overturned jeep, salvaged from the blast area, sits in the center of the eruption chamber where details of the explosion comes to life. Salvage activity in the months following the eruption and reforestation efforts that resulted in millions of trees being replanted is also exhibited.

Coldwater Ridge Visitor Center
Winds of Change Interpretive Trail
43 miles east of Castle Rock on Hwy. 504

The awesome power of nature, and its ability to heal itself can be observed at this visitor center. Mount St. Helens, with more than 1,300 feet of its peak blown-off and mud flows that brought destruction to everything in its path can be viewed from here. Visitors can also see the rebirth of plants, the return of deer and Roosevelt elk, and the newly-formed Coldwater Lake. Interactive exhibits, interpretive programs and the Winds of Change Interpretive Trail provide a wealth of visitor information.

Information about the formation of Coldwater Lake is available at the recreation area, 2 miles east of the Visitor Center. A boardwalk interpretive trail, "Birth of a Lake" and "Discovery Area" were opened to visitors in 1994.

Johnston Ridge Observatory
54 miles east of Castle Rock at the end of Hwy. 504

Visitors who want the closest, unobstructed view of Mount St. Helens' crater without hiking the Boundary Trail should drive to this western-most observation point. From the hillside observatory the view is overwhelming. Not only is the crater visible, but visitors can also see the 1,000-foot lava dome that was formed inside the crater by eruptions that occurred during the first six years after the eruption. To get the most from this experience, watch the 16-minute film that uses computerized animation and special effects to re-create the eruption on a 33-foot-wide screen. At the end of the film, the screen rises to reveal Mount St. Helens through the observatory's glass windows.

STELLA

Stella Historical Museum
Hwy. 4, 10 miles west of Longview, Stella (360) 423-8663

Stella was a busy port community on the Columbia River during the late 1800s and early twentieth century. Abundant salmon could be found in the waters near the mouth of Germany Creek, but the town was better-known for its massive "cigar-shaped rafts," some as large as 40,000 square feet, that were towed to the Pacific Ocean and used to transport logs south to San Francisco and San Diego. Two restored buildings are part of the museum complex: the 1907 blacksmith shop, that sits at its original site; and an 1871 home/post office that was relocated here. Photographs, relics from the region's logging and fishing industries, blacksmith tools and housewares are featured in this new museum's growing collection.

Stella Historical Museum

WOODLAND

Hulda Klager Lilac Gardens
115 S. Pekin Rd., Woodland (360) 225-8996

Hulda Klager's love for flowers led friends to give her a book on the American plant breeder, Luther Burbank. It sparked her imagination and her career as a hybridizer. At first she experimented with apples. She wanted a bigger apple so fewer had to be peeled to make a pie. In 1905, after succeeding with apples, she began working with lilacs. During the next 55 years, Mrs. Klager introduced 250 varieties. Her life's work with lilacs earned her many honors from local, state and national organizations. While spring is the best time to view her botanical gardens, the grounds are always open to the public during daylight hours.

Hulda Klager's restored hundred-year-old home has been designated a National Historic Site and is open to the public for two weeks every spring during the city's annual Lilac Festival. Her fine collection of antique dolls and period furnishings can be seen at that time.

Hulda Klager Lilac Gardens

Lewis County

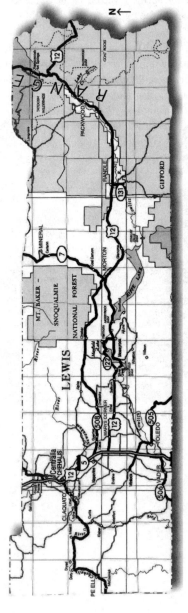

LEWIS COUNTY

CENTRALIA

Downtown Centralia Historic Murals
Area bounded by Maple, Rock, Cherry and Tower Sts., Centralia Guide available from the Twin Cities Chamber of Commerce, 500 NW Chamber Way, Chehalis (360) 748-8885

Sixteen outdoor wall murals depict the founding of the region and its transportation, industry and pioneers. Artists based their paintings on historic photographs from public and private collections. A description of each mural and its location is given in the Chamber's guide.

Mural of Centralia's Founder, George Washington On Pearl, between Main and Pine

George Washington Park
On Locust between Main and Pearl Sts., Centralia

A monument to Centralia's founder, George Washington, is the centerpiece of this memorial park. Washington, a freed slave, donated land for the city that is now Centralia. Throughout his life, Washington was a generous man; helping others who immigrated to this new land, and those who faced hardships once they arrived. His home became a way-station for many travelers, although anti-black laws prevented him from owning the land he farmed. His kindness to others was rewarded by the Oregon and Washington territorial legislatures and by an Act of Congress, which eventually granted him ownership of his land. His mural can be seen on Pearl between Main and Pine Sts.

Monument to Centralia's Founder, George Washington, near the city's Carnegie Library

Olympic Club Saloon
112 N. Tower St., Centralia (360) 736-5164

Attention to detail by the artists and craftsmen who worked to restore the interior of this turn-of-the-century establishment resulted in the rebirth of one of Downtown Centralia's famous landmarks. The saloon's original bar and large potbellied stove, an upstairs eatery overlooking the card room, and a dozen old-fashioned pool tables illuminated by early 1900s hanging lamps, are some of this establishment's more

notable features. Every element, from the beveled-glass entry doors to hand-painted wall stencils, have been authentically restored by the club's present owners, McMenamins Pubs & Breweries. Olympic Club has been listed on the National Register of Historic Places since 1980.

366

Centralia Massacre Site
Former IWW (Industrial Workers of the World) Hall
807 N. Tower St., Centralia

An Armistice Day parade commemorating the first anniversary of the end of World War I turned violent when four members of the American Legion broke ranks and raided the IWW (Wobblies) Hall. Three Legionnaires were killed at the Hall; another mortally wounded while chasing Wesley Everest who fled from the Hall. Everest and eleven other Wobblies were jailed. Vigilantes broke into the jail, seized Everest and lynched him from the Mellen Street Bridge. This black day in the state's labor history is marked at two sites in the city. Wesley Everest's gravesite is located at Sticklin Greenwood Memorial Park, 1905 Johnson Road, and is listed on the National Register of Historic Places. A monument to the fallen Legionnaires was erected in George Washington Park at Main and Pearl streets.

Borst Home
South end of Borst Park, 302 Bryden Ave., Centralia (360) 330-7688

Joseph Borst crossed the Great Plains from New York in 1846 to homestead 320 acres on the north side of the Chehalis River. During the 1855 Indian War, Joseph and his wife, Mary, moved to Fort Henness for safety. Later they lived in the blockhouse that now stands in Borst Park. Borst's home, which he erected in the early 1860s, was not only the finest in the region; it was built to last. Lumber came from Tumwater and was dried and seasoned for a year. Board ends were dipped in white lead to harden and waterproof them. Then wooden pegs were used to hold every board in place. Borst's well-constructed home is listed on the National Register of Historic Places.

Five of the Borst's young children (infant to 3 years old) were once buried in a small cemetery plot located just north east of their home. Wooden crosses identify the location of the original gravesites.

1916, the Daughters of the American Revolution placed a marker identifying a section of the Oregon Trail that passed by the Borst's home.

367

Borst Home

Borst Blockhouse
Borst Park, Harrison and Belmont, Centralia (360) 330-7688

Nestled among towering fir trees in this historic park is one of many blockhouses built in Western Washington during the 1855-56 Indian Wars. Joseph Borst built this blockhouse in 1855 near the confluence of the Skookumchuck and Chehalis Rivers. Flood waters later forced its relocation to this site. The well-preserved structure is good example of the precautions taken by these early settlers to protect their families during this period of unrest. Tours of the blockhouse interior are by appointment only.

CHEHALIS (chuh-HAY-lis)

Lewis County Historical Museum
599 NW Front St., Chehalis (360) 748-0831

The settlement that would eventually become the city of Chehalis and the seat of Lewis County started around a warehouse along the Northern Pacific tracks in 1873. Residents first called their town Saundersville (the town was built on Schuyler Saunders' donation claim), but renamed Chehalis in 1879. In 1912, Burlington

Northern constructed this 13,000 square-foot, Mission Revival-style, red brick depot. Today, the old depot serves as the county museum. It contains several galleries featuring exhibits of local historical significance, dioramas, and a replica general store, blacksmith shop, schoolroom, turn-of-the-century parlor, and railroad office. The region's logging, farming and mining history is also displayed. Chehalis Indian artifacts, pioneer relics, and an extensive collection of books, photographs and newspapers is preserved here. The depot is listed on the National Register of Historic Places.

Obadiah McFadden House
475 SW Chehalis Ave., Chehalis (360) 748-0831

Schuyler Saunders, on whose donation land claim Chehalis was founded, also built this two-story log home for the first Associate Justice in Washington Territory, Obadiah McFadden. McFadden also served in the state legislature, was a delegate to the U.S. Congress and was appointed Chief Justice of the territory. His 1859 home, which is listed on the National Register of Historic Places, is the city's oldest residence and the oldest continuously occupied home in the state.

Westminster Presbyterian Church
349 N. Market Blvd., Chehalis (360) 748-0091

The oldest Christian Church in the Chehalis Valley was organized during the 1855 Indian Wars, but it would be 27 years before they erected their first building (on State near Prindle). The present site was purchased in 1897; the "new" church dedicated in 1908. In succeeding years the church has been remodeled, enlarged and added on to, but still retains its original architectural style. One of the church's interesting features is the design of the beams that support the Sanctuary ceiling; they resemble a Greek cross. Two stained glass windows and the bell came from the 1882 State Street church building. On display is the foot-pumped organ that came from the 1882 church and the original pulpit Bible. Sunday services were cancelled only once in the history of the church. That was in 1980 when Mount St. Helens erupted and Chehalis was covered with a layer of ash.

Westminster Presbyterian Church,
Courtesy of Westminster Presbyterian Church

Pennsylvania Avenue - West Side Historic District
Primarily along Pennsylvania and St. Helens Aves., Chehalis (360) 748-0831

The homes that line the streets in this historic district were built in the late nineteenth and early twentieth centuries for the city's most prominent families. The "father of Chehalis," William West, who brought the railroad and County seat here and Noah Coffman, founder of the bank and land development company that shaped the town, are two of the city's elite who lived here. Most of the homes in this district, which is listed on the National Register of Historic Places, were constructed between 1900 and 1920 using variations of the popular Craftsman style. A guide to the homes in this district is available from the Lewis County Historical Museum.

McKinley Stump
Chehalis Recreation Park, 401 SW 14th St., Chehalis (360) 748-0271831

A giant 300-foot Douglas Fir was felled near Pe Ell in 1901 and its stump moved to Market Street in Chehalis for a reception in honor of President McKinley. The stump, which represented the region's rich lumbering industry, became a source of community pride. A number of visiting dignitaries, including President Theodore Roosevelt, used this natural stage to address local citizens. Today, the stump is preserved in an enclosed gazebo at this city park.

McKinley Stump

CLAQUATO (KLA-Kwa-toh)

Claquato Historic Marker
Claquato Rd., 2 miles west of Chehalis on Hwy. 6 (turn right on Chilvers Rd.)

"This pioneer town founded in 1853 on the donation claim of Louis H. Davis once was the county seat and an important stop-off for travelers between the Columbia River and Puget Sound. The sturdy little church built in 1858 with hand-forged nails and lumber sawed in a water-powered mill doubled as a school, Claquato Academy. The bronze bell in the belfry came around Cape Horn from Boston in 1857. In the 1870s, when the railroad by-passed Claquato, most of the town moved 3 miles east to Chehalis."

Claquato Church
Water St. off Chilvers Rd., near entrance to Claquato Cemetery, 2 miles west of Chehalis via Hwy. 6, Claquato (360) 748-0831 (Lewis County Community Services)

The founder of Claquato, Louis Davis, built a whip-saw type sawmill in 1857 and donated the mill's first lumber for construction of this church. The town's blacksmith, A.F. Gordon forged the squared-head nails. John Clinger, Mrs. Davis' brother, designed the church, made the door and window casings and built the unusual "crown of thorns" steeple. In the 1950s, Chehalis American Legion Post No. 22 authentically restored the 1858 church and rededicated it as a memorial to the

pioneers of Lewis County. Claquato Church was listed on the National Register of Historic Places in 1973 and is the oldest remaining Protestant Church in the Pacific Northwest still standing on its original location in its original structural form.

Claquato Church

Pioneer Fir
Claquato Cemetery, Water St. entrance, Claquato

In the early 1850s, Claquato was the largest community between the Columbia River and the capital city of Olympia. As a waystation on this overland route, travelers who couldn't afford or find room in one of the town's hotels camped under this giant fir tree. This tree, and the 1858 church are all that remain of the original pioneer town of Claquato.

MARY'S CORNER

John R. Jackson House State Park
Hwy. 14, 2 miles east of I-5, just south of Mary's Corner. For information and operating hours contact Lewis & Clark State Park, 4583 Jackson Hwy., Winlock (360) 864-2643

When you visit John and Matilda's 1845 log cabin today, it doesn't seem that such a small, unimposing building could have played a significant role in the development of the Territory. John, an English immigrant, was one of the first settlers north of the Columbia. He served as territorial sheriff, merchant, innkeeper, postmaster and judge. His modest cabin provided shelter for emigrants traveling the Oregon trail and for dignitaries such as Governor Stevens and Generals Grant, McClelland and Sheridan. The first district court north of the Columbia also convened here. Jackson helped form Washington Territory and was a representative in the first territorial legislature. Period furnishings, household items, and hand tools are preserved within this historic home.

John R. Jackson House

MINERAL

Mineral Lake Lodge
195 Mineral Hill Rd., 15 miles southeast of Mt. Rainier near Mineral Lake
(360) 492-5751

Few log structures match the grandeur of Mineral Lake Lodge. The 28-room, National Park-style inn was built by Scandinavians in 1906 as a resort for Tacoma's more affluent vacationers. It was one of the first resorts built in the area, and one of the largest all-log buildings west of the Mississippi. The lodge, which is listed on the National Register of Historic Places, is now a private residence, but is available for small parties and receptions.

MORTON

Old Settlers Memorial Museum
Gust Backstrom City Park, Hwy. 508, Morton (360) 496-5613

While the first to settle here cleared the land of trees, their interest wasn't in the value of the timber, but in the land they could farm. Arrival of the Tacoma Eastern Railroad in the early 1900s changed Morton to a logging and rail center by affording access to the region's rich timberlands. The community's ties to logging is celebrated every August when the city hosts its Logger's Jubilee; the granddaddy of all logging events. Displays of early logging equipment, historic photographs and artifacts are featured.

Old Settlers Memorial Museum

MOUNT ST. HELENS
Woods Creek Information Station
6 miles south of Randle on Forest Road 25

At this northern-most entrance to Mount St. Helens Monument, visitors can get information about places to see in the northeast section of the Monument. Adjacent to this information station is the Woods Creek Watchable Wildlife Trail, a one-mile nature trail through the area's woods and meadows. Nearby, at the Iron Creek Picnic Area, an easy half-mile trail can be followed through an ancient forest of old-growth trees. At Quartz Creek Big Tree Trail, enormous Douglas fir trees, some 10 feet in diameter and 750 years old, stand in a lush forest just one mile from where 150,000 acres of privately-owned, state and national forests were destroyed in the May, 1980 eruption of Mount St. Helens.

Windy Ridge Viewpoint, the closest eastern point to the volcano's crater accessible by car, is about an hour's drive from this Center.

PACKWOOD

Packwood Hotel
U.S. 12, Packwood

In the northeastern sector of the Gifford Pinchot National Forest is the community of Packwood, named for William Packwood, an explorer, trailblazer and pioneer who discovered coal in this region. Packwood Hotel was built by the Walter Combs' family in 1911, using locally milled lumber, and has been in continuous operation since its opening. Period and antique furnishings are featured in the hotel's guest rooms.

PE ELL (pee-EL)

Holy Cross Polish National Catholic Church
Third and Queen, Pe Ell

Polish settlers in the Pe Ell area built this Catholic Church from locally milled material in 1916. Although the small community already had a Roman Catholic Church (organized in 1892), the Polish community wanted a church where services could be conducted in their native tongue. Holy Cross is listed on the National Register of Historic Places.

RANDLE

"Some day I'm gon'a get me a piece of that there bottom land," said Sgt. Alvin York, the Tennessee back-woods farmer who became America's most decorated hero of WWI. York got his "bottom land" in Tennessee as a gift from the people of that great state, but many of his fellow Tennesseans had to make their way here to Randle's fertile Big Bottom country to get their "bottom land." Today, Randle serves as gateway to Mount St. Helen's Windy Ridge, the closest road to the east side of the volcano's crater that's accessible by passenger car.

TOLEDO

Cowlitz Landing Historic Marker
In mobile home sales lot on the frontage road adjacent to the northbound lanes of I-5 near the junction with Hwy. 506

"At this place, Hudson's Bay Company traders from Puget Sound loaded firs in canoes for transport to the Columbia River, in the years 1836-1846. Then American settlers came up the river, by bateau, barge and raft. A landing was built on the donation claim of F.A. Clarke, and a hotel on the adjoining land of E.D. Warbuss. American settlers held a convention here in 1851 and petitioned for a new U.S. Territory north of the Columbia River. Steamboats came in 1858. They served the Cowlitz Valley until 1917."

Cowlitz Mission Historic Marker
2½ miles northeast of Toledo on Jackson Hwy. at Spenser Rd.

"Venturesome frontiersmen, lured from civilization to the Oregon Country by the lucrative fur trade, so strongly besought leadership in religious worship for themselves and their families that Father Blanchet and Father Demers made the perilous westward journey and in 1838 founded here the Cowlitz Mission. This oldest mission in the Northwest now stands where then, in rude dwellings, the beneficent Fathers held service for the pioneers and with simple picture writings, not unlike their own, taught the Indians religious history and the blessings of devotion to the Great Spirit."

Cowlitz Mission
St. Francis Xavier Mission
139 Spenser Rd., one mile south of Jackson Hwy., 2 miles northeast of Toledo
(360) 864-4126 or (888) 846-2374

Fires took their toll on the first four missions built here. The first mission building, a log structure, was constructed in the late 1830s under the supervision of Fr. Blanchet, the first archbishop of the Pacific Northwest, and Father Demers who would become the first archbishop on Vancouver Island. When the first mission was built, it earned the distinction of being the first Catholic church in the state and the oldest mission in the Northwest. In 1932, St. Francis Xavier Mission was constructed of stone at the original mission site.

A Catholic Ladder, used by Fr. Blanchet in 1842 to teach the region's Native Americans the main truths of the Catholic faith, has been preserved on the grounds next to the church.

St. Francis Xavier Mission

Catholic Ladder at St. Francis Xavier Mission

VADER (VAY-der)

Ben Olson House
1026 "D" St., Vader (360) 295-3808

At the turn-of-the-century, Vader was a thriving community. Lumber, and related industry made it Southwestern Washington's commercial hub. Most of the city's business and industry is gone, but the beautiful 1903 Queen Anne-style Victorian home of Ben Olson remains. Olson was the president of Still Water Logging and Lumber Company, the city's largest. The fully-restored 12-room home features a corner tower and wrap-around porch. The privately-owned home is listed on the National Register of Historic Places and is shown by advance appointment only.

Ben Olson House

Little Falls Jail
"A" St. between 5th and 6th Sts., Vader (360) 748-0831

Between 1896 and 1950 this building served the city of Vader (formerly Little Falls) as both city hall and jail. If restoration efforts prove successful, the jail will be one of the few early jails remaining in the state.

Little Falls Jail

Pacific County

PACIFIC COUNTY

BRUCEPORT

Bruceville-Bruceport Historic Marker

Two miles west of South Bend on the north side of U.S. 101 overlooking Willapa Bay, Bruceport

"The deserted site of a famous pioneer village, once a county seat, is westward on Willapa Bay, formerly called Shoalwater Bay. The crew of the oyster schooner "Robert Bruce" settled here in December 1851, after that craft had burned. Crewmen built cabins, filed land claims, and named the settlement "Bruceville." It was changed to "Bruceport" in 1854. This site recalls the lively oyster industry of 1851-1880, when enormous quantities of native oysters were gathered by local Indians for San Francisco bound schooners."

CHINOOK (shi-NOOK)

Washington State's First Salmon Hatchery
Sea Resources
One mile off U.S. 101, Chinook

The first state-run salmon hatchery was established at this site in 1893 and is now operated by Sea Resources, a non-profit corporation. Local school children are bussed to the hatchery on field trips to learn about the role hatcheries play in preserving this precious resource.

Columbia River Historic Marker
On U.S. 101, 2 miles west of Astoria Bridge, Chinook

"Here the mighty Columbia River ends its journey and flows into the Pacific Ocean. Although all others doubted this river's existence, the American explorer, Captain Robert Gray, attempted to enter its mouth but was repelled by the current until, on May 11, 1772, with all sails set to a favorable wind, he boldly raced his ship "Columbia" through the breakers and over the perilous bar. The discovery of this river, named for his vessel, proved of great value to the United States in establishing its claim to the Pacific Northwest.

Chinook Point National Historic Landmark
On U.S. 101, 5 miles southeast of Fort Columbia State Park, Chinook

Captain Robert Gray's entry into the Columbia River from the Pacific Ocean in 1792 is commemorated at this site. It was on Captain Gray's second journey to the Pacific Northwest that he was able to successfully navigate his ship into the mouth of the Columbia River. Gray's discovery was documented by Captain George Vancouver in 1798 and gave the United States the right to claim the Oregon territory.

Fort Columbia Historic Marker
At the entrance to Fort Columbia State Park, on U.S. 101, south of Chinook

"Here was the home of the Chinook Indians and their great chief, Comcomly. Capt. Robert Gray dropped anchor near here after his discovery of the Columbia River in 1792. In the days of the fur trade this area was witness to many stirring events, and in 1843 Capt. Scarborough here became the first permanent settler to the north of the Columbia. For years this promontory served as a vital landmark for the safe crossing of the Columbia's bar. Finally, as a coastal fort, its guns here guarded the mouth of the river from 1896 until the end of World War II."

Fort Columbia State Park
U.S. 101, 2 miles east of Chinook (360) 642-3078

For more than 50 years, 27 coastal defense installations, such as Fort Columbia, protected the West Coast of the United States. History of the fort, from the outbreak of the Spanish-American War in 1898 to the end of World War II; the Lewis and Clark Expedition who camped nearby; and the Chinook Indians who lived here generations before the first white man arrived, is displayed in several of the Fort's preserved buildings. The Daughters of the American Revolution and Pacific County Historical Society jointly furnished the 1902 Commanding Officer's house with period pieces and operate it as a house museum. An interpretive center located in the former enlisted men's barracks tells the military history of the Coast Artillery. The old Quartermaster's Storehouse houses the Chinook Observer Printing Museum. A youth hostel is located in the building that served as the post hospital. Three defense batteries that once held three Endicott Period six and eight-inch guns, bunkers and searchlight stations can also be toured.

Fort Columbia State Park

Battery Jewels Ord, Fort Columbia State Park

MCGOWAN

St. Mary's Church
U.S. 101, 1/2-mile southeast of Fort Columbia State Park, McGowan

The tremendous volume of salmon netted in the surrounding waters during the early 1900s led to the establishment of canneries in the town of McGowan. In 1904, construction of St. Mary's Catholic Church was financed and built on land donated by Patrick McGowan, for whom the town was named. Mass is now observed on Sundays only during the month of August.

St. Mary's Church

Lewis and Clark Campsite
U.S. 101, 1 mile southeast of Fort Columbia State Park, Chinook

Travelers can now picnic in the same spot where Lewis and Clark camped for ten days in November, 1805. The site is commemorated by a statue of Lewis and Clark gazing across their campground to the Columbia River. From here the expedition headed northwest to Cape Disappointment and their final destination, the Pacific Ocean.

ILWACO (il-WAH-koh)

Ilwaco Heritage Museum
115 SE Lake St., Ilwaco (360) 642-3446

History of Southwestern Washington, from the Native Americans who preceded the European setters, to the island's early explorers, missionaries, and pioneers is exhibited in the galleries of this impressive museum. An authentic Chinook basket display, carved duck miniatures, a scale-model replica of the turn-of-the-century town of Seaside Village, a model of *Sector,* the boat that was rowed across the Pacific from Japan to Ilwaco in 1991, and an actual 26-foot cedar surfboat, one of the first used at the Klipsan Lifesaving Station, are featured in the museum's major exhibit areas. A marine compass from Fort Columbia, equipment once used in the region's cranberry industry and a scale model of the railroad used to build the jetty across the mouth of the Columbia River are just some of the museums' interesting displays from their extensive collection.

Next door to the museum is a **restored depot** from the Ilwaco Railroad & Navigation Company, the narrow-gauge railroad that once ran down the main street of the town and served the island communities from Ilwaco to Nahcotta. Inside the depot is a 50-foot scale-model of the Long Beach Peninsula as it was in the early 1920s.

Ilwaco Heritage Museum

Nautical Display inside Ilwaco Heritage Museum

The Inn at Ilwaco
120 Williams St. NE, Ilwaco (360) 642-8686

Ilwaco's Presbyterian Church, built in 1928 on a former school site, was converted into a bed & breakfast inn in 1988. Sunday school rooms are now guest rooms; the sanctuary is The Playhouse Theatre featuring traveling shows and local talent. Although the interior has changed considerably, hints of the old church remain. The original church bell that hangs in the belfry was shipped around the Horn and period antiques fill the rooms of the inn.

Fort Canby
Fort Canby State Park, Hwy. 100, 3 miles south of Ilwaco (360) 642-3078

When Fort Canby was established in 1862 to protect the entrance to the Columbia River it became the first defense installation on the West Coast located north of San Francisco. The initial armament consisted of three, 10-inch Rodmans placed near the Cape Disappointment Lighthouse in 1864. Two, 300-pounder smoothbore cannon were added in 1890. In 1903, three gun batteries were installed in concrete bunkers. Battery Guenther had four, 12-inch guns that were previously located at Fort Stevens across the river in Oregon. Batteries O'Flyng and Allen both had

6-inch guns. Fort Canby was deactivated in 1950 following the end of World War II. None of the fort's original buildings remain, but the concrete bunkers, observation platforms and magazines, with their heavy iron doors, can be explored. Although the guns, which were never fired in battle, are long gone, the painted insignia of the 249th Coastal Artillery Unit remains on a Battery Henry Allen wall, evidence of the strong military presence that once protected the state's Pacific coastline.

Ammunition Magazine, Fort Canby

Cape Disappointment Lighthouse

Fort Canby State Park, Hwy. 100, 3 miles south of Ilwaco (360) 642-2382

Before this lighthouse was built at Cape Disappointment in 1856, settlers would use a white flag by day and bonfires at night to guide ships entering the Columbia River near this perilous point. More than two hundred ships were wrecked, stranded or sunk and hundreds of lives have been lost in the vicinity of the mouth of the Columbia River. Construction of Cape Disappointment Lighthouse, one of the first on the Pacific Coast, was delayed when one of the ships that was bringing building materials for the lighthouse sank off the Cape and lost its cargo. The loss of that vessel further underscored the need for this light station. The original oil lamp burned more than 5 gallons of whale oil a night and produced a light that could be seen 20 miles out to sea.

Access to the lighthouse can be made by hiking the trail from the Lewis and Clark Interpretive Center or by walking up a steep road from the Coast Guard Station. First established as a Life Saving Service at Cape Disappointment in 1873, the station is today one of the busiest motor lifeboat stations on the West Coast and home to the U.S.C.G. Motor Lifeboat School.

North Head Lighthouse
Fort Canby State Park, Hwy. 100, 3 miles south of Ilwaco (360) 642-3078

Forty years after Cape Disappointment Lighthouse was put into service to guide mariners into the Columbia River a second light station was erected on the ocean side to assist skippers approaching Cape Disappointment from the north. A combination of heavy fog and gale-force winds added to sailors woes as they navigated the Pacific along Long Beach Peninsula. Winds at North Head, the third windiest place in the Nation, have been clocked in excess of 150 mph; winds fierce enough to flatten trees. North Head's original light, a first-order Fresnel lens that was first installed at Cape Disappointment Lighthouse, is now displayed at the nearby Lewis and Clark Interpretive Center.

North Head Lighthouse

Lewis and Clark Interpretive Center
Fort Canby State Park, Hwy. 100, 2 miles south of Ilwaco   (360) 642-3029

It was here, at Cape Disappointment, in November, 1805, that the Lewis and Clark
Expedition first saw the Pacific Ocean, 18 months after beginning their 4,000-mile
trek from St. Louis. The events of their epic 28-month journey is chronicled in
exhibits, murals, journal excerpts, interactive displays and multimedia presentations.
A half-scale replica of the type of dugout built by members of the expedition is
exhibited along with a video demonstrating how dugouts were made by hand. Other
exhibits at the Center include the original first-order Fresnel lens from the North
Head Lighthouse, coast artillery items and Coast Guard artifacts.

*Fresnel Lens from the North Head
Lighthouse, Lewis and Clark
Interpretive Center*

KLIPSAN BEACH

Klipsan Beach Life Saving Station
Hwy. 103 and Klipsan Beach approach, Klipsan Beach

This station was one of nineteen life saving stations manned along the Pacific Coast
by the Life Saving Service, a non-military division of the Treasury Department.
Established in 1889, the station provided salvage help and navigational assistance
to mariners for nearly 60 years. As navigation systems improved the number of life
saving stations were reduced. The only station remaining in the former "graveyard
of the Pacific" is located at Cape Disappointment. The former Klipsan Beach station,
which is listed on the National Register of Historic Places is now a private residence.

LONG BEACH

Lewis and Clark Monument
Lewis and Clark Square, 3rd St. South and Hwy. 103, Long Beach

The northwestern most point reached by the Lewis and Clark Expedition is commemorated at this site by a bronze statue of the two Captains along with more than 40 plaques from cities and towns along their historic trail. A statue depicts Clark carving his initials in a tree at the end of their trail in Long Beach on November 19, 1805. The compass used by Lewis and Clark to map their westward journey to this point is preserved at the Smithsonian in Washington, D.C.

Lewis and Clark Monument

Marsh's Free Museum
Antique and Gift Shop, 409 S. Pacific, Long Beach (360) 642-2188

An array of antiques and collectibles greet visitors to this unusual 1921 store before they even step inside its front door. Buoys, farm implements, a hand-made cranberry separator, whippet wheel, old coffee grinder, bone crusher, German sausage stuffer, and an old pot-belly coach heater from the O.W.R. & N. Railroad are some of the interesting articles displayed here. One of the most historically significant objects exhibited is the bell from St. Francis X Mission, the Northwest's first Catholic Church (founded near Toledo in 1838).

Bell from St. Francis X Mission, Marsh's Free Museum

Weigel's 1893 cottage is being preserved on the property next door to Marsh's Free Museum. And, across the street, is the world's largest fry pan. It was used years ago to promote the city as a popular clam digging destination.

Weigel's Cottage

World Kite Museum & Hall of Fame
3rd St. NW, Long Beach (360) 642-4020

America's only museum dedicated exclusively to the history of kites, kitemakers and famous kiteflyers is located in this town where, every August, thousands attend the Washington State International Kite Festival. The 2,500 year-old history of kites is told here; from how they were used to win wars to their role in celebrating birth, death, planting and harvests. Special exhibits include: sport kites, the Asian heritage of kites, the city's kite festivals; and a hall of fame honoring exemplary personalities in kiting including Lawrence Hargrave, who invented the box kite in 1893, and Peter Travis, the Australian who's famous for his theatrical kite tales.

In addition to the kite enthusiasts who meet on the beach to participate in the various kite festivals that are held here every year, motorists can also enjoy a drive along the beach. The 28-mile beach, the longest in the world, has designated areas where motorists can drive their cars on the beach's hard-packed sand.

MENLO

Willie Keil's Grave
Hwy. 6, 2 miles northwest of Menlo

Dr. William Keil promised his 19-year-old son, Willie, that he could be in the lead wagon when he brought his followers west from Bethel, Missouri in 1855 to establish a colony at Menlo. Willie died before the trip, but was brought on the 2,000-mile trek in a lead-lined coffin for burial here.

NAHCOTTA (NAH-KAH-tuh)

Ilwaco Railroad and Steam Navigation Company Depot,
Nahcotta Store, Hwy. 103, Nahcotta

Narrow-gauge steam locomotives no longer travel up and down the town's main street, but the train's 1888-1930 schedule between Nahcotta and Ilwaco can still be seen on the side of the post office building that once served as both post office and train depot. The train's schedule wasn't as predictable as the sign may suggest. Schedules had to coincide with the tide, since steamers could only dock at Ilwaco at high tide. A working model of the Clamshell Railroad, as it was affectionately called, is exhibited at the Heritage Museum in Ilwaco.

Ilwaco Railroad and Steam Navigation Company Depot

OCEAN PARK

The Wreckage
256th Pl., Ocean Park

Its name came from the source of material used in its construction. Author and educator, Guy Allison, built the house in 1912 from wreckage salvaged from a barge that broke-up off the Columbia River bar. Allison designed the house based on an Alaskan blockhouse. The "Wreckage" is listed on the National Register of Historic Places.

Nearly 2,000 vessels have wrecked near the mouth of the Columbia River in the past 300 years. Among them is the French ship *Alice*, that went aground off Ocean Park in 1909. During times of extreme low tides, the wreck of the *Alice* is visible north of Pacific Pines Park; its cargo of cement anchoring it to the ocean floor.

S.A. Matthews House
262nd and "U" Sts., Ocean Park

Ocean Park was originally a settlement established by an association of the Methodist Church in 1883. One of the community's early residents was S.A. Matthews, a skilled carpenter. Among the houses Matthews constructed in the Ocean Park area was his 1889 home. It's known as, "Whalebone House" for the whale bone decorating the front lawn. Matthews' home is listed on the State Heritage Register.

OYSTERVILLE

Oysterville Historic District
An 80-acre area roughly bounded by Territory Rd. (formerly 4th St.), Pacific St., Nelson St. and Willapa Bay. A walking tour guide is available in the vestibule of the Oysterville Church at Territory and Clay Sts., Oysterville

Robert Espy and Isaac Clark came to this region in 1854 on the recommendation of the Chinook Indian Chief Nahacti who told them of tide beds covered with small Ostrea Lurida oysters. Clark laid out the town of Oysterville on donation claims that he and Espy filed and together they ran a successful business shipping Willapa Bay oysters to San Francisco. Their success brought an influx of new settlers and, in 1855, Oysterville, one of the oldest communities in Western Washington, became the county seat. Descendants of many of the town's first settlers live here in the seaside homes that have been preserved for more than a century. Among the places listed in the walking tour guide of this nationally registered historic district are:

W.D. Taylor House - 1870 - Home of an early stage driver who built the Taylor Hotel.

The Red Cottage - 1863 - Site of the first county courthouse and oldest surviving structure in Oysterville.

Schoolhouse - 1908 - third school built at this site. Constructed from California redwood carried as ballast by oyster schooners. The one-room schoolhouse was used until 1957. South of the schoolhouse is a plaque identifying the site of the first courthouse in Pacific County.

Oysterville Post Office - 1858 - The oldest continuously operating post office under the same name in the state.

Oysterville Cemetery - 1858 - Final resting place for many pioneer families. Chief Nahcati, who led Espy and Clark to the oyster beds, saved them when they were lost at sea, and for whom the town of Nahcotta was named, is also buried here.

Tom Crellin House - 1869 - Tom Crellin, who came from the Isle of Man, built the home but R. H. Espy bought it in 1892 to serve as the parsonage for the church.

Big Red House - 1871 - Home of Robert Espy, co-founder of Oysterville.

Oysterville Schoolhouse

Crellin/Espy Home

SEAVIEW

Shelburne Inn
4415 Pacific Way, Seaview (360) 642-2442

Seaside resorts were popular vacation destinations at the turn-of-the-century where families would often spend the entire Summer. The Craftsman and late Victorian-style Shelburne Inn, built in 1896, is the oldest continuously run hotel in the state and the last of the Peninsula hotels from that era. Art Nouveau stained-glass windows from an old English church, genuine artwork, and original beaded-fir paneling are some of special touches that keep history alive at this bed & breakfast inn. In 1978, the Shelburne Inn was added to the National Register of Historic Places.

Many old homes can be seen along the town's back streets. Two of the better known are the 1888 Schulderman Collie House on 37th St. (on the National Register of Historic Places) and the Sou'wester Lodge off the Seaview beach access road. The Sou'wester was built by U.S. Senator Henry Winslow Corbett of Oregon in 1892 as a country estate.

Shelburne Inn

395

SOUTHBEND

Pacific County Historical Museum
1008 W. Robert Bush Dr., South Bend (360) 875-5224

Harvesting and processing oysters from Willapa Bay began on a commercial scale in the early 1850s with oyster schooners ferrying their precious commodity to the Gold Rush boom town of San Francisco. The hot and cold cycle of the oyster business, due primarily to rapid depletion of the supply, made ghost towns of such places as Bruceport. But South Bend's economy was bolstered by its lumber industry and position as the seat of Pacific County. Today, a number of oyster companies remain in South Bend, the "oyster capital of the west." Indian artifacts, maps, photos, pioneer tools, works of art and textiles are displayed in collections organized by theme in this museum of county history. Pre-history and pioneer periods, maritime and logging industries, and community life is demonstrated in the museum's fine exhibits.

Pacific County Historical Museum, Courtesy of Pacific County Historical Society

Several of South Bend's older buildings are historically interesting or being preserved because of their architectural value. The old drug store, with its pressed tin ceiling, is now home to the Pacific County Museum. The 1910 Lumber Exchange Building, which is listed on the National Register of Historic Places, now houses retail shops and apartments.

Lumber Exchange Building, Courtesy of Pacific County Historical Society

Pacific County Courthouse
On Memorial Dr. 2 blocks south of U.S.101, South Bend

One of the grandest courthouses in the Pacific Northwest was built at the top of "Quality Hill" in 1910-11 after the county seat was moved here from Oysterville. A

29-foot, stained-glass rotunda crowns this majestic structure and tasteful ornamental trim accents the building's exterior. Murals within the courthouse portray the early history of Pacific County. Not only is the view of the city and Willapa River impressive from the steps of the courthouse, but the view of the courthouse itself, especially near sunset, is worth the visit.

397

TOKELAND (TOHK-luhnd)

Tokeland Hotel and Restaurant
100 Hotel Rd., Tokeland (360) 267-7006

Instead of taking U.S. 101, the more direct route between Raymond and Aberdeen, try Hwy. 105, the scenic coastal route that follows the north shore of oyster-rich Willapa Bay to Tokeland. This small peninsula community was named for Chief Toke, who camped here during the Summer months with his family. Lizzie Brown, daughter of the island's first settlers George and Charlotte Brown, and her husband, William Kindred, built their farmhouse at this site in the 1880s. In 1889, they expanded the house and opened it as the Kindred Inn. The present owners reopened the refurbished hotel and restaurant in 1990 replete with original and turn-of-the-century furnishings. Tokeland Hotel, one of the oldest resort hotels in the state, is listed on the National Register of Historic Places.

East of the hotel, at the end of North St., is an early 1920s Coast Guard Station. The Coast Guard's old boat house, which is listed on the National Register of Historic Places, can be seen on the beach near Emerson and Kindred streets.

Tokeland Hotel and Restaurant, Courtesy of Tokeland Hotel and Restaurant

Willapa Bay Light
Cape Shoalwater, 7 miles west of Tokeland off Hwy. 105

At Cape Shoalwater, where Willapa Bay meets the Pacific Ocean, a skeleton frame lighthouse guards the channel entrance. The first lighthouse, known as Cape Shoalwater Light, was constructed in 1858 about 3/4-mile from the present light. Eroding sands undermined that structure in 1940 and washed it out to sea. As the ocean claimed more of the Cape, summer cabins, the Coast Guard's lifeboat station, and the replacement lighthouse had to be moved. In total, the lighthouse has been relocated four times.

Other sites in the Tokeland area include: the North Cove Pioneer Cemetery; old cranberry bogs; and the one square-mile Shoalwater Bay Tribe Reservation, the nation's smallest Indian reservation.

Skamania County

SKAMANIA COUNTY

CARSON

Carson Mineral Hot Springs Resort
St. Martin Rd., Carson (509) 427-8292, (800) 607-3678

Isadore St. Martin, who discovered these hot springs in 1876, built the present three-story resort hotel between 1897 and 1901. Stories of the relief from pain Mrs. St. Martin experienced brought a large number of guests to the springs. Tents were originally erected to accommodate all the visitors. The cabins and bathhouse were added in 1923. Original turn-of-the-century furnishings, iron beds, and rocking chairs fill the rooms. But noticeably missing are television sets and phones.

COOK-UNDERWOOD-WILLARD

Broughton Lumber Company Flume
North side of Hwy. 14 near Underwood and the side road to Willard

Remnants of what was once the world's largest operating log flume can be seen extending north from Underwood to Willard, some nine miles to the northwest. Harold Broughton bought the flume and used it to float rough-cut lumber from his mill in Willard to his finishing mill in Underwood. On an average day, 125,000 board feet of lumber took the 55-minute trip down the flume. It ceased operating in the 1980s.

MOUNT ST. HELENS

Mount St. Helens National Volcanic Monument

On May 18, 1980, Southwestern Washington was rocked by the mammoth eruption of Mount St. Helens. Life in this part of the state changed forever. Fifty-seven people perished, 150 square miles of forest were destroyed, hundreds of homes were lost or damaged, and mud and debris flowed into rivers, lakes and streams. Travelers to this National Monument can learn about its history by stopping at the visitor center east of Castle Rock, or at the many park information stations, view points or interpretive trails. Four state highways lead to the monument.

Pine Creek Information Station
17 miles east of Cougar on Forest Rd. 90

A short movie and information on road conditions, hiking trails, and camping, prepares travelers for their Mount St. Helens experience. Fifteen miles west of this information center is Ape Cave, one of the longest intact lava tubes in the continental United States. The 12,810-foot cave was formed by another volcanic eruption nearly 2,000 years ago, but wasn't discovered until 1946.

NORTH BONNEVILLE (BAHN-uh-vil)

Bonneville Dam
Hwy. 14, southeast of Stevenson

Harnessing the power of the mighty Columbia River to create electricity brought an army of workers here during the Great Depression for the jobs that could be had building Bonneville Dam. The original town of North Bonneville was razed to make room for construction of the dam's second powerhouse. The town was reconstructed on the site of the former town of Lower Cascades, once the largest town in the territory. The visitor center on the Washington side of the dam features hydropower exhibits and the history of the Columbia River. A second visitor center on the Oregon side offers a look into the history of the dam.

Those who want to experience the Columbia and hear about this region's history, geology and Native American legends can take a two-hour cruise on the Columbia

Gorge Sternwheeler which departs from the Bonneville Dam Visitor Center on the Washington side and from the Cascade Locks on the Oregon side. Phone (503) 374-8427 for schedule.

Bonneville Dam, Photo by Judy Menish

402

Fort Cascades National Historic Site
West of the Bonneville Dam Second Powerhouse on Hwy. 14, North Bonneville

U.S. Army troops provided protection from Indian ambush to immigrants who were forced to detour by land around the Columbia River Cascades at this site. A kiosk describes the history of Fort Cascades, which actually comprised three sites. One of the fort's blockhouses was named for Major General Rains, whose troops fought near here in 1858. Remnants of an old fish wheel can be seen by following a two-mile gravel trail to the banks of the Columbia.

SKAMANIA (skuh-MAY-neeuh)

Beacon Rock
Beacon Rock State Park, on the bank of the Columbia River, 2 miles east of Skamania via Hwy. 14

At 848 feet, Beacon Rock is the largest geologic formation of its kind in the United States, and the second largest in the world. Although there's no written record that the volcanic rock was ever used as a landmark, as its name implies, its presence was recorded by Lewis and Clark when they camped at its base in November, 1805, and again on their return trip in April, 1806. When an attempt to quarry the rock was made in the early 1900s, it was purchased by Charles Ladd, a Portland banker, to preserve the landmark for future generations. Henry Biddle bought Beacon Rock

from Ladd in 1915 and hired a crew to cut a trail to the top. Visitors who hike the steep 3/4-mile twisting trail (with 52 switchbacks) to the top of this ancient volcano core are treated to an unmatched and unforgettable view of the Columbia Gorge.

Beacon Rock, Photo by Judy Menish

Trail to the top of Beacon Rock

STEVENSON

Columbia Gorge Interpretive Center
990 S.W. Rock Creek Dr., Hwy. 14 east of the Bridge of the Gods, Stevenson
(503) 427-8211

Long before the arrival of white settlers, this region was the site of Native American
Villages; a focal point for socializing, trade and fishing. Immigrants following the
Oregon Trail in the mid-1800s would have to disassemble their wagons in order to
get around the nearby Upper Cascades. They would reassemble them at this site
and then continue rafting down the Columbia River. In the early 1900s giant fish
wheels, some as tall as 40 feet, were used by scores of fishermen as revolving nets
to catch salmon heading upstream to spawn. The history of these events is preserved
in the historical society's collections on display in this outstanding interpretive center.
A full-scale 37-foot high fish wheel, local Native American artifacts, the world's
largest rosary collection, a 1921 Mack log truck and restored Corliss steam engine
are among the museum's featured collections. Other exhibit areas demonstrate the
creation and future of the Gorge, the development of hydroelectric power, and the
history of the many cultures of the Gorge. An outside exhibit features a replicated
1910 railroad depot and restored Spokane, Portland & Seattle Railway Caboose.

Columbia Gorge Interpretive Center

Wahkiakum County

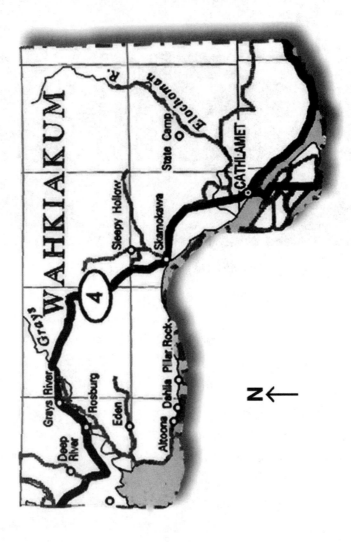

WAHKIAKUM COUNTY

CATHLAMET (KATH-LA-muht)

Wahkiakum County Historical Museum
65 River St. at Division, Cathlamet (360) 795-3954

Logging and salmon canning were major Cathlamet industries as early as the 1860s. The first commercial salmon cannery site was established just east of town in 1866 and major logging operations remained until 1959. Logging equipment, Chinook Indian artifacts, pioneer items and an extensive photo collection are displayed. Outside the museum, under a protective canopy, stands "Six Spot," a 20-ton, 1923 steam locomotive that was specially geared to meet the unique operating needs of the logging industry.

The ground on which this museum stands was the site of a Chinook tribal village in the early 1800s. Judge William Strong's home was also erected here in the 1850s. Judge Strong was the first American settler in Wahkiakum County and the first Federal Judge in Oregon Territory.

Wahkiakum County Historical Museum

Antique Machinery in Wahkiakum County Historical Museum's Outdoor Exhibit Area

Pioneer Church
Congregational Church, Alley St., Cathlamet

Just above the town, in a rocky outcropping, stands Pioneer Church, erected in 1895. The church, which features unusual architectural features such as fish scale shingles, is listed on the National Register of Historic Places.

A number of older buildings grace the town including: the 1927, two-story brick Cathlamet Hotel; and the Kimball-Butler home, the former residence of Congresswoman Julia Butler Hansen that was originally built by the town's founder, James Birnie in 1857. The Kimball-Butler home is listed on the State Heritage Register.

DEEP RIVER

Deep River Pioneer Lutheran Church
East River Rd., Deep River

Generally, the first to settle or establish a pioneer community shared a common faith. And, once their homes were built, or the first industry started, the community would come together and build a church; each adding his or her skills to the effort. The farmers who cleared the land in Deep Harbor and the Europeans who came to log the forest joined together in 1898 to build this Lutheran Church. The church, which is listed on the National Register of Historic Places, has survived a hundred years in the wilderness. A testament to the pioneers who built it.

GRAYS RIVER

Grays River Covered Bridge
Hwy. 4, 1 1/2 miles east of Grays River

The town, river and bay it empties into were named for Captain Robert Gray, the American explorer who discovered and named the Columbia River in May, 1792. The town's best-known landmark is its covered bridge built in 1905. When first built, the bridge was an uncovered span across Grays River. The cover was added three years later. Today, it stands as the state's oldest covered bridge still in public use. It was placed on the National Register of Historic Places in 1971.

SKAMOKAWA (skuh-MAH-kuh-way)

Skamokawa Historic District
Hwy. 4, Skamokawa

Homes and businesses built here during the 1880s and 1890s faced the meandering Skamokawa Creek and a number of sloughs that were the lifeline of the community. Like the canals of Venice, the community was linked by its waterways. It wasn't until the early part of the twentieth century that roads connected the town to the outside world. But, in spite of their apparent isolation, those who settled here prospered. Many of the town's pioneer buildings can be seen in the historic district which is listed on the National Register of Historic Places.

Redmen Hall
River Life Interpretive Center, Hwy. 4, Skamokawa (360) 795-3007

For 30 years, this 1894 building was Skamokawa's schoolhouse. In 1926, when the school district consolidated, members of the Fraternal Order of Redmen acquired the old school as a meeting hall and renamed it "Redmen Hall." The restored, century-old building overlooking the Columbia River is now home to the River Life Interpretive Center.

Redmen Hall

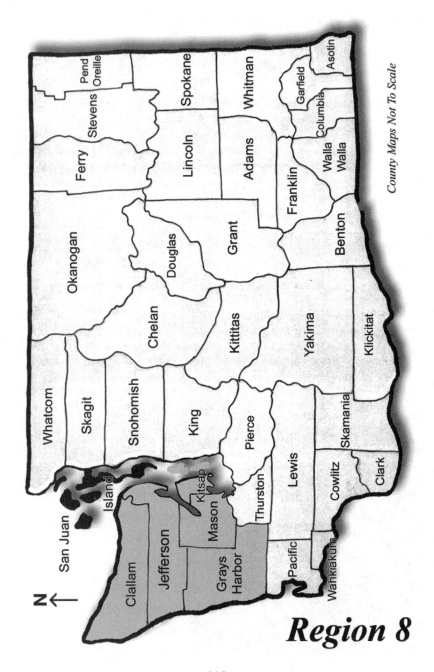

County Maps Not To Scale

Region 8

Clallam County

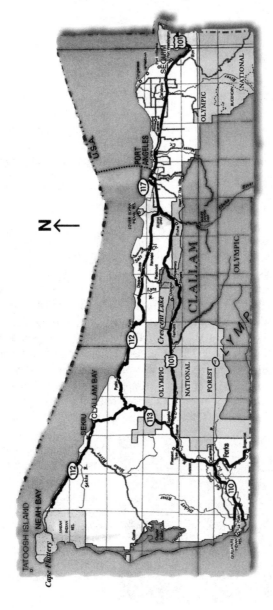

REGION 8

CLALLAM COUNTY

CLALLAM BAY

Slip Point Lighthouse
Northeast side of Clallam Bay

When the lighthouse at Slip Point was erected in 1905, it was the last major station to be built on the American side of the Strait of Juan de Fuca. Automation claimed the traditional lighthouse building in 1951 when it was replaced with the simple tower that stands here today.

FORKS

Forks Timber Museum
1421 S. Forks Ave., on U.S. 101, Forks (360) 374-9663

No monument to the community's cultural and economic ties to the timber industry is more fitting than the log structure that houses Forks Timber Museum. This great source of civic pride was a high school carpentry class project that got support from volunteers who donated both material and labor. A logger's bunkhouse, camp cookhouse stove, saws used in the industry and scale models of large logging equipment are featured. While exhibits focus on Forks timber history, the region's roots aren't forgotten. The story of early fur trappers, farmers and Native Americans is also presented. One of the museum's prized objects on display is an original, full-size cedar canoe from a Makah Coastal Indian tribe.

On the grounds at the rear of the museum is an outdoor exhibit area containing a fire lookout tower, two old growth forest nature trails, the Forks Loggers Memorial and memorial gardens.

Logger's Bunkhouse, Courtesy of Forks Timber Museum

Adam Copeland House
First Federal Savings and Loan, 131 Calawah Way, Forks (360) 374-6122

The bungalow Craftsman-style log home of early Forks pioneer Adam Copeland was modified for use as a bank in the 1980s. Copeland's original floor plan and some of the home's main features have been incorporated into the design of this modern banking facility. Care was taken to insure that any building additions would complement the original structure. Copeland's home is listed on the State Heritage Register.

Olympic National Park
Hoh Rain Forest Visitor Center
Entrance is 14 miles south of Forks on U.S. 101

Interpretive nature trails that lead from this Visitor Center give guests a glimpse into the natural history of a temperate rain forest that's been preserved and protected as part of this 915,000-acre World Heritage Park. Water flows so clear you can see pebbles at the bottom of creek beds. Thick, green moss and ferns cover virtually everything. Old growth spruce trees, some reaching heights of 300 feet, dot the landscape. And rainfall that averages more than 130 inches a year makes this one of the state's most exotic places to visit and explore.

LAKE CRESCENT

Morgenroth Cabin
Storm King Information Center
Olympic National Park
U.S. 101, between Rosemary and Singers, 3 miles from east end of lake, 20 miles west of Port Angeles

The log structure that serves today as a park information station was built in 1905 by Chris Morgenroth as a guard station and home. Morgenroth, an early forest ranger, was known as a crusader for preservation of old growth forests and for implementing the Forest Service's first reforestation program.

Two popular trips for visitors who want to learn more about the natural history of this region originate here. They can hike an easy 3/4-mile nature trail from the Center that leads to the base of 90-foot Marymere Falls or schedule a narrated cruise on Lake Crescent.

NEAH BAY

Makah Museum
Makah Cultural and Research Center
Hwy. 112 at the entrance to Neah Bay (360) 645-2711

The nation's only collection of relics from the ancient Makah coastal whaling village of Ozette are being preserved in this combination museum, research and cultural center. Archaeologists began excavating the perfectly preserved Ozette site in 1970 when tidal erosion uncovered homes that had been buried under a massive landslide for 500 years. In addition to the ancient Northwest Coast Indian artifacts on display, the museum also features a full-size replica of a fifteenth century cedar longhouse, Makah dugout canoes, and whaling and sealing implements.

The Ozette site, 15 miles south of Neah Bay at Cape Alava, is one of the most significant archaeological sites in the Pacific Northwest and is listed on the National Register of Historic Places.

Cape Flattery

The mile and a half round-trip hike from the parking area to the 100-foot cliffs of Cape Flattery, the Northwestern most point in the contiguous United States, once presented a number of challenges and risks for those who came to this remote spot to enjoy its breathtaking view. Fallen trees across twisting, uneven, primitive trails led to the unprotected edge of the Cape. Today, the hike is much easier and safer. Although the walk still leads through thick forest and wetlands, the completely refurbished trail now includes footbridges and cedar observation decks with guardrails.

Cape Flattery Lighthouse
Tatoosh Island (Can be viewed from the Cape Flattery observation deck)

This light may be one of the most observed, but least visited of all the West Coast lighthouses. Located one-half mile off Cape Flattery on rockbound Tatoosh Island, the 1857 lighthouse guards the entrance to the Strait of Juan de Fuca. Its remote location and inaccessibility during rough seas and bad weather required the dozen families who lived here (before the light was automated) to stockpile a 6-month supply of food and provisions. In addition to the lighthouse, the little community's buildings housed a school, post office, meteorological facility and naval station.

Cape Flattery Lighthouse on Tatoosh Island

PORT ANGELES

Olympic National Park Visitor Center
Pioneer Memorial Museum
L. L. Beaumont Cabin
3002 Mt. Angeles Rd. (via Race St.) south of Port Angeles (360) 452-0330 or (360) 452-4501

At more than 1.5 million acres, Olympic National Park and Forest covers nearly half of the Olympic Peninsula and offers visitors visual treats that range from ocean shores to glacier-clad mountains, sub-alpine meadows and temperate rain forests. At this Center guests can learn about the Park's history and get information and directions to the parks natural attractions. Hurricane Ridge, the Hoh Rain Forest, Sol Duc Hot Springs are some of the park's popular destinations. Other areas of interest include the trails that follow the old Spruce Railroad and lead to remote spots such as: Olympic Hot Springs, Marymere Falls, and Bailey Ridge, home of the world's largest sub-alpine fir.

Displays at the **Pioneer Memorial Museum** tell the history of Clallam County through artifacts on loan from the Clallam Historical Society Museum. Indian whaling tools and logging exhibit are part of this museum's permanent collection. Behind the museum is a restored and authentically furnished 1887 homesteader's log cabin. It was home to the L. L. Beaumont family for nearly 40 years.

Hurricane Ridge Visitor Center
2800 Hurricane Ridge Rd. (360) 452-0330

A short drive to mile-high Hurricane Ridge is the beginning of an unforgettable venture. Dioramas at the Center tell the natural history of the Park and identify the mountain peaks in the Olympic Range that can be seen along the trails. While the spectacular view of the Olympic Mountain Range by itself makes the trip worthwhile, a hike on one of the placid nature trails through the sub-alpine meadows will add even more enjoyment to the excursion.

The Museum of Clallam Historical Society
Clallam County Courthouse
223 E. Fourth St., Port Angeles (360) 417-2364

Early 1770s explorers were attracted to the natural harbor of present-day Port Angeles, but most settlers headed to the well-established town of Port Townsend. When the customhouse was moved here from Port Townsend in 1862, President

Lincoln set aside area for the town and a military installation. He also signed an executive order establishing Port Angeles as the nation's second National City, second only to Washington, D.C. The rich history of this "National City" and the county that borders the Strait of Juan de Fuca is displayed in this historical society museum.

The 1914 redbrick, Georgian-style building that houses the museum's collections is one of the city's finest early-twentieth century architectural gems. It served as the county courthouse for 65 years and is listed on the National Register of Historic Places.

Photo by Judy Menish

416

Arthur D. Feiro Marine Laboratory
Port Angeles City Pier

This Peninsula College laboratory was opened to the public to give visitors an opportunity to have an up-close experience with local marine life. Volunteers are on-hand to explain the history of the sea, its flora and fauna, and the region's marine life. Large "touch tanks" offer many a rare opportunity to handle marine animals that are usually only available to view from behind glass.

Other places of historic interest in the Port Angeles area include:

Crown Park at W. Fourth and "M" Sts. where a **multi-ton flywheel** from Crown Zellerbach's original mill is on display.

The **Federal Building** at First and Oak Sts. was built at a site President Lincoln reserved for Federal use on June 10, 1862. The building, which is listed on the National Register of Historic Places, was formerly a post office and is now used for government offices.

A replica of the **Liberty Bell** can be seen in Veterans Park at Second and Lincoln Sts. The bell, forged in the same English foundry as the original Liberty Bell, was purchased by Port Angeles' residents to celebrate our nation's bicentennial.

An authentic **Indian longhouse** of the type erected by Northwest tribes and a few pioneer log cabins are preserved in Lincoln Park at W. Lauridsen and Bean Sts.

For more information about these sites, and other places of interest in the area, contact the Port Angeles Visitors Center, 121 E. Railroad (360) 452-2363.

Juan de Fuca Historic Marker
5 miles west of Port Angeles on U.S. 101

"In Venice, an old Greek mariner, Apostolos Valerianos, told of the trip that he had taken up the Pacific Coast on a Mexican expedition in 1592 under the name of Juan de Fuca and of his discovery of a passageway leading to an inland sea, his description of which fitted closely that of Puget Sound, lending credence to his story. Mapmakers of Europe marked this unknown inlet with his name, and while the career of the old Greek mariner ends in historical darkness, in 1788 Captain John Meares, on discovery of this inlet, named it the Strait of Juan de Fuca."

Juan de Fuca Historic Marker

SEKIU (SEE-Kyoo)

Sekiu School
Rice St. just off Hwy. 112, Sekiu

One of the town's most noticeable landmarks is its 1916 schoolhouse. For 30 years children from the Sekiu-Clallam Bay area attended school here. Today, another generation comes here, but this time its for community activities. The exterior of this Nationally Registered Historic Place remains virtually unchanged; its Craftsman and bungalow detailing still evident.

SEQUIM (SKWIM) (Sequim-Dungeness Valley)

Museum and Arts Center
175 W. Cedar, Sequim (360) 683-8110 (formerly the Sequim-Dungeness Museum)

Evidence of a 12,000-year-old link between man and a Mastodon was uncovered in 1977 on the farm of Emanuel Manis just south of Sequim. The pair of Mastodon tusks Manis found led Washington State University archaeologists to one of the decade's most important discoveries, a bone spear point embedded in the Mastodon's rib. It was the earliest validation of human existence in the Pacific Northwest. Artifacts from the Manis Mastodon Site, a Nationally Registered Historic Site, is exhibited here along with the history of the Sequim-Dungeness Valley from early Indian days to the twentieth century. Another of the museum's unique exhibits features the story of Sequim's 1895 irrigation system, the largest irrigation system west of the Cascades, and the Sequim Irrigation Festival, the oldest continuing community event in the state.

Old Dungeness Schoolhouse
Near the mouth of the Dungeness River on Sequim-Dungeness Ave., north of downtown Sequim

One of the city's most impressive turn-of-the-century landmarks was erected on this site in the 1890s as a public school for the children of the Dungeness Valley. The two-story building, with its distinctive bell cupola, remained an active school until 1955. Today, the restored building, which is listed on the National Register of Historic Places, is used as a community center.

McAlmond House
On the bluffs west of the Old Dungeness Schoolhouse, north of Sequim

Ship's carpenters built this Gothic Revival-style frame house for Captain Elijah McAlmond in 1861 from materials shipped here from Oregon. It was one of the finest structures in the region and first house in the county built from sawed lumber. It stands today as the last original building remaining from the community of New Dungeness. The home, which is not open to the public, is listed on the National Register of Historic Places and can only be viewed from the exterior.

New Dungeness Light Station
At the end of the Dungeness Spit north of Sequim in the Dungeness National Wildlife Refuge (360) 683-5847

Near the tip of the Dungeness Spit, one of the longest natural sand promontories in the nation, is the 1857 New Dungeness Light, the oldest lighthouse north of the Columbia River. Like other locations where lighthouses were erected, the spit was once the site of numerous shipwrecks, earning it the nickname "Shipwreck Spit."

419

But this lighthouse filled another need not shared by other lights. It served as a beacon for warring Indian parties from Canada and New Dungeness who often fought on this narrow strip of land to settle their differences.

Today, the white clapboard, red-roofed lighthouse, which is listed on the National Register of Historic Places, is about half its original 100-foot height. Visitors who want to see this historic site up close need to note that the lighthouse is a 10-mile round trip hike from the mainland. Certain activities are prohibited along the Spit to protect the thousands of migrating shorebirds, waterfowl and various forms of sea life that inhabit the Refuge.

Other sites in Sequim:

Pioneer Memorial, 300 block of E. Washington St. (Hwy. 101) contains historic tombstones, recreated Indian canoe, and a homesteader's cabin.

Two older buildings worth visiting are the **Opera House**, 119 N. Sequim Ave., and **Town Hall**, 152 W. Cedar St., which are both listed on the State Heritage Register.

Dioramas of Olympic Peninsula birds, wildlife and plants are some of the featured exhibits at the **Sequim Natural History Museum**, 503 N. Sequim Ave.

Grays Harbor County

GRAYS HARBOR COUNTY

ABERDEEN

Aberdeen Museum of History
111 E. Third St., Aberdeen   (360) 533-1976

When settlers first came to this land in the 1860s, they found a forest so dense that travel between Aberdeen and the neighboring city of Hoquiam, a mere 3 miles away, was only possible via a water route along Grays Harbor. The abundance of timber fed the twin lumbering cities, spawned their growth and continues to play a major role in their economy today. Photographs on display in this old 1922 National Guard Armory building capture the history of the community and its growth. Also displayed are pieces of antique fire-fighting equipment, farm and logging equipment, household furnishings from the 1880s to 1940s, and replicas of a general store, one-room school, blacksmith shop, and pioneer church.

National Guard Building

Grays Harbor Historical Seaport
813 E. Heron St., Aberdeen   (360) 532-8611

A distance of only 100 miles separates the modern Navy's sleek nuclear-powered submarines at Bangor from the Ports at Aberdeen, but, when measured in time, two centuries separate their ships. Replicas of tall sailing ships of the type that sailed

422

into Grays Harbor in the late 1700s can be seen here today. Gifted shipwrights at this historical seaport constructed a full-size operating replica of the 170-ton square-rigged tall ship "Lady Washington" and the "Columbia Rediviva," the ship Capt. Robert Gray sailed from Boston to Grays Harbor in 1788. Capt. Gray's 105-foot brig was the first American vessel to make landfall on the West Coast and the first to visit Japan. Capt. Gray was also the first American to circumnavigate the world.

Tours of the tall ships are conducted by costumed crewmembers when "Lady Washington" is in port. Three-hour voyages and port-to-port passages can be booked by calling (800) 356-2972.

Aberdeen Historic Building Walking Tour
Main Street Association 214A E. Wishkah (360) 538-1165

Several early twentieth century commercial buildings are preserved in Aberdeen's historic downtown district. The building styles represent Romanesque Revival, Renaissance Revival, and Beau Arts architecture designs with terra cotta ornamentation and Art Deco detail. The city's Main Street Association publishes a walking tour brochure that includes a description of the wide range of businesses that once operated here. Some of the buildings along Heron Street were once part of the city's "red-light" district. The upper floor at today's "Billy's Restaurant" housed the fabled Elnora Rooms during the 1950s.

COSMOPOLIS (Kahz-MAH-poh-lis)

Neil Cooney Mansion
Cooney Mansion Bed and Breakfast, 1705 Fifth, Cosmopolis (360) 533-0602 or (800) 9-SPRUCE

When Lumber baron Neil Cooney built this exquisite 10,000 square-foot, three-story mansion in 1908 it was to showcase the lumber produced by the giant Grays Harbor Commercial Company, the company he managed and would later own. The extensive use of Sitka spruce paneling and other fine woodwork in the Craftsman-style, 37-room mansion earned it the nickname, "Spruce Cottage." Today, Cooney's Mansion is operated as a bed & breakfast inn with many original turn-of-the-century American Arts and Crafts Period furniture and fixtures. The inn's owners have assembled a family scrapbook filled with old photos and stories of Cooney, his mill and restoration of the mansion.

Neil Cooney Mansion

Cosmopolis Treaty Site
Represented by mural on water storage tank off South U.S.101 in Cosmopolis

Territorial Governor Isaac Stevens negotiated with several tribes of Chehalis, Quinault, Chinook and Quileute Indians at a clearing near this site in February 1855

in an effort to relocate them to a reservation away from this area. The treaty that established the Quinault Reservation for the Coastal Indians was signed a year later. A monument commemorating the treaty signing can be seen at 1st and "H" Streets.

424

ELMA

Historical Murals
Downtown Elma

Forty murals, depicting the region's history and rural life, blanket the town's storefronts and civic buildings. They recall early life in the region; pioneer farming, logging, and ranching endeavors; the coming of the railroad; and other important events in the community's history. Elma's collection of murals outnumbers those of any other city in the county. Old-fashioned gas lamps in the downtown district add to the turn-of-the-century charm of this 1880s village.

HOQUIAM (HOH-Kwee-hum)

Arnold Polson Museum
1611 Riverside Ave., Hoquiam (360) 533-5862

Vast timber reserves in the Grays Harbor region attracted experienced loggers from around the world. Among the immigrants was Alex Polson, who homesteaded this site in 1894. Polson was a member of the crew that logged off the famous "21-9" forest (an extremely dense 6-square-mile tract by the harbor that was logged for 30 years). Eventually he established his own lumbering business. Alex's son, Arnold, built this 26-room Colonial Revival mansion on his father's original homestead in 1923. Arnold Polson's home, which is listed on the National Register of Historic Places, houses a collection of Grays County artifacts including: antique furniture, Native American relics, collectible dolls, logging memorabilia and a photo history of the region.

Museum staff can provide information about other historic sites in Hoquiam including: the historic ship *Mamala*, docked at the 8th St. Landing; the city's **eight historic murals**; and **Bowerman Basin**, a natural harbor whose wetlands are home to thousands of shorebirds who migrate here in the spring and fall.

425

Linn Dump Truck, Arnold Polson Museum

Hoquiam's Castle
515 Chenault Ave., Hoquiam (360) 533-2005

Robert Lytle's elaborate 20-room, Queen Anne-style home reflects the fortune he earned as one of the area's turn-of-the-century lumber barons. Majestic oak columns and paneling line the entry hall, hardwood floors are made of maple and pecan, exquisite hand-carved antique furnishings fill the rooms, and Tiffany lamps, cut-crystal chandeliers, and stained glass windows illuminate this well-maintained 1897 mansion.

The privately owned home, known locally as "Hoquiam's Castle," is listed on the National Register of Historic Places and is open to the public for guided tours.

Lytle House Bed & Breakfast
509 Chenault Ave., Hoquiam (360) 533-2320

Next door to Robert Lytle's "Hoquiam Castle" is another Queen Anne-style home from the same era. This one was built in 1890 for Robert's Brother Joseph and his wife, Mary, and is also listed on the National Register of Historic Places. Joseph also made his fortune in the lumber industry, but that wasn't his original plan. He was a grocer who turned a small logging business he received in payment of a debt into one of the largest cedar shingle mills on the West Coast. Restored antique furniture and period collectibles create an authentic atmosphere for guests who stay at this quaint inn.

Lytle House Bed and Breakfast

Seventh Street Theater
313 Seventh St., Hoquiam (360) 532-6058 or (360) 533-3531

Embossed sailing ships and Egyptian chariot races enhance the exterior facade of this 1928 Renaissance Revival-style theatre. But its real beauty lies beyond the theatre's massive entry doors. The wooden-beamed foyer, with its colored glass fixtures and marble terrazzo floor, prepares patrons for the visual treat that awaits them in the large 1,100-seat auditorium where special effects create the impression of an open-air playhouse. A simulated evening sky with twinkling stars, the recreated upper stories and rooftops of an old Spanish Village and behind-the-scenes lighting were used in creating the Pacific Northwest's first atmospheric theatre. In the early years of the twentieth century, many of the country's top entertainers and artists performed on its stage. The ongoing restoration effort of this Nationally Registered Historic Place has helped maintain the Seventh Street Theatre as a first-class performance center.

Seventh Street Theatre

Hoquiam Carnegie Library
Hoquiam Timberland Library, 621 "K" St., Hoquiam (360) 532-1710

Frank Lloyd Wright's architectural style can be seen in the design of this 1911, 2-story, redbrick Carnegie building, which is listed on the National Register of Historic Places. Its wood-paneled interior, with its many fireplaces, makes it one of the coziest libraries in the state.

1911 Carnegie Library Building

McCLEARY

McCleary Museum at Carnell House
314 Second St., McCleary (360) 495-3670

An abundant supply of Western Red Cedar brought Henry McCleary to this area in 1897. He built a small lumber mill and grew his business over the years. In 1910 he started construction on a door plant that would become one of the largest in the world. To insure that his employees had a place to live, McCleary also began building a "mill town," with homes for more than ninety families. He sold his business and town to the Simpson Logging Company in 1941 after all near-by lumber had been cut. A fine collection of artifacts and old photographs from the McCleary and Simpson eras are exhibited in this historical society's museum.

Old McCleary Hotel
42 Summit Rd., McCleary (360) 495-3678

Special business visitors to Henry McCleary's town once stayed in the founder's 1912 guesthouse. At the time of its construction, it was considered to be a state-of-the-art hotel. Today, guestrooms contain brass beds, oak dressers and other period furnishings. Claw-foot tubs are still used in the private and shared baths. Original paneling and Victorian wallpaper cover the walls of the dining room where family-style meals are served in an early-twentieth century setting. Reservations are required for both hotel stays and dining.

Simpson Timber Company Locomotive
Across from City Hall in Beerblower Park, McCleary

In 1962, the Simpson Timber Company donated the locomotive Henry McCleary purchased in 1905 to the city. The locomotive, nicknamed "Dink" was put on display to recognize the role that McCleary and Simpson played in the history of this community.

MONTESANO (mahn-tuh-SAY-noh)

Chehalis Valley Historical Museum
703 W. Pioneer Ave., Montesano (360) 249-5800

Initially the town was known as Scammon's, for its founder, Isaiah Scammon, who sailed around the Horn from Maine to this area in 1852. His home was the county seat and courthouse until 1886, when Montesano became the center of government for Grays Harbor County. Exhibits inside this former 1906 wood-frame church building cover the early history of the valley and the growth of the region's forest products industry. Pioneer logging relics and early farming equipment are also displayed.

Chehalis Valley Historical Museum

Grays Harbor County Courthouse
100 Broadway W., Montesano

Since 1886, Montesano has been the seat of Grays Harbor County government. For its first 25 years, county business was conducted in temporary quarters. Then, in 1910, construction of this magnificent Beaux Arts Roman Revival-style sandstone courthouse building began. The domed building, with its picturesque clock tower, is a testament to the civic pride demonstrated by the city's forefathers. Inside are several murals depicting events in local history and general themes such as the timber industry, justice, truth, science and art.

430

Grays Harbor County Courthouse

Abel House B&B
117 Fleet Street St., Montesano (360) 249-6002 or (800) 235-ABEL

One of the state's leading trial and defense lawyers, William Abel, built this three-story home in 1908 using locally quarried sandstone blocks. Original Douglas fir woodwork can be seen throughout the home which is now operated as a bed and breakfast inn.

Abel House Bed and Breakfast

431

Lake Sylvia State Park
Exit 104 off U.S. 12, 1 mile north of Montesano

Before Lake Sylvia became a state park, it was the site of the county's first sawmill. Although the mill no longer exists, visitors to this popular recreational area can see how a working forest operates by following the park's 2-mile Sylvia Creek Forestry Interpretive Trail.

Other sites of interest in the Montesano area include: the **Mission Revival-style City Hall**, 104 N. Main, which is listed on the State Heritage Register; and the 200,000-acre **Clemons Tree Farm** established by Weyerhaeuser in 1941 as the nation's first commercial tree farm.

OAKVILLE

Historic Oakville
U.S. 12, Oakville

False-front stores on a turn-of-the-century Main Street and Victorian homes lining streets in the city's older residential area grace the western border of the Chehalis Indian Nation. The town's quaint main street boasts an 1889 hardware store, a number of antique and craft shops, and the 1912 Key Bank, reputed to be the last bank in the state to be robbed on horseback.

OCEAN SHORES

Ocean Shores Environmental Interpretive Center
1013 Catala Ave. S.E., Ocean Shores (360) 289-4617

The diverse history of this six-mile peninsula that's seen Native Americans, fur traders, pioneers, cattle ranchers, land developers and a brisk tourist trade is described in the exhibits at this North Beach interpretive center. Other displays focus on the ecology of the region; its native plant and animal life.

QUINAULT

Lake Quinault Lodge
South Shore Dr., 2 miles east of U.S. 101, Lake Quinault (360) 288-2900

It was President Franklin Roosevelt's love of nature that brought him here in 1937 to study the feasibility of establishing a National Park in the area. A year later, Olympic National Park was born. On that trip, President Roosevelt was a guest at this famous lodge. Today it serves as a peaceful place for guests to rest and relax, or as a jumping-off point for the many adventures that await travelers to the southern region of this National Park. Inside the lodge are many of its original 1920s furnishings and one of the state's largest private collections of Northwest Indian art and baskets.

A short distance from the lodge is the **Quinault Ranger Station**. From here visitors can stroll along a short nature trail, get information on longer hikes to the Enchanted Valley and Anderson Glacier, or begin their drive around the lake to the temperate rain forest on the north shore.

Lake Quinault Lodge, Photo by Judy Menish

Enchanted Valley Chalet
East fork of the Quinault River, an easy 26-mile round-trip hike from the Quinault Ranger Station (360) 288-2444 (Quinault Ranger Station)

This three-story backcountry chalet was built in the early 1930s to compete with the larger Lake Quinault Lodge. While no longer an inn, the restored chalet houses

433

a ranger station and offers emergency shelter to hikers who journey to this valley of 1,000 waterfalls.

WESTPORT

Westport Maritime Museum
2201 Westhaven Dr., Westport (360) 268-0078

In 1939 this 3-story, 18-room, Nantucket-style building was constructed by the U.S. Coast Guard and commissioned as the Westport lifeboat station. It remained an active station until the Coast Guard moved down the street in 1973 to larger quarters. Since 1985 it has been operated as a maritime museum by the Westport-South Beach Historical Society. Exhibits emphasize Coast Guard, Pacific maritime and local history and include old photographs, marine artifacts, and sea mammals. The story of the state's large cranberry industry that thrives south of Westport along the "Cranberry Coast" is told in the exhibits displayed in the Day Room.

Two glass-enclosed display cases on the grounds of the museum contain mammal skeletons including that of a medium-size gray whale and partial skeletal remains of a blue whale. An authentic scale model of the old Coast Guard Station is also housed in one of the cases. A new structure on the museum grounds houses a 100-year-old, six-ton, 17-first order Fresnel lens from the Destruction Island Lighthouse.

Westport Maritime Museum

Grays Harbor Lighthouse
Westport Light State Park, Ocean Ave. Beach Approach, off Hwy. 105, Westport

At 107 feet, this octagonal watchtower soars higher than any lighthouse in the state and is one of the tallest on the Pacific Coast. Built in 1897-98, it replaced the first lighthouse and life-saving station originally constructed south of Westport at North Cove. Although a coastal light has been here as a beacon to ships for over a century, more than fifty deep-sea vessels have still been lost to the fierce squalls that often turn the waters at this entrance to Grays Harbor. Radar and other electronic navigation aids have greatly reduced these losses, but the light still remains a visual guide to mariners. Visitors can arrange for tours of the lighthouse by signing up at the Westport Museum.

Maritime History Trail
A bike and pedestrian pathway that leads from the Westport Museum to the Grays County Lighthouse

A 6,000-foot-long, 8-foot-wide cement trail runs on top of the dune along the shore from the Grays County Lighthouse to Westport's south jetty. Three observation platforms and interpretive signs explaining the local flora and habitat line the length of the Dune Trail. Dune Trail is one section of Westport's interesting **Maritime History Trail.**

Westport-South Beach Historic Murals

Artists murals commemorate local historic events and scenes of yesteryear at several places in South Beach's Cranberry Coast region. The walk along the Westport Marina Esplanade features murals of historic ships. Turn-of-the-century beach-goers are painted on the side of the Grayland Volunteer Fire Department. The old

Warrenton Cannery is depicted on the side of the grocery store at Warrenton Cannery Rd.

While traveling through the area watch for these interesting sights: **Fishermen's Monument** at the end of Neddie Rose Dr., dedicated to those who lost their lives at sea; an observation deck and three-story tower at two sites along Neddie Rose Dr.; **cranberry bogs** east of Hwy. 105 and southeast of Grayland Beach and Cranberry Rds.; the **Westport Aquarium** on Harbor Street in Westport, and an old **5-inch coastal defense gun mount** in Westport's City Park.

Jefferson County

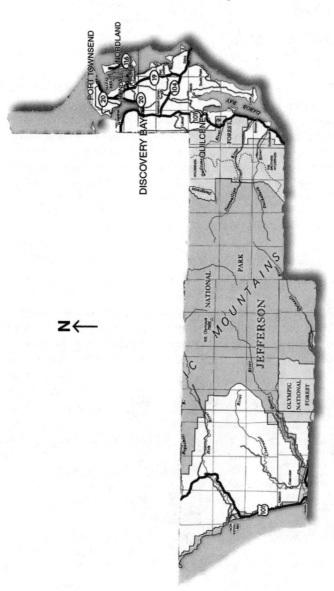

JEFFERSON COUNTY

DISCOVERY BAY

Discovery Bay Historic Marker
4 miles north of Discovery Bay on the east side of U.S. 101

"On May 2, 1792, the intrepid English explorer, Captain George Vancouver, in search of a northwest passage, sailed his sloop Discovery and the armed tender Chatham down the Strait of Juan De Fuca and into this sheltered harbor. The bay Vancouver named Port Discovery for his ship, and the small island guarding the entrance he appropriately called Protection Island. While at anchor here Vancouver set out in small boats for further exploration of this vicinity and discovered nearby the harbor of Port Townsend, so named by him for the Marquis of Townshend."

HADLOCK

The Old Alcohol Plant
310 Alcohol Loop Rd., Hadlock (360) 385-7030

After the Washington Mill Company closed in 1907, its owners began construction of a half-million dollar plant that would turn the area's plentiful sawdust into alcohol using a process patented in France. Eastern competitors kept the plant's alcohol out of their market and, when the plant switched from sawdust to Hawaiian molasses,

the Hawaiian Sugar Trust bought a controlling interest in the plant and forced it to close. For 65 years the buildings sat empty until they were converted into this first-class hotel, restaurant and marina.

The Old Alcohol Plant,
Photo by Judy Menish

438

Across the bay at **Port Hadlock** is the **old downtown district** where retail stores and restaurants cater to visitors to this tri-city area. The **Methodist Episcopal Church** at Randolph and Curtiss and **Captain Peter Shibles home** on Curtiss are two remaining early-day Hadlock properties that are listed on the National Register of Historic Places.

IRONDALE

Irondale Historic District
Moore St., Irondale

Little remains of the town's iron smelter or steel mill that employed hundreds of workers between 1881 and 1915. Several homes built at the beginning of the century for the mill's superintendents and the Irondale Jail, which is listed on the National Register of Historic Places, can be seen today in this bedroom community.

NORDLAND

Fort Flagler
Fort Flagler State Park, northern end of Marrowstone Island, north of Nordland
(360) 385-1259

One of the initial elements of our country's first national defense program was established in the 1890s with the construction of three coastal artillery installations at Forts Worden, Casey and Flagler. Their combined batteries of 3- to 12-inch guns and mortars formed an effective "triangle of fire" defense that guarded the Admiralty Inlet entrance to Puget Sound and provided protection for the Navy's yard at Bremerton and the cities of Seattle and Tacoma. Construction at Fort Flagler, the last of the three forts, began in 1897 and took ten years to complete. At Battery Wansboro, one of the nine Endicott period batteries installed here, two, 3-inch, disappearing guns are displayed. After World War I, coastal artillery units were disbanded and Fort Flagler was deactivated. It was reactivated during World War II as a base for training engineers and other troops in amphibious military maneuvers and remained in use until the Korean War ended in 1954. An interpretive exhibit across from the park office gives the fort's history and tells the coastal defense story.

Today, in the shadow of the once-powerful coastal armament, some of our country's largest warships can be seen as they head for the Navy's ordnance center on Indian Island. Indian Island has been a U.S. Naval base since 1941 when it was commissioned as a high-explosives storage, seaplane arming area and submarine net depot.

Historic Fort Flagler Military Hospital Photo by Judy Menish

Marrowstone Point Lighthouse
Fort Flager State Park, northern end of Marrowstone Island, north of Nordland

When the first light was installed here in 1888, it was little more than a fixed red light lantern suspended from a 12-foot high post. The station became a more typical lighthouse in 1918 when a light tower was built on top of a newly constructed foghorn house. The automated signal is not open to the public.

PORT TOWNSEND

Jefferson County Historical Museum
210 Madison St., Port Townsend (360) 385-1003

Puget Sound's second oldest city was founded by Alfred Plummer and Charles Bachelder in 1851 and was destined to become the "key city of Puget Sound." The hope that the city would become the terminus of the transcontinental railroad fueled real estate speculation and a building boom. In 1890, when Tacoma was chosen as the terminus, Port Townsend's boom collapsed, its population dwindled and the city was frozen in time. The city, while it survived economically, never again saw the rapid growth it experienced in the 1880s and 1890s. That lack of progress saved many of the city's Victorian homes and late 1800s buildings from the wrecking ball. Today, more than seventy places of historic interest can be explored within the Port Townsend district, the largest Victorian seaport north of San Francisco. The seaport, a National Historic Landmark, is a gateway to many historic districts within the city, as well as a number of early Victorian homes and businesses that have been listed on the National Register of Historic Places.

The Museum of the Jefferson County Historical Society honors the rich heritage of its people. Rare and historical artifacts tell the history of the region's native Indian tribes, explorers, settlers, Victorian-era families and military that came here. By preserving and displaying a wide-ranging collection of relics, Victorian and pioneer furnishings, early tools, equipment, antique appliances and 7,000 photographs, life in the county has been well documented.

The restored, Old English Revival-style building that houses the Society's collections was dedicated in 1892. It has served the community as its City Hall, Municipal Courtroom, Jail and Fire Station. The century-old building is listed on the National Register of Historic Places.

1892 City Hall Building, Courtesy of Jefferson County Historical Museum

441

Port Townsend's Historic Points of Interest, free guide available at the Chamber of Commerce Visitors' Center, 2437 E. Sims Way (360) 385-2722, and from many of the town's merchants

The highest concentration of the city's historic sites are located in the Port Townsend Historic District, a registered National Historic District roughly bounded by Scott, Blaine, Walker, Taft Sts. and the waterfront. Within this district are fifty-three places of historic interest, including nearly twenty that are recognized for their individual historic value with a listing on the State Heritage Register or the National Register of Historic Places.

Port Townsend had its start in 1851 when two settlers, Alfred Plummer and Charles Bachelder, built a log cabin at what is now the corner of Water and Tyler Sts. Water Street became the town's main street where many of its pioneer business began. A sampling of sites to see in this historic district begins with buildings on this famous street.

Lewis Building, Water and Madison, est.1889. Was originally the Clarendon Hotel. Was converted into an Emporium in 1934. Old, hand-painted advertisements can still be seen on the side of the building facing city hall.

Lewis Building

Franklin House, Water and Quincy, est.1886. Enlarged from a 1869 wooden building into the town's first fireproof brick hotel.

N.D. Hill Building, Water and Quincy, 1889. Originally was N.D. Hill and Sons Drug Company, a family drugstore with offices and apartments on second floor. Now a popular tavern with a carved wooden Victorian bar.

N.D. Hill Building, Photo by Judy Menish

C.F. Clapp Building, 700 Block of Water, est.1885. One of town's first banks and first in town with a cast iron facade. Originally a dry goods store; once the third largest in Washington Territory.

Enoch S. Fowler Building (a.k.a. Leader Building), Adams between Water and Washington, est.1874. State's oldest remaining 2-story, all-stone, commercial building. Served as county courthouse before Washington became a state and, since 1916, has housed *The Port Townsend Leader*, the oldest continually published newspaper in the state.

443

Mount Baker Block, Water and Taylor, est.1890. The original blueprints for this Renaissance/Romanesque Revival-style building, which called for four or five stories, were changed when plans for the transcontinental railroad's terminus fell apart and the country slipped into a National Depression. The upper floors were never completed, as was the case for others built during this era in the Port Townsend area.

James and Hastings Building, 900 block of Water, est.1889. Italian Renaissance-style originally built to house a dry goods store with offices and apartments upstairs.

James and Hastings Building

Capt. Tibbals Building, 1004 Water, est.1889. Restored Richardson-Romanesque building now operated as the Palace Hotel replete with Victorian furnishings and antiques. When first built, had three saloons on first floor with "boarding house" upstairs. Some of the rooms were named for the ladies who worked here. The madam's room is now the honeymoon suite.

Lighthouse Cafe Building, 955 Water St. (360) 385-1165, est. pre-1880. One of few original wood-frame buildings remaining downtown. Once served as the Custom House but was best-known when it housed the Axtel Saloon.

Sterming Block, 925 Water, est.1889. George Sterming's popular Belmont Restaurant and Saloon that operated here before the turn-of-the-century once again offers waterfront dining in this restored building.

Union Wharf, Foot of Taylor, est.1867. Wharf was constructed by the Union Dock Company and incorporated in 1867 as Washington Territory's first corporation. It had a 340-foot dock where scores of tall-masted ships anchored at this port of entry for all of Puget Sound.

Hastings Building, 839 Water, est.1889-on State Register. Was one of city's largest and most lavish buildings. Constructed by Lucinda Hastings and her children in an Italian Renaissance period style with a facade sheathed in sheet metal to appear like masonry.

Hastings Building

Haller Fountain, Taylor and Washington at foot of stairs to Jefferson. Dedicated in 1906 to memory of early pioneers. Its bronze statue of Venus was cast in New York and first appeared in the Mexican exhibit at the 1893 Chicago Exposition.

Francis Wilcox James House, 1238 Washington, est.1891-on National Register. This 3-story Victorian shingled house is one of city's finest homes. Hand-carved, wild cherry banisters, inlaid parquet floors of oak, walnut and cherry woods, and five chimneys are some of its most notable features. It became the Northwest's first Bed & Breakfast Inn in 1973 and is currently operated as the James House B&B.

Customs House and Federal Building, Washington and Harrison, est.1893-on State Register. Houses post office and other federal offices. Inlaid stone floors, curved glass windows, wrought iron staircases and a wood-paneled lobby reflect the elegance of this building, the most expensive structure in town. Pillars at the entrance are capped by the likeness of Indian Chief Chetzemoka and his wife. (See Chetzemoka Park listing.)

John Fuge House, 305 Pierce, est.1880. John Fuge, a Welsh ship's carpenter, built this Italianate-style house for a Port Townsend customs agent. The award winning, restored home, is operated as the Heritage House Inn and features original Victorian antiques in its six guestrooms. Fuge also built a row of homes in the 1500-block of Washington.

Frank W. Hastings House, 313 Walker, est.1889-on National Register. Turreted Queen Anne-style Victorian home of former German Consulate, August Duddenhausen. Operated today as the highly rated Old Consulate Inn B&B.

Jefferson County Courthouse, Jefferson and Case, est.1892-on National Register. This combination Romanesque- and Gothic-style courthouse is one of the oldest in the state. Its 100-foot clock tower was a visual landmark for mariners approaching the port.

Hiram Parrish House, Lawrence and Calhoun, est.1878-on State Register. His home was the city's first brick house.

George Down's House, Polk between Clay and Franklin, est.1886-on State Register. Built by owner of early sawmill. Fine attention to detail. Features beautiful stained-glass windows.

R.C. Hill House, 611 Polk, est.1872. Was family home for nearly 100 years. Now named the Holly Hill House, a B&B for all the Holly trees that surround the old Victorian.

Colonel Henry Landes House, 1034 Franklin, est.1872. Former Kentucky Colonel, Henry Landes, stated the first banking service in the city. Landes established the First National Bank of Port Townsend, served on the city council and was elected to the Washington State Senate.

Capt. Enoch S. Fowler House, Polk and Washington, est.1860-on National Register. The city's oldest remaining home, designed in a New England Classic Revival-style, was built for retired sea captain, Enoch Fowler. Capt. Fowler, an immigrant from Lubec, Maine, constructed the town's first dock and operated the first mail service between Port Townsend, Victoria, Olympia and Seattle.

Frank A. Bartlett House, 314 Polk, est.1883-National Register. Frank Bartlett, a town merchant and county treasurer, constructed this 14-room, French Provincial-style house. The house features a well-proportioned French mansard roof and an impressive interior with large rooms and tall, first-floor ceilings.

St. Paul's Episcopal Church
1020 Jefferson (360) 385-0770, est.1865-on National Register. St. Pauls was the third Episcopal congregation in the state, and the first to build its own church building. It remains the oldest Episcopal Church in the diocese of Olympia. Originally built on a bluff overlooking Point Hudson, the Carpenter Gothic-style church building was moved to its present site in 1882. A ship's captain donated the church bell on the condition that it be rung in foggy weather to warn passing ships.

Old Bell Tower, Jefferson and Tyler, est.1890-on State Register. Volunteer firemen were once summoned by the ringing of the bell that's still mounted atop this restored, one-of-a-kind fire tower. Antique, horse-drawn vehicles on display include a hearse, cab and fire apparatus.

Rothschild House State Park, Taylor and Franklin, est.1868-on National Register. David Rothschild, a prosperous early Port Townsend entrepreneur, built this Federal-style home on a bluff overlooking his general store. The restored 8-room home is filled with original family furnishings, housewares and clothing. Some rooms contain original wall and ceiling papers, carpets and fine woodwork. It's Washington's smallest state park.

Rothschild House

Lucinda Hastings House, 514 Franklin, est.1889. Lucinda Hastings, the first white woman in the region, arrived here in 1852 with her husband, Loren. She was one of the city founders and one of its most prominent citizens. At the time this house was constructed it was the most expensive built in the city. That same year, Lucinda, and her six children built the giant Hastings building at Water and Taylor Sts.

Ann Starrett Mansion/George Starrett House, 744 Clay (360) 385-3205, est.1889-on National Register. A classic, 4-story, Queen Anne, Stick-style Victorian home. There are many interesting interior features in this 12-room mansion including the tower's free-hung, spiral staircase that leads to a domed ceiling. The 2-tiered staircase is believed to be the last of its kind in the United States. The fully restored home is furnished in period antiques and is operated as a bed and breakfast inn.

1889 Photo of Ann Starrett on the balcony of the Starrett Mansion, Courtesy of Ann Starrett Mansion

Trinity Methodist Church, 609 Taylor (360) 385-0484, est.1871-on State Register. State's oldest remaining Methodist Church. First minister's Bible among artifacts exhibited.

Edward Sims Home, Taylor and Lawrence, est.1886. Home of former State Legislator and world affairs counsel to President Woodrow Wilson during World War I.

Carnegie Library, 1220 Lawrence, (360) 385-3181, est.1913. Nestled among Port Townsend's nineteenth century homes and businesses is its beloved city library. Its wood-burning fireplace and upholstered furniture has helped create a comfortable home library-type atmosphere for patrons in this turn-of-the-century community.

Captain Thomas Grant House, 731 Pierce (360) 385-4168, est.1887. Lizzie Grant, one of the city's well-to-do women, commissioned the construction of this Italianate Villa-style residence. Wallpaper from Paris, silk wall decorations from the original Broadway production of the "Flower Drum Song," and period antiques grace the rooms of the home that has become known as "Lizzie's," one of the city's bed and breakfast inns.

449

H.L. Tibbals House, 1208 Franklin, est.1877. Tibbals was city councilman, sheriff, and postmaster. Restored home contains fine art and antiques and is run today as the Chanticleer Inn B & B.

John C. Saunders House, 902 Sims, est.1891-on National Register. One of the largest homes in Port Townsend was owned by J.C. Saunders, an elected customs collector and president of Commercial Bank. The grand size of his Victorian home and the extensive grounds earned his estate the name "Holly Manor."

Manresa Castle, 7th and Sheridan (360) 385-5750 or (800) 732-1281, est.1892-on National Register. The town's first mayor, Charles Eisenbeis, built this 3-story

castle for his wife, Kate, using brick from his own brickyard. The commanding appearance of this structure, with its towers and turrets, resemble castles in Eisenbeis' native Prussia. Jesuits priests converted it into a training college when they acquired the building in 1927. The brick exterior was covered with stucco when the Jesuits added a wing to the building. Since 1968, the building has been extensively restored and returned to a Victorian style. Hand-painted wall coverings, carved oak woodwork and European antiques adorn the interior. The present owners operate the castle as an inn and restaurant and conduct free tours.

Point Hudson
End of Water St., Port Townsend

An original Makah Indian cedar canoe is displayed under a protective canopy at this point where, for centuries before the arrival of white settlers, Indians from many tribes would camp and fish while en route to the Puget Sound region. In 1792, on his famous voyage of discovery, Capt. George Vancouver landed here and named the bay Port Townsend.

Original Makah Indian Cedar Canoe

Chetzemoka Park
Jackson St. between Blaine and Garfield, Port Townsend

On a summer day in 1904, nearly 200 residents met here to clear land for the city's first park. The Civic Improvement Club, which spearheaded development of the park, named it as a memorial to Chetzemoka, the S'Klallum Indian chief who befriended the city's first settlers. (The sculpted faces of Chetzemoka and his wife

can be seen at the top of the columns outside the old Customs House on Washington St. Chief Chetzemoka's final resting place is in Port Townsend's Laurel Grove Cemetery along side the graves of many of the city's pioneer families.) The 8-acre park embraces meandering creeks, a rose garden, several arbors and a 1905 bandstand.

451

Fort Worden
Fort Worden State Park, 200 Battery Way, at the end of Cherry St., Port Townsend (360) 385-4730

Between 1896 and 1911, three forts were built to protect the Admiralty Bay inlet into Puget Sound and the U.S. Navy shipyard at Bremerton. Each of the three forts, Casey, Flagler and Worden, had batteries of coastal guns and mortars that formed a "triangle of fire" defense for the Bay. Fort Worden was the headquarters of the Harbor Defense of Puget Sound and had the distinction of being the only Army fort to be named after a navy man, Admiral John L. Worden. Admiral Worden commanded the ironclad battleship *Monitor* in the Civil War battle with the Confederate ship, *Merrimac*, and later served as superintendent of the U.S. Naval Academy. Victorian homes on Officers Way, early twentieth century barracks, a restored balloon hangar, parade ground, army cemetery, artillery bunkers, and searchlight tower are among the sites preserved within this National Historic Landmark. The lighthouse at Point Wilson and two museums are also on the grounds of this 443-acre state park. Movie buffs might recognize many of the fort's buildings and sites from the film, "An Officer and A Gentleman" that was shot here in 1980.

Searchlight Tower, Fort Worden

248th Coast Artillery Museum
Fort Worden State Park, Bldg. 201, 200 Battery Way, Port Townsend (360) 385-0373

None of this fort's forty-one guns were ever fired at an enemy vessel, but the importance of the coast artillery is undisputed. The strong defensive position of these units, and the dedication of the military personnel, who served at these installations, insured the protection of our shores from attack and invasion through two world wars. This 1904 enlisted men's barracks now houses seacoast artillery artifacts, a military small arms collection, regimental flags, uniforms from the turn-of the-century to World War II, and scale models of Fort Worden's massive fortifications and the 12-inch disappearing guns that once stood here. A fine collection of historic photographs gives visitors a look at the large guns that were once mounted on the fort's dozen batteries.

Enlisted Men's Barracks, 248th Coast Artillery Museum, Fort Worden

Artillery Shell at Entrance to Former Enlisted Men's Barracks

Fort Worden's Commanding Officer's House
Fort Worden State Park, Port Townsend (360) 385-4730

Italian marble sinks, 10-foot high pressed-tin ceilings, an 1898 Ispahan Persian rug, Maddox English China, an Empire sofa, a Beckwith organ from 1889, and hundreds of other features and furnishings makes this the finest building on the grounds of

453

this historic fort. Completed in 1904, the 5,979-square-foot, Jeffersonian Classical-style building was home to twenty-seven of the fort's thirty-three commanding officers and their families. A portrait of Admiral John L. Worden, for whom the fort was named, hangs in the front hall of this beautifully restored and furnished home.

Balloon Hangar
Richard F. McCurdy Pavilion, Fort Worden State Park, Port Townsend

An airborne defense system that used manned balloons was launched from this site in 1920 and remained operational until the end of World War II. The balloon hanger, built by the 24th Battery Balloon Company to house its fleet, was remodeled in 1991 for use as a performing arts facility. It was named for Richard McCurdy, a pioneer publisher and founder of Centrum, a non-profit arts center. The balloon hanger is one of only two remaining in the United States.

Balloon Hangar, Fort Worden

Alexanders Castle
Fort Worden State Park, Port Townsend

The brick, castle-like structure that stands atop the hill behind the old HQ Barracks seems out of place among the fort's white wooden buildings. It was constructed as a retreat in the early 1880s, a dozen years before Fort Worden was established, by a minister named Alexander from St. Paul's Episcopal Church in Port Townsend.

Alexanders Castle

Point Wilson Lighthouse
Fort Worden State Park, Port Townsend

Two lighthouses have served as warning beacons at Point Wilson where the waters of Puget Sound and the Strait of Juan de Fuca meet. The first was a frame tower, erected in 1879, with an oil lamp illuminating a fourth-order Fresnel lens. But the point's high tides eroded the beach, forcing replacement of the first structure. In 1913, this 46-foot, reinforced concrete octagonal tower replaced the original lighthouse. The light, which is visible for 17 miles under clear conditions, is now completely automated.

Point Wilson Lighthouse

455

Port Townsend Marine Science Center
Fort Worden State Park, 532 Battery Way, Port Townsend (360) 385-5582

Touch tanks at this marine science center lets visitors experience first-hand the marine world that lies off the beach in Port Townsend Bay. Events from guided beach walks and interpretive programs to workshops and summer camps make this an interesting, educational and fun stop for family member of all ages. The center's Puget Sound Timeline Exhibit is a 70-foot "ribbon of time" with exhibit cases and interpretive panels that trace the biological and geological history of the earth from 4.6 billion years ago.

Fort Townsend
Old Fort Townsend State Park, off Hwy. 20, 4 miles south of Port Townsend

Concern for the safety of the region's settlers during the Indian wars of the mid-1850s led the U.S. Army to establish Fort Townsend at this site in 1856. The area's natural resources were used to construct the fort. Buildings were erected using timber from the nearby forests and plaster made from ground clamshells. Troops that were sent from this fort to the San Juan Islands in 1859 during the "Pig War" boundary dispute with England were withdrawn in 1861 at the outbreak of the Civil War. The fort was rebuilt in 1874 and remained an active military post until the

barracks were destroyed by fire in 1895. Its last military use was during World War II when the fort was used as an enemy munitions defusing station. The only military building remaining today is the 65-foot-tall U.S. Navy Explosives Laboratory. Interpretive signs mark the site of the old fort's original building.

QUILCENE (KWIL-seen)

Quilcene Historical Museum
151 Columbia St., Quilcene (360) 765-4848

A historical account of the region's Indian conflicts, mining and railroad ventures, and its successful logging and seafood industry are recorded in the exhibits displayed at this museum of local history. Information can be obtained from museum staff about the successful local oyster industry that started in the tranquil waters of Quilcene Bays. The well-known oysters that are grown here get their start in the hatchery that follows Linger Longer Road along the Bay. It's the world's largest oyster hatchery.

Earl Oatman House
40 Muncie Ave., Quilcene

Earl Oatman and L.G. Seitzinger operated the first store in lower Quilcene. Oatman was also affiliated with the First National Bank in Port Townsend. In 1913, he constructed this Colonial Revival-style bungalow, the only one of this style that remains in the county from the early 1900s. Oatman's home is listed on the National Register of Historic Places but is not open to the public.

RUBY BEACH

Destruction Island Historic Marker
One mile south of Ruby Beach on the west side of U.S 101

"In 1775, while at anchor under the lee of this island the Spanish explorer, Bodega y Quadra, commanding the schooner Sondra, sent seven men ashore for wood and water, all of whom upon landing were killed by the Indians. In memory of this incident, Quadra named the island "Isla De Dolores," the Island of Sorrows. In 1878, Captain Barkley anchored here in the Imperial Eagle and landed six men who met a similar fate at the mouth of a nearby river, which Barkley called Destruction River. This island has since been named Destruction Island, and the Indian name of Hoh restored to the river." Three miles offshore on Destruction Island is the 98-foot **Destruction Island Lighthouse**. Construction of the station, which took three years to build, was competed in 1891. Its first-order Fresnel lens contains 1,176 prisms and has a replacement value in excess of $4 million. The fully automated station, and the island, is closed to the public.

Kitsap County

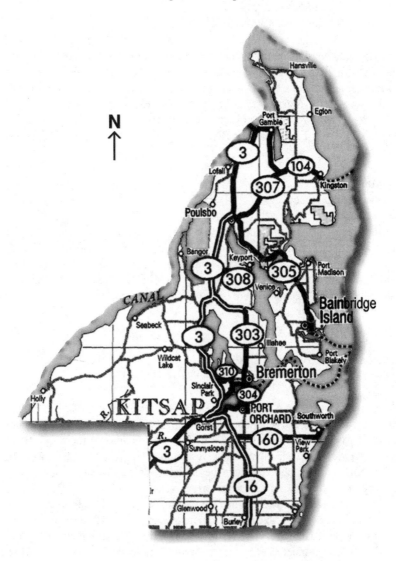

KITSAP COUNTY

BAINBRIDGE ISLAND

Bainbridge Island Historical Museum
Strawberry Hill Park, 7650 NE High School Rd., Bainbridge Island (206) 842-2773

A little more than 200 years ago, Capt. George Vancouver, the first white man to command a vessel into Puget Sound, landed here to cut tall trees for masts. Seventy years later, Port Blakely, at the island's southeast shore, continued to be a source for timber. It became one of Puget Sound's leading lumber centers. Shipbuilding and agriculture were also prominent early island industries. But today the island is primarily a residential community. Thousands of artifacts and old photographs along with the written, oral and video history of the island are preserved by the Bainbridge Island Historical Society in this restored 1908, one-room Island Center Schoolhouse. Every inch of space within its walls is utilized to display the Society's collection; an extensive and comprehensive accumulation of treasures from the island's past.

Antique Pump Organ, Bainbridge Island Historical Museum

The Bloedel Reserve
7571 NE Dolphin Dr., Bainbridge Island (206) 842-7631

Preserved within the boundaries of this 150-acre estate are more than 80 acres of second-growth forest and a series of gardens, ponds, meadows and wildlife habitats.

The Bloedel family established this reserve in 1984 to "provide people with an opportunity to enjoy nature through quiet walks in the gardens and woodlands." Their large family home, replete with original furnishings, now serves as the reserve's visitor center. Reservations are required to tour the reserve.

BANGOR

Naval Submarine Base (SUBASE) Bangor
West of Keyport on the west shore of the Kitsap Peninsula

During World War II, the Korean War and the war in Vietnam, this base was named the U.S. Naval Magazine at Bangor. Ships bound for duty in these wars stopped here and were loaded with conventional munitions. In 1973, the Navy selected Bangor to be homeport for the first squadron of Trident nuclear submarines. The eight, 540-foot-long Trident subs based here, each with the capability to carry up to twenty-four long-range, nuclear-armed missiles, can occasionally be seen in the Hood Canal.

BREMERTON

Bremerton Naval Museum
130 Washington Ave., Bremerton (360) 479-7447

In 1954 this museum was established for the purpose of depicting and preserving the history of the U.S. Navy with an emphasis on the Puget Sound Naval Shipyard at Bremerton. Artifacts from the shipyard and some of the Navy ships that were serviced here, an extensive collection of historical photographs, large-scale ship models, old uniforms and ship bells are displayed.

Puget Sound Naval Shipyard
Bremerton   (360) 476-7111

Since September 1891, the U.S. Navy's shipyard at Bremerton (Puget Sound Naval Shipyard) has been one of the most important installations of its type in the United States. It was here that battleships, destroyers and submarines were built, overhauled or repaired. Among the ships repaired here were some that were damaged by the Japanese in the December 7, 1941, attack at Pearl Harbor. The dry dock at this National Historic Landmark is the largest in the world where up to four destroyers could be constructed at the same time. Its 5-acre machine shop is the best equipped and one of the largest in the world.

Today Bremerton is homeport to the nuclear aircraft carrier *USS Nimitz*, the largest warship in the world, and sixty other active and mothballed ships including carriers, battleships, nuclear submarines, cruisers, destroyers, and frigates. One of the Navy's best-known ships was once mothballed here, the *USS Missouri*. It was on the deck of this famous ship that representatives of the Japanese government surrendered to the Allied Powers in Tokyo Bay on September 2, 1945, officially ending World War II. The *Missouri* is now moored next to the *USS Arizona* Memorial at Pearl Harbor, Hawaii.

A narrated, 45-minute, water-based tour of the shipyard and mothball fleet is available through Kitsap Harbor Tours, 290 Washington Ave. #7 (360) 377-8924.

USS Turner Joy (DD-951)
Docked at the north end of the Bremerton Waterfront Boardwalk, Bremerton
(360) 792-2457

For 23 years, from 1959 through 1982, this Seattle-built, Forrest Sherman-class destroyer cruised the waters of the Pacific Ocean as part of the Navy's Pacific Fleet. She saw extensive action during the Vietnam War where she earned nine battle stars. In 1990, the decommissioned ship was donated to the Bremerton Historic Ships Association for restoration and preservation as a floating museum and public Naval Memorial. Most spaces on board the ship are included in a self-guided tour including the engine room, bridge, and berthing spaces. A replicated POW cell from Hoa Lo Prison (Hanoi Hilton) is part of the ship's Vietnam Prisoner Of War exhibit.

USS Turner Joy

Kitsap County Historical Museum
280 4th St., Bremerton (360) 479-6226

The history of Kitsap County from the birthplace of Chief Seattle, to the 1850s New England-style logging town of Port Gamble, to the Navy warships at Bangor and Bremerton is recorded at this historical society museum. Thousands of photographs covering county, Naval, and Puget Sound transportation history; a large archive of county records and maps; local Indian artifacts; hand-carved furniture and other pioneer memorabilia is housed in the museum's new and larger quarters (was formerly located in Silverdale). The museum's permanent "County Time Line" exhibit traces the geological, industrial and military beginning of Kitsap County.

HANSVILLE

Point No Point Lighthouse
Hansville Recreation Area, East of Hansville

Puget Sound's pea soup-thick fog, that often obscures this remote beach, contributed to several shipwrecks before a warning light and fogbell became operational here on January 1, 1880. That original 10-foot-square, 27-foot-tall masonry lighthouse structure, which is listed on the National Register of Historic Places, has remained basically the same since its construction, with the exception of a change in its fog signal. Two other noteworthy events in the region's history took place before the light was installed. Lieutenant Charles Wilkes moored here in May, 1841, while exploring the region's inland waters and named this entrance to Puget Sound, "Point No Point." And, in 1855, Governor Issac Stevens and 1,200 members of the Chimakum, Clallam and Skokomish Indians met here on the eve of the 1855-56 Indian Wars to sign a treaty establishing reservations in exchange for Indian lands.

KEYPORT

Naval Undersea Museum
Garnett Way, 3 miles east of Hwy. 308, Keyport (360) 396-4148

"Torpedo Town, U.S.A." was founded at Keyport in 1914 when the U.S. Navy determined that the waters offshore would be ideal for operating a still-water range for testing torpedoes. The Naval Undersea Warfare Engineering Station that stands here today is now the Navy's only depot for torpedoes and mobile targets. Outside the station's gates is the $6.5 million Naval Undersea Museum, with the Nation's largest collection of naval undersea technology exhibits. Artifacts and ordnance from World Wars I and II, an underwater salvage and rescue operation exhibit, actual undersea vessels including mini-subs and the 95-ton Deep Submergence Vessel Trieste II, a display depicting the development of torpedoes from the 1800s to present, underwater mines, and a simulation of the control room of a nuclear submarine, are included in the museum's permanent collection.

Deep Submergence Vessel

FORT WARD

Fort Ward
Fort Ward State Park, southern end of Bainbridge Island (206) 842-4041

Protecting the Navy's interests at its Bremerton Shipyard from hostile warships was a prime concern in the 1890s. In 1900, Fort Ward was added to the trio of coastal artillery forts defending the entrance to Puget Sound at Admiralty Bay. Fort Ward was equipped with five gun batteries to guard the Rich Passage entrance to Bremerton and Port Orchard.

Armament at the fort included 3- and 5-inch guns and one battery with three, 8-inch disappearing guns. The Navy took control of the fort in 1938 and installed antisubmarine barrier nets across Rich Passage. At the end of World War II, officers' homes became private residences and the fort was deeded to the state for use as a park.

PORT GAMBLE

Port Gamble National Historic Site
Hwy. 104, 1 mile northeast of the Hood Canal Floating Bridge, Port Gamble

Visitors to this 1850s New England-style village will find a noticeable lack of the typical tourist attractions. Instead, they'll find a quiet, picture-postcard community, with a main street lined with Victorian gas lamps and three dozen meticulously restored original homes and shops.

The town got its start in 1853 when Andrew Pope and William Talbot, natives of East Machias, Maine, established a lumber mill at this site; founded Port Gamble, one of the state's oldest company towns; and built their business into one of the Northwest's major forest products firms. The sawmill, which, until the end of 1995, was the oldest continuously operating sawmill in North America, no longer produces lumber. But the city of Port Gamble, a National Historic Landmark, remains intact and is being preserved and maintained as a company town.

Community Hall Building, Port Gamble National Historic Site

Walker-Ames House
Next to the General Store, Port Gamble

Puget Mill Company's building number 14 was the former residence of mill superintendent, William Walker. Walker could observe the activities of the mill from a vantage point that overlooked the bay. The residence is one of the city's fifteen places of historic interest that are listed in a guide available from the Port Gamble General Store and Historic Museum.

465

Port Gamble General Store
Rainier Ave., Port Gamble (360) 297-7636

One of the first buildings erected when the town was established in 1853 was its general store. The crew of the "Julius Pringle" originally constructed the store as a trading center near the original mill site. In 1916, the store was rebuilt at its present location (remodeled in 1972 and 1996). It remains the town's general store, selling everything from groceries to clothing, and is listed on the State Heritage Register. The **Of Sea and Shore Museum** occupies the store's second floor and mezzanine (see following listing).

Port Gamble General Store and Of Sea and Shore Museum

Of Sea and Shore Museum
Upper level of Port Gamble General Store, Rainier Ave., Port Gamble
(360) 297-2426

Mollusks (shells) collected from more than a hundred countries are displayed from the 25,000-shell collection accumulated by this museum's curator, Tom Rice. His collection, one of the largest in the United States, also includes several thousand specimens of other marine life, shark jaws, glass balls, and objects gathered from ocean shores.

*Of Sea and
Shore Museum*

Port Gamble Historic Museum
On the downhill side of the General Store, Rainier Ave., Port Gamble (360) 297-8074

Imagine the courage it took in the 1850s for men and women to leave the comfort and security of a well-established East Coast city, travel west to the rugged and untamed shores of the Pacific Northwest, and start their lives and businesses anew. The history of two such men, Andrew Pope and William Talbot, who came here in 1853, built a lumber mill and founded the company town of Port Gamble, is chronicled in this museum of local history. Replicas of Pope's San Francisco office, Captain Talbot's cabin from the "Oriental," a turn-of-the-century scene from the lobby of the Puget Hotel, the Victorian bedroom from Admiralty Hall, an Indian cedar house, and an early 1900s saw filing room from the mill are among the exhibits. Family heirlooms, photographs, artifacts from the early days of Port Gamble, and original Land Grant Deeds signed by Presidents Abraham Lincoln and Andrew Johnson are also displayed. A grindstone removed from Pope and Talbot's mill in 1895 stands

across from the museum's entrance.

Andrew Pope's San Francisco Office

Pope and Talbot Mill Grindstone

The Thompson House
Hwy. 104, south end of Port Gamble

This private residence is the state's oldest continuously occupied house. James Thompson constructed this Victorian-style home in 1859 and, for 99 years, his descendants lived here. An addition was built in 1872 and the home completely restored in 1969.

St. Paul's Episcopal Church
Hwy. 104, south end of Port Gamble (360) 297-3800

Parishioners still worship at this 1870 New England-style church, a copy of the church in Andrew Pope's and William Talbot's hometown of East Machias, Maine. The church's bell is original, an 1879 gift donated by the officers' wives from Pope and Talbot's San Francisco office.

Port Gamble Cemetery
Walker St., Port Gamble

Among the burial plots in this restored pioneer cemetery is the gravesite of Gustav Englebrecht, the first U.S. Navy man to die in action in the Pacific. Englebrecht was a sailor on board the U.S. Navy Warship *Massachusetts* that arrived here in 1856 to defend the mill's workers from Indian attacks during the 1855-56 Indian Wars. He was killed by an Indian in a minor skirmish and laid to rest in this small cemetery. His gravesite is a Registered National Historic Site.

Gustav Englebrecht Gravesite

Hood Canal Floating Bridge
Hwy. 104 across the Hood Canal, one mile northwest of Port Gamble

Captain George Vancouver named this body of water "Hood's Channel" during his exploration of the Puget Sound region in 1792. One hundred and seventy years later the Hood Canal Floating Bridge, the longest floating bridge over tide water in the world, was constructed across this two-mile-wide section of the channel. In 1979, 18 years after the bridge opened, a raging storm caused the western half of the bridge to break loose and sink severing the link between the north end of the Kitsap Peninsula and the Olympic Peninsula. It reopened to traffic in 1982. Trident Nuclear Submarines, homebased at Bangor, 12 miles south of the bridge, can occasionally be seen in the canal.

PORT ORCHARD

Log Cabin Museum
416 Sidney Ave., Port Orchard (360) 876-3693

Sidney Stevens platted the town of Port Orchard (originally named Sidney) in 1886. It was incorporated in 1890 and became the county seat of Kitsap County in 1893. Within the walls of this c.1913-14 log cabin are furnishings, housewares, relics and family memorabilia representative of the type of articles found in South Kitsap County's homes during the first half of the twentieth century.

Sidney Art Gallery
202 Sidney Ave., Port Orchard (360) 876-3693

Street scenes from "Old Town Port Orchard" have been recreated and can be visited on the second floor of the city's 1908 Masonic Lodge Building. Artifacts on loan from the Log Cabin Museum add to the authenticity of the setting. The gallery on the first floor showcases art and crafts of local and regional artists. In the surrounding civic and business district are more than a hundred antique dealers; making this the "antique capitol" of the Kitsap Peninsula.

Horluck Foot Ferry
At the foot of Sidney Avenue in Port Orchard, and next to the Bremerton Ferry Terminal in Bremerton (360) 876-2300

Water taxi transportation via a small Mosquito Fleet provided a quick means of passenger travel between Port Orchard and Bremerton before the turn-of-the-century. Today, the historic fleet still offers passengers a 15-minute ferry across the Sinclair Inlet between the two cities.

POULSBO (PLAZ-boh)

Historic Downtown Poulsbo
Front St., and the area between Third, Jensen and the Marina, Poulsbo

"Velkommen til Poulsbo" greets visitors to the town that's fondly referred to as "Little Norway on the Fjord." Its population remained mostly Norwegian from the time of its founding in the late 1880s until the outbreak of World War II, with Norwegian the predominant language in the homes and on the streets. The area offered many fjord-like harbors and opportunities for typical Scandinavian occupations: fishing, logging and farming. Evidence of the rich heritage of this community can be seen in almost every shop along the city's business district; from the native foods, clothing and merchandise to the Norwegian folk art designs painted on the buildings.

First Lutheran Church
Poulsbo

One of the first community buildings erected by the town's settlers was the First Lutheran Church. Its commanding design reflects the strong religious belief of its founders. The white spire that crowns the church has been a city landmark since the parish was erected in 1886.

Marine Science Center
Marine Science Society of the Pacific NW, 18743 Front St. NE, Poulsbo
(360) 779-5549

Living displays of marine life in "touch tanks" and aquariums at this Center gives visitors of all ages a hands-on look at life under the waters of Puget Sound as it exists today. But the Center is more than just a place to view beautiful specimens, its a place to learn. Staff at the Center have received national acclaim for their outstanding program of teacher training.

471

SILVERDALE

Jackson Hall Memorial Community Hall
9161 Washington Ave., Silverdale

Those who have been involved in the Scouting program, either as a participant, parent or leader, will appreciate the history behind this community building. In 1932, Boy Scout leaders from Troop 552 purchased the land this building stands on for $38 from the county as tax title property. Then they, and the troop committee ladies auxiliary, embarked on fund-raising efforts for the building fund. Part of the funds ($203) came from the estate of the late Jackson Hall. Banquets, card parties, raffles and other events raised another $1500. The WPA provided the labor and, on July 24, 1937, the Hall was dedicated. Since then this log building has served as a Scout hall for Boy Scout Troop 552. It contains an outstanding collection of Scouting memorabilia including uniforms, merit badges, banners, pennants and camporee exhibits that date from the late 1920s.

SUQUAMISH (soo-KWAH-mish)

Suquamish Museum
Suquamish Tribal Center, 15838 Sandy Hook Rd., Suquamish (360) 598-3311, Ext. 422

The outside world seems a distant memory as you walk through the doors of this museum where the sights and sounds of an ancient time surround you. The realism of the exhibits, life-size and hands-on, lets you experience a walk in the footsteps of those who lived on these lands for over 15,000 years. Chief Seattle, through a multi-media exhibit, "The Eyes of Chief Seattle," is your tour guide as you learn the history of Puget Sound's original inhabitants. Another outstanding presentation, "Comes Fourth Laughing, Voices of the Suquamish People," is a documented visual interview with tribal elders who give entertaining accounts of their life during the last 100 years. Suquamish Museum is internationally acclaimed and rated by the Smithsonian Institute as best historical museum of Native Americans in the Pacific Northwest.

Suquamish Museum

Chief Sealth Historic Marker
On the beach at Suquamish, just north of the Agate Pass Bridge on Hwy. 305

"Born in 1786, his life spanned the period from the exploration of Puget Sound by Europeans to its settlement. He represented the Duwamish and Suquamish tribes in the Treaty of Mukilteo with Governor Stevens in 1855. Chief Sealth showed his friendship for the new settlement of Puget Sound during the Indian disturbance of 1855. In gratitude for this stand and respect for his leadership, the new city was named Seattle. He died in 1866 and is buried in the Suquamish Memorial Cemetery near St. Peter's Church."

Chief Seattle Burial Place
Suquamish Memorial Cemetery by St. Peter's Catholic Church, South St., west of Augusta Ave., Suquamish

He was called Tsu-Suc-Cub by the six tribes of Salish Indians he led, and Chief Sealth or Chief Seattle by the many white settlers he befriended. This man of vision, for whom the city of Seattle is named, was buried here in June 1866, not far from Old Man House where he was born in 1786. His gravesite is marked with a granite memorial inscribed with the words: "Seattle, Chief of the Suquamish and Allied Tribes, died June 7, 1866, the firm friend of the Whites and for him the City of Seattle was named by its Founders." An Indian dugout canoe rests on top of the posts that frame his burial site. Chief Seattle's final resting-place overlooks the waters of Puget Sound and the village where he lived.

Chief Seattle Burial Place

Old Man House Historic Marker

At the foot of McKinstry St., overlooking the beach north of the Agate Pass Bridge, Suquamish

"On the beach below this point is the site of a famous Indian house, home of Chief Sealth, for whom Seattle is named. It was built of hand-adzed cedar slabs, and was the largest known Indian house in the region. Its length, quoted variously as up to 900 feet, was probably achieved by joining together several separately built units. Its site was ideal for an Indian village and archaeological work shows that it was so used before the house was built. Chief Sealth died in 1866. Soon after 1870 the house was razed on order of the United States Army."

Old Man House (Site)

Old Man House State Park, at the foot of McKinstry St., above the beach over-looking Agate Pass (follow signs through town), south of Suquamish (360) 842-3931

Native Americans call the Indian dwelling that once stood here "Oleman House," loosely translated as "strong man house." For it was the birthplace and home of Chief Seattle, the elected leader of six tribes, and Chief Kitsap, for whom the county was named. Several families lived here in what was believed to be the largest longhouse in the Pacific Northwest, and perhaps the largest Indian communal home in North America. Estimates of the building's size range as high as 54,000 square feet. In 1870, the U.S. Army burned the home to the ground to discourage communal living.

Chief Joseph Hillaire Story Pole

South St. and Augusta Ave., Suquamish

This pole was carved by Chief Joseph Hillaire from a one thousand-year-old tree as a memorial to Chief Seattle (Sealth) and Chief Kitsap, the last of the great Indian chiefs in the Puget Sound region. Every symbol on a totem pole has a meaning and together they tell a story. A description of these symbols and their meaning appears on the nearby State Historic Marker (see next listing).

Totem Symbols Historic Marker
South St. and Augusta Ave., Suquamish

"Thunderbird—Indian tribal crest
Beaver—tribes of water area-vigor
Blackfish—annual expedition for oil
Clam and Salmon—basic food of area
Anchor—first meeting with white men from ships in the area
Paddle—symbol of transportation
Profiles—Chiefs Kitsap and Sealth
Handclasp—friendship of Indian and white man—signing of treaties
Deer—hunting, food and clothing
Flame Spiral—camp, potlatch, feast"

WINSLOW

Eagle Harbor Congregational Church
Winslow Way and Madison Ave., Winslow

Schooners, steamers, and minesweepers were built at the 15-acre shipyard that dominated this harbor between 1902 and 1959. Although the shipyard, once one of the largest in the Pacific Northwest, is gone, many of the community's original buildings remain, including this 1896 church.

Bainbridge Island Winery and Museum
682 State Hwy. 305, 1/2-mile north of the Ferry landing, Winslow (206) 842-9463

Antique crystal, glasses and wine-related objects fill the small museum in this island's historic winery. Its the only winery in Western Washington that produces all of its wines from locally-grown grapes and strawberries.

Mason County

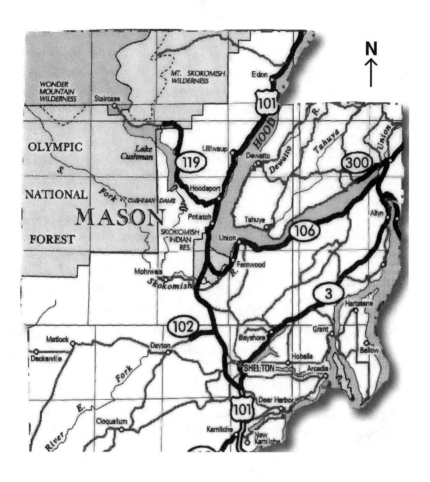

MASON COUNTY

SHELTON

Historic Shelton
Roughly bounded by Adler, Front, Kneeland and 7th Sts., Shelton

David Shelton settled here in 1853 and farmed the land for 32 years before he platted his farm for a town. A monument on the grounds of the city's Public Safety Building marks the site of Shelton's log cabin, one of 15 historic sites in this district. Other noteworthy places are:

Sol Simpson House, Adler and 4th. Simpson came to Shelton in 1887 and started the Simpson Lumber Company in 1900. Eventually his company became the state's second-largest timber holder.

Mark Reed Home, Adler and 3rd. Mark Reed, Sol Simpson's son-in-law, was an innovator in the logging business and is credited with the success of the Simpson Company.

Grant Angle Home, Cota and 7th. Angle founded the county's first newspaper, the *Mason County Journal*, in 1886.

Doyle's Hall, Kneeland and 2nd. Many of Shelton's social events took place in this building's second-floor ballroom. The building was also home to the International Woodworkers of America union.

Shelton Public Library and Town Hall, Cota and 5th. Another of the Simpson Company's founders, A.H. Anderson, along with Mary Simpson endowed this building in 1914. Its the city's oldest existing civic structure and is listed on the National Register of Historic Places.

Simpson Logging Co. Train
Visitor Information Center and Chamber of Commerce, Railroad Ave. between 2nd and 3rd, Shelton (360) 426-2021

Tracks that led west from this site went into the area's timber where this 1924 Shay locomotive pulled log cars, such as the one displayed here. Both the Simpson Logging

Co. Engine No. 7, that was named "Tollie" in honor of Mary (Tollie) Simpson, and the Peninsular Railway Caboose No. 700, that now houses the Visitor Center and Chamber of Commerce, are listed on the National Register of Historic Places.

Simpson Logging Co. Train

UNION

Hood Canal Historic Marker
Fir St. and Hwy. 106, Union

"While charting northwest waters for the British Admiralty in May, 1792, Captain George Vancouver anchored his two ships in Discovery Bay for repairs. Taking three small well-stocked boats, he set forth to view more closely the surrounding region and found a narrow inlet to the south which proved to be both extensive and picturesque. After sailing its entire length, he retraced his course to resume his comprehensive charting of the coast. In honor of the right honorable Lord Hood, Vancouver named the newly-discovered inlet Hood's Channel, known to all as Hood Canal."

BIBLIOGRAPHY

Atkinson, Allegra & Ashley, Rose, *In and Around Seattle With Children,* **Craftsman & Met Press, Seattle, WA 1972**

Avery, Mary W., *Washington A History of the Evergreen State,* **University of Washington Press, Seattle, WA 1967**

Bard, Rachel, Killeen, Jacqueline, and Miller, Charles C., *Country Inns of the West,* **101 Productions, San Francisco, CA 1982**

Bower, Donald E., *Roaming the American West,* **Stackpole Books, Harrisburg, PA, 1971**

Brewster, David, *Northwest Best Places,* **Sasquatch Books, Seattle, WA 1985**

Burley, George & Evans, Lynette, *Roche Harbor, A Saga in the San Juans,* **B & E Enterprises, Everett, WA 1972**

Cochran, Barbara Fleischman, *Exploring Spokane's Past, Tour to Historical Sites,* **Ye Galleon Press, Fairfield, WA 1984**

Cohen, Marvin H., *Steam Passengers Service Directory,* **Empire State Railway Museum, Inc., Middletown, NY 1985**

Clark, Norman H., *Milltown,* **University of Washington Press, 1970**

Darvill, Jr., Fred T., *Stehekin-A Guide to the Enchanted Valley,* **Signpost Books, Edmonds, WA 1981**

Davidson, Nancy, Sunset Magazine, *The Beautiful Northwest,* **Lane Magazine & Book Co., Menlo Park, CA**

Dungeness: The Lure of the River, **Sequim Bicentennial History Book Committee, Port Angeles, WA 1976**

Editors of the American West, *The Great Northwest,* **American West Publishing Co., Palo Alto, CA 1973**

Ferris, Robert G., Editor, *Lewis and Clark, Historic Places Associated With Their Transcontinental Exploration (1804-06)*, United States Department of the Interior, Washington, DC, 1975

Fish, Byron, *Guidebook to Puget Sound*, Ward Ritchie Press, Los Angeles, CA 1973

Fish, Byron, *60 Unbeaten Paths*, Superior Publishing Co., Seattle, WA 1972

Florin, Lambert, *Ghost Town Album*, Superior Publishing Company, Seattle, WA

Florin, Lambert, *Ghost Towns of the West*, Promontory Press, 1970

Fodor's Far West 1986 & 1987, Fodor's Travel Publication's, Inc., New York & London

Fuller, George W. *History of the Pacific Northwest*, Alfred A. Knopf Publishing, NY 1931

Glassley, Ray Howard, *Visit the Pacific Northwest*, Binfords & Mort, Publishers, Portland, OR 1948

Great Historic Places, Simon and Schuster, New York, 1973

Gray, William R., *The Pacific Crest Trail*, National Geographic Society, Special Publications Division, Washington, DC 1975

Hart, Herbert M., *Tour Guide to Old Forts of Oregon, Washington & California*, Pruett Publishing Co., Boulder, CO 1981

Henning, Robert A., *1987 Northwest Mileposts*, Alaska Northwest Publishing Co., Edmonds, WA 1987

Highway Heritage Markers, Heritage Corridors Program, Washington State Department of Transportation, Olympia

Historic Houses of America, Editors of American Heritage-The Magazine of History, American Heritage Publishing Co., Inc., New York 1971

Jollota, Pat, *Naming Clark County,* **Fort Vancouver Historical Society of Clark County, Vancouver, WA 1993**

Keithley, Malcolm, *State Museum Guide,* **Wenatchee, WA 1963**

Kirk, Ruth & Alexander, Carmela, *Exploring Washington's Past,* **University of Washington Press, 1990**

Klein, Barry T., *Reference Encyclopedia of the American Indian, 4th Edition,* **Todd Publications, NY, NY 1986**

Krenmayr, Janice, *Foot-Loose in Seattle,* **Seattle Times Company, Seattle, WA 1973**

Lord, Suzanne, *American Travelers' Treasury,* **William Morrow & Co., Inc., NY 1977**

Lyons, Dianne J., *Washington Handbook,* **Moon Publications, Inc., Chico, CA 1989**

Mace, William H., *A Beginners History,* **Rand McNally & Company, USA 1924**

Martin, Cy & Jeannie, *Gold! And Where They Found It, A Guide to Ghost Towns & Mining Camp Sites,* **Trans-Anglo Books, Corona Del Mar, CA**

Morgan, C.T., *The San Juan Story,* **San Juan Industries, Friday Harbor, WA 1966**

Morgan, Murray, *The Northwest Corner,* **The Viking Press, NY 1962**

National Register of Historic Places, **Washington State Department of Community Development, Office of Archaeology & Historic Preservation, Olympia, WA 1989**

Official Museum Directory, **R.R. Bowker, New Providence, NJ 1992, Pages 994-1015**

Phillips, James W., *Washington State Place Names,* **University of Washington Press, Seattle, WA 1988**

Poppleton, Louise Ross, *There is Only One Enumclaw,* **Enumclaw, WA 1981**

Preserving Washington's History, A Bicentennial Report, **The Washington State Parks & Recreation Commission**

Reynolds, R. Moland, *Byways of the Northwest,* **Graphics Arts Center Publishing Co., Portland, OR 1976**

Roberts, Bruce and Jones, Ray, *Western Lighthouses, Olympic Peninsula to San Diego,* **The Globe Pequot Press, Old Saybrook, CT 1993**

Salisbury, Albert & Jane, *Here Rolled the Covered Wagons,* **Superior Publishing Co., Seattle, WA 1948**

Scofield, W.M., *Washington Historical Markers,* **The Touchstone Press, Portland, OR 1967**

See America's Other Washington, The State, Museums & Interpretive Centers, **Washington Museum Associations, William E.** Steward, **Wenatchee, WA 1963**

Skagit County Centennial Almanac 1883-1983, **Skagit County Centennial Committee**

Sunset Books & Sunset Magazine, *Washington Travel Guide,* **Lane Publishing Co., Menlo Park, CA 1987**

The Buildings of Old Skagit County, Ten Self-guided Tours-1977, **Skagit County Historical Society, Mt. Vernon, WA 1977**

Trails West, **National Geographic Society, Prepared by Special Publications Division, Washington, DC 1979**

Vokac, David, *The Great Towns of the West,* **West Press, San Diego, CA 1985**

Washington State Parks Heritage Sites, **Washington State Parks and Recreation Commission, Olympia, WA**

Woodbridge, Sally B., Montgomery, Roger, *A Guide to Architecture in Washington State,* **Roger, University of Washington Press, Seattle, WA 1980**

Workers of the WPA in the State of Washington, *Washington: A Guide to the Evergreen State, Federal Writers' Project – The New Washington*, **Binsford & Mort, Portland, OR 1950**

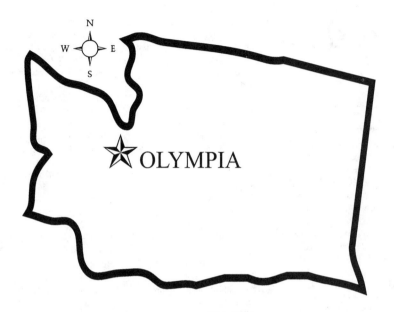

★ OLYMPIA

State Flower
Coast Rhododenron

State Bird
Willow Goldfinch

State Flag

Index

Z

Y